MISSION: MOTHERHOOD

MISSION: MOTHERHOOD

WRITING A NEW FAIRY TALE OF LOVE AND FAMILY

CHERI BERGERON

The names and identifying characteristics of individuals in this book have been changed. Some dialogues have been re-created and dramatizations have been added based on real events.

The mention of specific organizations or authorities in this book does not imply endorsement by the author, nor does it imply that such organizations or authorities have endorsed the author. The author is not responsible for changes to third-party websites.

COPYRIGHT © 2025 CHERI BERGERON
All rights reserved.

MISSION: MOTHERHOOD
Writing a New Fairy Tale of Love and Family

FIRST EDITION

ISBN   978-1-5445-4605-6   *Hardcover*
       978-1-5445-4607-0   *Paperback*
       978-1-5445-4606-3   *Ebook*

To my mother, for passing down her ability to love unconditionally and live selflessly.

To my amazing, chaotic, imperfect, unconventional family. You are living proof there is beauty beyond the bounds of biology. Thank you for your acceptance and unwavering support. You are my sunshine!

To all the faceless girlfriends who share a silent desperation and longing to become mothers but find themselves trapped inside an outdated fairy tale. I pray my story brings strength and hope to help you achieve your mission and fulfill the desires of your heart.

CONTENTS

Introduction 9

PART 1: THE DEMISE OF THE FAIRY TALE

1. Reality Check 23
2. The Messages of Childhood 31
3. Married to My Career 41
4. Homecoming 53
5. Looking for Love (in All the Wrong Places) 65
6. Ticking Clocks 85

PART 2: THE ROADS TO MOTHERHOOD

7. Becoming a Foster Parent 99
8. A Better Life for Aurora 111
9. The Road to Fertility 125

10. Rachel's Story 145
11. Ripple Effects of Loss 167
12. Finding Worth 181
13. Into the Woods with Baby A and Baby B 201
14. Brandon's Story 209
15. Lauren's Battle for Survival 229
16. Genetic Russian Roulette 255
17. Brayden and the Gift of Normal 261
18. The Daddy Box 285
19. The Measure of a Father 299

PART 3: THE MEANING BEHIND YOUR MISSION

20. Healing the Past 311
21. Tender Mercies 327
22. A Girlfriend's Advice on Writing Your Own Fairy Tale 339

    Epilogue 351
    Acknowledgments 355
    About the Author 359

INTRODUCTION

NO ONE COULD TAKE THIS CHILD AWAY FROM ME. AT LEAST, that's what I'd told myself over and over for the last four years. But now I was standing in my kitchen with a cell phone to my ear, consulting with Jimmy, my divorce lawyer. We'd just been ambushed…again.

"I'm so sorry, Cheri," he started, his voice ominous, "the amicus attorney for your son just called to say he's going to recommend Gaston be named Brayden's legal father."

That male chauvinist bastard!

Breathe, Cheri, I told myself, bracing as if I was about to parachute out of a plane at ten thousand feet. *Just breathe.* The world tilted a little. I darted my eyes around the darkened kitchen, using my senses to find my center as I steadied myself against my custom Carrara marble countertop.

I loved my Tuscan-inspired kitchen. From the dark walnut cabinets to the natural limestone accent walls, wrought iron fixtures, and vibrant, hand-painted ceramics, it had always been my happy place. It reminded me of the spectacular adventures I'd had in Italy. But at this moment, my carefully curated sanctuary felt cold and empty.

Ours wasn't the typical attorney-client relationship. Jimmy and I were on a first-name basis. The weight of my high-stakes, precedent-setting legal case had formed an unbreakable bond between us. I gripped my iPhone harder, but the lifeless device gave me no glimpses of the future.

"How much weight does the amicus's opinion carry?" I wondered aloud. The pit growing wider in my stomach didn't bode well, but I needed to know. "Does a judge ever go against an amicus's recommendation?"

Jimmy's tone was somber, but I'd hired him to be honest and not treat me like a wilting flower. "Almost never," he said. "As the child's representative in court, their opinion is supposed to be impartial."

Impartial, my ass.

The whole thing felt rigged from the start. We'd planned so carefully. For three months we'd methodically collected our documents and assembled an array of witnesses. Made our case that Gaston wasn't acting in the role of a father. I'd worn my power suits to preliminary hearings and could prove that I was a good mother and sole provider. And now, because the misogynistic legal system wanted to force fit someone into the daddy box, I was about to lose sole custody of my own son.

There wasn't supposed to be any drama on the eve of the trial. All the legal theater was to start the next day in court. I would be prepared for battle then, but I wasn't prepared for battle now. I was in my home. My safe place. It was Sunday night and the kids were in bed. I was on my third glass of Cabernet, trying to settle my nerves before the big day. My preference in wine resembled my personality—big, bold, and sometimes overbearing. I'm definitely an acquired taste, or so I'm told.

Damn him! It seemed to me that my ex had a knack for waylaying me when I was most vulnerable.

If Gaston was named my son's legal father, that meant joint custody. He would be a permanent fixture in my son's life. He would be a role model imposed upon my family against our will. It meant I'd have to pretend I was okay with him getting time alone with my son after he'd spent years—*years*—playing Mr. Nice Guy before suing me at the exact moment an amicus was legally appointed in a custody battle.

Brayden wasn't his. Against all odds, I'd conceived him on my own. I carried him on my own. Birthed him on my own. And, finally, I parented him on my own. Gaston was going to become my son's father over my dead body.

But that's exactly what was happening, a small voice inside me said. Out of all the ways I'd lost children, losing one by way of a legal technicality straight from the heart of Texas's patriarchal establishment was too much to handle.

"I know this isn't the news we'd hoped for," Jimmy continued. I could feel him searching for encouraging words across the miles between our houses and not finding any. "Look, it's not over yet. I'll see you in court tomorrow. Get some rest." As I said good-night and ended the call, I felt my core crunch along old fault lines.

Somehow, I made it to my mother, who was in her bedroom. "The amicus is going to rule against us," I said, the desperation in my voice palpable. She was as stunned by the news as I was and I saw pain, a similar kind to mine, flash across her normally serene face as she watched her child suffer. All she could do is what she'd done my entire life: swaddle me in her warmth and compassion and hope her love would give me some shield against the monsters lurking in the dark.

In my mother's arms, in that moment of utter despair, I sent up a prayer. Or, maybe, a plea. *Why does this keep happening to me? Why is this so hard?* Memories swarmed me. My head swam with fragments of faces and feelings I still couldn't fully confront. Numbness crept through my muscles. Helplessness gathered strength from my anxiety and *squeezed*.

Ten years of fighting to be a mother. Ten years of disappointments and pain. What could the universe possibly be trying to tell me? Why was I going through all this? *What does it all mean?*

Then, peace. And a message. *You're going through this so you can help other women go through this.*

Where I live in Austin, the earth gets parched in the one-hundred-degree summers. Seeing the ground crack from extreme dryness and everything wilt, even the trees, you wonder if anything will live. Then a thunderstorm comes, dumps buckets of water, and suddenly brown lawns become lush green canopies adorned with delicate white rain lilies. The message from deep within pulled me out of my despair and my tears flowed like a summer downpour. It was a torrent that brought new life and healing. In that brief moment, all the anger and bitterness of decades fell away to make room for a new purpose.

I'd share my mission of motherhood to help future mothers plan and execute their own.

MOTHERHOOD IS A MISSION

I use the word *mission* instead of the popular word *journey* to describe my experience because, for me, motherhood *is* a mission. It's a visceral calling that grips you to the point that you have no choice. A *journey* sounds so benign, like something you'd do across Europe or on a weekend yoga retreat. To me, *mission* is the relentless pursuit of something so meaningful that failure is not an option. It's not a matter of *if* you'll accomplish your goal but *when*. It's a commitment, a sense of militaristic duty. That's the way I viewed my mission to become a mother.

While motherhood ultimately became my mission, it took a while for me to get the message. My first mission was that of a career woman. As I pursued my dream of becoming a marketing executive, I became very comfortable exuding a determined, take-no-prisoners persona to achieve the results I wanted. Some who encountered me at work would characterize me as one "bad bitch." Rather than a derogatory term, I like the way hip-hop culture defines "bad bitches" as confident, independent, mission-driven women who control their own destinies, deftly maneuvering their way to success in a male-dominated world. In that context, I wear the label of "bitch" as a badge of honor.

Our society in the mid-2020s is getting more comfortable with women being bad bitches in the boardroom. I spent twenty years as a high-tech executive, achieving VP of Marketing with a publicly traded software firm, before stepping back from the career ladder to be the mother I wanted to be. I knew how to handle obstacles in my profession. But I had no idea how hard it would be to overcome the obstacles to becoming a mother.

As products of the postfeminist era, women's expectations to have it all—education, career, money, life partner, and the latest trendy styles pushed by social media influencers—push the pitter-patter of little feet further and further out. But science is supposed to have our backs and iron out any biological issues we may face as mature mothers. Right? Well, maybe not as much as we want to believe.

Compounding the issue, the last forty years have seen an explosion of advancements in human fertility and baby making as medicine gets a better and better picture of what leads to a healthy baby and what doesn't. But even as the professional fertility conversation gets more complex, the fabric of our culture is still rooted in traditional definitions of family and motherhood and recoils from talking about the hard realities of infertility, pregnancy complications, and birth defects. When we do talk about it, the rhetoric is often full of shame and ignorance.

Part of the mission of this book is to challenge the social gag order surrounding the topics of fertility, birth, and motherhood. I'm well aware that some of my story and the way I go about telling it may step on some toes, but I believe these ugly truths lose their grip on us when they are brought into the light of day. Don't be surprised if I find humor in unlikely places because, as women, there are times we need a good laugh so we don't cry.

Based on my experience, becoming a mother in the modern world sometimes means getting into bad bitch mode and ruffling some provincial feathers. Our mothers were also bad bitches, they just did it quietly. It wasn't always afghans and rocking chairs for them. Then and now, motherhood can be a fight against social expectations, the legal system and its outdated views of fertility and parenting, our families, our partners, even our own freaking bodies.

And like any war, this mission is going to take all your mental power, all your physical strength, all your emotional resilience, and all your faith.

It's going to take all of you.

TRADITIONAL MOTHERHOOD IS A FAIRY TALE FOR MANY WOMEN

Motherhood, as our culture teaches it, is a fairy tale. It can be a beautiful fairy tale when the carriage never turns back into a pumpkin. As young women, we know the proper steps to achieve the fairy tale all too well. We are to get a good education, make good money, find a good man and marry him, have good sex, and make good babies. But held as a rigid formula for success, this traditional fairy tale disenfranchises a growing number of women who discover the tiara and glass slipper don't fit. I was one of those women.

For twenty-first century women used to being in power in our education and careers, we are still somehow powerless in the realm of motherhood, sticking by the old, tired fairy tales dependent on the fatalistic meeting of a Prince Ryan Reynolds who has it all: looks, ambition, intelligence, chivalry, a sense of humor, and a scruffy dog that genuinely seems to like him.

That story sounds like a fantasy. And it is. But we keep telling ourselves that story, even when we know it isn't true. At least for me, it wasn't. Raised in a conservative household, I thought marrying Prince Charming was my only option. Instead, mine was a sad romantic version of Monopoly. Every time I passed Go, I collected one man who was worth far less than $200. But I kept going around the gameboard anyway, despite all the failures, thinking I needed to get myself a man before I could get myself a child. In same-sex households the vision is still a pair of complementary people raising a child together. The mommy and daddy boxes still exist, no matter the gender of the person who checks them off. We still get trapped in the fantasy of two parents against the world.

I learned firsthand that trying to force fit myself into a one-size-fits-all fairy tale can do more harm than good. That's the problem with standard sizes: only a few people match the measurements and look good in them. But my mission taught me there's more than one way to write a fairy tale, and it's high time for a new one. Your own. Because let's face it, the only story that works for you is the one that fits your situation, needs, and dreams.

This book is two parts memoir, one part activism, and a dash of self-help mixed with a sprinkle of reality TV. My story, a rarity in the public eye, challenges the traditional fairy tale and provides a rallying cry of solidarity and support for women, like me, who desperately want to be mothers but don't see how it's possible. This is my Norma Rae moment, one voice standing on a box on a busy factory floor holding a sign that says "Union" like in the 1979 movie starring Sally Field—a call for a group with a similar experience and goal to come together to change the way things are done. Only, my sign would read "Screw the Fairy Tale," a mantra mothers should put on repeat as they navigate their own missions.

When the fairy tale storylines failed to give me the future I dreamed about, I rejected all of them to create a family on my own terms. And I went after my goal with the dogged determination of a soldier. I believe you can do the same.

MOTHERHOOD IS A RAW AND PERSONAL EXPERIENCE

This book is not a "how to," and it doesn't give medical or legal advice on what to expect while you're expecting to get pregnant or adopt a child. There are other books I'm happy to recommend on my website **missionmotherhoodbook.com** and doctors you can seek out to diagnose and offer solutions for your unique situation.

In preparing for my mission, I trained as a life coach with the Life Purpose Institute to get more skilled at guiding people through their struggles; however, I don't pretend to be a therapist. It took me years to process the trauma of my mission with my own therapists and I highly recommend getting one for your own mission.

No, this book is not a generalization or prescription. It's about one woman's mission to become a mother—*any* kind of mother—through options ranging from the traditional family unit, to fostering and adoption, to fertility procedures involving donors and in vitro fertilization (IVF). The results of these options were both joyful and devastating—sometimes both—and included a landmark child custody case that would set legal precedent for the definition of parentage in the state of Texas.

My thoughts come mostly from my own experiences, and while I tried many paths on my way to becoming a mother, I didn't try them all. But it doesn't really matter how many motherhood options I've gone through. Yours will be different from mine. What matters is showing what I did and how it felt going through my trials and tribulations so you can get a glimpse behind the curtain at the Things Nice Women Shouldn't Discuss. I've done my best to be as candid, vulnerable, and honest as I can in telling all that I endured to achieve my mission. At times, as a reader, it may be difficult to bear, because that's the way it felt to live it.

My story contains an in-depth description of events throughout my mission of motherhood, but I have changed many of the names and specific details of individuals into fairytale characters as a way to protect the innocent, the guilty, and all the shades in between. But I have stayed true to my experience of becoming a mother. That is accurate and expresses the truth as I know it.

Since my experience is also meant to show how the motherhood mission affects all parts of a woman's life and being, I have to express my personal values and beliefs, including my faith. I'm a product of both pragmatism and spiritualism, progressive and conservative ideas, and it wouldn't be my authentic story without those parts. Readers who fall too far on either side of the political spectrum may not like what I have to say. I accept that. I don't ask you to agree with my choices; I ask you to witness them. Then, you can use that knowledge to make your own choices.

MOTHERS ON A MISSION DESERVE THE SUPPORT OF A GOOD GIRLFRIEND

I went to hell and back to become a mother, but I didn't walk the path alone. There were many people who helped me get through the excruciating and the unimaginable.

Unfortunately, many friends came in and out of my life as I pursued my mission of motherhood. I wish I'd had one girlfriend, just one, who understood and fought by my side at every step. But this is not *Sex in the City*. Sisterhood sometimes fails in the pursuit of motherhood. For some of my girlfriends, my experiences may have been too painful. Or, perhaps my difficult choices offended their values. And for a few, the whole ordeal took more time and energy than they could spare. So I was often left to face the emotional turmoil that comes with complicated fertility experiences by myself. At times, the sound of isolation was deafening.

I don't want that to be your experience.

Women often face the nightmares of fertility problems alone. It's our quiet despair, something not talked about publicly because it rubs up against the core thing that makes us women: the ability to conceive and carry a child. And everyone and their lawyer is quick to tell us what vision of motherhood is acceptable and judge us when it doesn't line up with their ideals.

Know that you don't have to carry that burden alone. For you, the main role I want to play is friend.

This book strives to create an intimacy similar to one girlfriend talking to another over a glass of wine when the lights are dim enough to make speaking uncomfortable truths doable. Talking about vaginas is uncomfortable. Talking about abortion is uncomfortable. Talking about the loss of a child is uncomfortable. Together, I know we can get through it.

There's one thing I know about motherhood for sure. There is no one way; there is just my way. And her way. And your way. While each path to motherhood will and should be different, one truth remains the same: there will be struggle. Small or large, one or many, there will be moments that bring you to your knees.

No mission worth fighting for is accomplished easily or without cost. Success comes from a lot of trial and error, twists and turns, and dead ends. If you have any old wounds left to discover, trust me, this mission will rip them open. When you go on your mission of motherhood, you go with your whole self: body, mind, feelings, and soul. It tests all of you.

But you don't have to go through it alone.

My purpose, made clear one Sunday night in my mother's bedroom, is to be a confidant and coach—the girlfriend I didn't have that would share advice, joy, grief, and a glass of good wine—with those who have the same driving desire to become a mother that I did but who don't yet know how to get there. Most of all, I want to share hope with women who are feeling hopeless.

At this moment, I think about you. Yes, you, the person reading this book. I can only imagine what you've experienced, what led you to pick up the story of another woman struggling to create a family of her own. I wonder if what you're going through is anything close to what I've gone through. If it's better. If it's worse. Or something in between.

Even from this side of the page, I see you. I don't know who you are, but we are kindred spirits. I know what the emptiness inside feels like. I know the pain of realizing I am, yet again, alone. I know the grief that saturates the word *childless*. I know the single-minded mission the search for motherhood becomes. And I want you to know, if motherhood is truly your desire, then there is no amount of tricky biology, imperfect partners, or limiting mindsets that can come between you and the family you dream about.

With knowledge, courage, determination, and a village that loves you, nothing is impossible. As a community of women on a mission, we can figure this out together.

So let me show you how I became a mother.

My mission started with a reality check—one that caused my old fairy tale of motherhood to come tumbling down.

PART 1

THE DEMISE OF THE FAIRY TALE

In an unexpected moment of clarity, some women realize they've been living their lives by a set of societal rules and assumptions that don't work for them. That newfound awareness can be jolting, disorienting, and terrifying, but from it can emerge moments of clarity about what really matters.

CHAPTER 1

REALITY CHECK

THE OFFICE WAS CLASSICALLY MALE. DARK WOOD PANELing everywhere. A tastefully weathered brown leather couch positioned across from a three-hundred-pound traditional mahogany desk. Oversized diplomas in thick black frames graced the walls. Sports memorabilia from the University of Texas at Austin signed by the legendary Darrell Royal perched proudly on a floor-to-ceiling bookcase. On the wall beside me hung a huge photo panorama of Austin at night, the Colorado River a dark ribbon as it flowed silently under the First Street and Congress Avenue bridges, reflecting the lights of a vibrant downtown. It was a stately office to match a stately doctor. But even with these personal touches, my nose still detected a hint of antiseptic and prophylactics that was typical of a fertility clinic.

I was there to see Dr. Babymaker. He was an older gentleman in his late fifties or early sixties, enjoying the time of life when a lot of middle-aged men seem to pause in their aging, after their hair goes steely gray but their wrinkles haven't deepened yet.

His clothes always matched his dignified, clean-shaven face: tailored, refined, and flawless. Somehow, he managed to be distinguished and reserved without being aloof. A warm charm and quiet confidence rolled off him in a way that put his female patients at ease. My mother thought he was hot stuff.

Dr. Babymaker had a habit of being late to appointments. The fertility business was booming, and he was one of the top fertility doctors in the state of Texas with thousands of patients and babies under his belt. Today was no different. I tapped my foot impatiently while my hands fiddled with a magnetic fidget toy that sat on the coffee table next to me. I was not accustomed to waiting for anyone. My impatience was legendary. But in this case, I knew I was not the one in control or in any position to make demands. I was desperate and at his mercy.

My long dark hair was pulled back in a bun, a pair of slick ebony sticks holding it in place. My circa 2008 Donna Karan black blazer was complemented by matching sleek midrise black pants that flared with just the right amount of femininity around my stylish but practical Prada loafers. One of my mentors was a lesbian, and I'd picked up the loafer habit from her. A Mark Jacobs white silk camisole peaked out from the blazer's notched collar. A little bit of bedroom to go with my boardroom, which was enough to keep my male colleagues and clients a little bit off balance, making it impossible to be stereotyped as either girlie or butch. I found power in being an enigma.

These were my battle clothes. Clothes like this had won me many deals in my fifteen years as a high-tech marketing executive. Maybe I thought wearing my best threads to a fertility clinic would somehow stack the deck in my favor.

I had no issue throwing money at a problem. That's what you do in the business world, and it almost always works. Anything's possible with the right amount of money, and I'd earned my fair share of it. I was fully prepared to spend tens of thousands of dollars to make my motherhood dream a reality. If I was willing to go to those lengths, then surely the doctors and I could work something out.

Instead, I got a reality check.

"Honestly, Ms. Bergeron, considering your age, it's going to be difficult for you to get pregnant on your own. Not impossible, but difficult."

Not impossible? I thought to myself. How could my situation be that bleak?

He brought out a couple of well-worn publications from the Centers for Disease Control with official-looking charts and numbers on them. While I often spent my workdays poring over numbers and statistics, I'd never seen these stats before. Most of the lines and numbers blurred together, but I got the important stuff.

The numbers laid out the hard truth in unmistakable terms. As a woman ages, her fertility doesn't decline in a graceful, gentle curve. It falls off a freaking cliff! Things start going downhill at thirty. By age thirty-five, you're in a freefall that gets steeper with each passing year. At age forty, a woman's chances of conceiving and delivering a healthy baby without medical intervention hovers around 10 percent.

"With all the risk factors, a woman who is pregnant over age thirty-five is considered a geriatric pregnancy," Dr. Babymaker explained, his normally gentle tone bearing an unintentionally jagged edge. "The risks go up significantly, so you'll need to be monitored closely to make sure that both you and the baby stay in good health."

I sat expressionless, trying not to break down. My outside exuded control and professional power. Inside, my world was falling apart. Apparently, biology didn't give a crap about Prada.

Is he serious? I thought. I was turning forty in two months. I knew I might have some challenges getting pregnant at my age, but I was convinced I could be transformed into a virtual spring chicken with the help of advanced medical science. It felt like someone had punched me in the stomach. I thought I'd been right on time to become a mother. Everything else in my life was set. But it seemed the train had already left the station and I'd had no idea I was late.

The office walls caved in on me while the roof crumbled down slowly, little by little, and a sinking, desperate feeling welled up in my gut. I strained to get air in my lungs as beads of sweat collected on my brow. Maybe the AC had quit running.

"The odds are improbable that you will be able to conceive naturally," said Dr. Babymaker. "We also need to be concerned about whether your eggs are viable."

Did he say viable? I thought in disbelief. I pictured three sad little old lady eggs huddled together in the corner of my ovaries shriveling away to nothing. It made me cringe. I rubbed my forehead to clear the fog that seemed to be descending over my eyes. There was a list of concerns after that. If my eggs *were* viable, would I produce enough of them? Would they implant? Would they grow a healthy child? Would I be able to carry the baby to term? Dr. Babymaker's words sounded far away, as if coming from a place I could no longer reach.

While I climbed the corporate ladder and gained financial independence. While I traveled and explored exotic cities and enjoyed fancy restaurants. While I bought a house in the best suburb. While I loved, and failed at love, more than once—through all my incredible experiences, I'd clung to the thought that I HAD TIME. *I am only forty years old, after all!* I'd read *People* magazine and *Cosmopolitan* like everyone else. I heard scores of stories about celebrities having babies in their late forties and fifties. Screw it, I'd even heard of rare cases of women delivering in their sixties! Hadn't medical science advanced to the point where everyday miracles were possible for women like me?

And it wasn't just science selling me a lie. I started hearing echoes of voices in my head from the feminist movement I'd listened to for the last three decades. "Choose to be a mother when you are ready," the opinion pieces said. "Figure out who you are first." "Prioritize your career; you'll have plenty of time for a family when you're financially stable." "Don't worry, sweetie, modern medicine will have your back." Now that "I Am Woman Hear Me Roar" anthem sounded like a steaming pile of Texas bullshit.

Just as the self-loathing and inner recrimination started to reach a fever pitch, a dissenting voice rang out in my defense. *But it took you forever to find a man good enough to have kids with.* Fair point, inner voice. What was I supposed to do if I didn't meet the perfect Prince Charming in high school or college that caused the pieces of my motherhood ambitions to fall magically into place? How could it be all my fault?

These were the messages that I'd heard over and over my whole life, although I couldn't recall exactly where or when. But the messages had been clear as day. There were steps to go through before having kids so you could have a good family life. Loving parents. Picket fences. Happy children. I believed the whole fairy tale.

It took a long minute for me to realize that's what all those stories were—fairy tales.

My designer clothes, the travel, the fine art—bought with all the money I'd made over the years when I only had myself to support—now revealed themselves as the lifeless accessories they were. Outward signs I had it together as I tried to fill the hollowness in my womb. A hollowness that now ached with the possibility it would never be filled with life.

Where and when did I go so far wrong?

This was not the way my day was supposed to go. Before coming into Dr. Babymaker's office, life seemed full of promise and possibility. The flashes of motherhood I'd seen driving to this appointment now mocked me.

Mothers in stylish athletic gear pushing jogging strollers down quiet neighborhood sidewalks, their napping babies dressed in pastels to match Texas's perfect spring weather.

Children carefully navigating their way through carpets of bluebonnets in a roadside field so they didn't squish them before crouching down so their mom could get a snapshot on her phone.

Toddlers making their slow but determined way up the steps of a rainbow-colored playscape as women in cardigans and capris hovered protectively behind them, arms ready to catch them if they fell.

A blond-haired little girl skipping out of Chuck E. Cheese, her red balloon bobbing merrily over flyaway hair as fine as silk, and a woman laughing and batting at the balloon as it danced around her, using her body to shepherd the little sprite away from any cars that dared move in the parking lot.

These women were living my dream. A dream that science was supposed to help me achieve. Somewhere I heard a fizzle, like my dream of motherhood was imploding like a doomed star burning its way through the atmosphere, leaving a massive black hole in its wake. Dr. Babymaker's charts had let all the air out of my naïve mommy-wanna-be balloon.

I summoned my strength and tried to wake myself up from this nightmare. My eyes went back to the charts. Their titles were long and clinical but all I could see written boldly above their stark numbers was "You're Screwed."

Sorrow and self-loathing came first as the room went fuzzy around the edges for a heartbeat, as if my soul were trying to escape. This bottom-falling-out-of-the-world feeling quickly gave way to something else. Seething anger and betrayal. I lived my whole life up to this point expecting the fairy tales to be real. Would this be the price I paid for believing them? I liked to think of myself as a savvy, streetwise woman who could spot a con job from a mile away. But in this case, I had been sold an ideological bill of goods and I'd bought it hook, line, and sinker. I was not going to take this news lying down. I tried to figure out who to blame, but all I saw were faceless strangers.

I white knuckled the roller coaster ride of my emotions for a few more moments. Just when I felt all hope was lost, out from a remote corner of my mind walked a little girl. Curly brown hair several shades lighter than mine. The ruffles on her powder-pink spring dress flounced as her legs worked busily, the sunshine making her sparkly miniature Converses twinkle. Her creamy skin was like rose petals. My own outfit was softer now, light chiffon in a paisley pattern of blues and greens and whites, flowing like water around my arms and hips. I cradled her hand in mine as we walked on the endless trails down by Lady Bird Lake. Big spreading live oaks formed canopies of dappled shade as we strolled along the manicured gravel trails. Suddenly, my daughter pointed and giggled, her blue eyes shining in delight, as an early monarch butterfly came to pay us a visit, flitting around our heads before it went off in search of the pink and white milkweed that would be its nursery...

In an instant, I was jerked back to reality. Dr. Babymaker was speaking to me again. Seeing the distraught look on my face, his rumbling voice tried to be reassuring. "Of course, results vary mother to mother. You may still have a chance at a healthy pregnancy, but we'll need more tests to find out."

I was deflated—but not defeated. I marveled at the whole process of bringing a child into the world, and I couldn't wait to experience it for myself. It was God's finest miracle. My inner voice was trying to tell me something. I would not lose hope. I was not ready to let my little girl go. She was mine. I knew I must become a mother.

No matter the cost.

Steady yourself, Cheri, I thought to myself, girding my loins. *You can do this.*

"Okay, Dr. Babymaker," I said, determination in my voice, "what's it going to take to get me pregnant?"

Inwardly, other thoughts waged an epic battle in my head like mortar shells hitting scorched earth. One question beat down the others to claim the hill of my attention.

How the hell did I get here?

CHAPTER 2

THE MESSAGES OF CHILDHOOD

I CRAWLED ACROSS THE BEDROOM FLOOR, THE NIGHT-mare still fresh and causing my young heart to race. The blue and green shag carpet was both a comfort and a bane as it silenced my creeping but also gave my tender knees slight rug burns. The tall pile that swayed every which way in the dim light reminded me of the harmless grass in my expansive backyard. And yet, it was as if I was crawling through the jungle like the soldiers I'd seen on the evening news. I did not want to wake my father, whose loud, rumbling snores made him sound like a hibernating bear. At six-foot-one and 230 pounds, my father was imposing even when he slept.

My mother opened her eyes as I found my way to her side of the bed and gently tapped my tiny fingers on her shoulder. She didn't complain or seem upset with me. She slid out from beneath the olive-green and beige bedspread, took me by the hand and helped me up. Then, she calmly walked me back to my darkened bedroom.

In the corner sat an old wooden rocking chair painted light blue with animal appliques on it, just visible in the soft moonlight coming through the window. As if I was a baby again, she picked me up and cradled me in her arms, gathering my coltish legs up so they wouldn't dangle too far over the edge of the armrests. I was six and growing like a weed. My mother began to sing. Soft strains of "You Are My Sunshine" hummed up from her breast where my head lay... *I love you.* Her heartbeat and the rhythm of the song melded together with the melodic creaking of the chair as she rocked back and forth, back and forth, until I fell asleep.

In that moment, despite the lingering shadows of my fear, I felt warm, safe, and protected. It's my earliest memory of pure love and showed me the kind of mother I wanted to be.

We lived in a classic Dutch Colonial house in an upscale suburb of Columbus, Ohio, known as Upper Arlington. The house was huge for the 1970s and smelled like it'd been around for two hundred years. Three stories of square footage but only one full bathroom. Hand-me-down oak furniture graced wallpapered and faux wood paneled rooms with nondescript olive-green and blue artwork. A pale yellow velvet couch dominated the formal living room in a "sit on me if you dare" kind of way. It was the only fancy piece of furniture my parents owned, and it was reserved for "adults only."

Like most marital unions born in the 1960s, my parents' marriage was very traditional. My grandmother didn't give my mother a middle name because she theorized it would become obsolete when she got married. It was expected that her maiden name would become her middle name when she took her husband's name for her last. My mother had been groomed from birth to be a dutiful housewife and mother. She had studied home economics in college to prepare herself to be the "good wife" and got the coveted MRS degree—she was now MRS. Bergeron.

She cooked, cleaned, and kept the house immaculate while her husband worked six days a week in a nine-to-five job as an HR manager for the oil and gas industry. When my brother and I were born a couple years later, she poured herself into her role as caregiver. Summer days at the pool, afternoons at the library, and winter mornings dancing around the house to Bobby Sherman and playing cards as we sat on heated floor vents. In many ways my childhood was idyllic. When I played house with my little friends, the example of motherhood I imitated was hers.

My brother and I were normal siblings. At least, that's what I told myself. We were born fourteen months apart, and my mom says we were raised like twins because Phillip could barely walk when I was born. My arrival must have stolen the attention away from his toddler utopia, and it seemed to me he never got over that first blush of sibling jealousy.

My brother didn't play with me often, but when he did, he liked to "roughhouse." He'd pin my body down and put both his hands over my mouth and nose so I couldn't breathe. Only when I started to turn blue and struggle in panic would he ease up. Then he would do it again. Other times, he'd ambush me while I was playing with my Barbies. I'd be planning a trip to Malibu one moment and be crushed by a squirming tangle of boy limbs the next. Occasionally, I would get a good shot in, but I always lost the battle. I complained to my parents, but they seemed disinterested in what they saw as harmless sibling squabbles. As we stepped into adolescence and I gained some curves, my brother's friends often wanted to spend time in my company rather than his, which seemed to outrage him. I only wanted my brother to accept me, but I often felt powerless to stop the growing divide between us.

If my relationship with Phillip was rocky, the one with my father was a granite wall. I remember as a little girl feeling uncomfortable riding in the car alone with him because I couldn't take the awkward silence between us, let alone the secondhand cigarette smoke. I know he tried to take an interest in the things that I was doing, like the time he took me out for a special father-daughter dinner or attended the occasional softball game, but any closeness achieved in those moments didn't last. I often thought I was more of an annoyance to him than anything else.

As I got older, I felt the weight of my father's judgment. For starters, he wasn't fond of the way I dressed. It was the era of Madonna, and I'd bought a coveted pink miniskirt. I wore it with those white fold-down ankle socks with the band of lace around the hem that flirted with the top of my black kitten heels just so. I'd pose in front of my full-length bedroom mirror, pointing one toe into the floor as I cocked one knee and put my opposing hand on my hip as I twirled the long pink pearls that grazed my lacy pink top. A curled-out side ponytail held with a pink pom-pom fuzzy scrunchie bobbed every time I tilted my head, striking a pose like I'd seen in the music videos. I thought it was one of my best looks.

My father hated it.

I didn't know or suspect what men and women did together behind closed doors, but I was old enough at thirteen to realize I could attract male attention if I looked a certain way. I started to taste the kind of power women could wield even if they were physically weaker than men. I liked how that power felt.

At the age of fourteen, we moved to Plano, Texas, where the oil and gas industry was booming. In Plano, a burgeoning suburban sprawl was emerging out of the desolate, flat farmland that had been owned by a small group of Texas families for generations. Fast-built, newly constructed houses that looked like barns adorned with scrawny stick trees were popping up amid the pastures of horses and cows as an estimated fourteen hundred new families moved into the area each month. Unlike the close-knit community of Upper Arlington where everyone knew everyone else and a new kid in school was rare and exciting, new classmates were descending on my school in droves. There was nothing special about being the new kid there. Nothing about the place felt like home.

I was at that awkward age when self-esteem is fragile, and a girl starts to figure out how boys see her. A sixteen-year-old boy from school, whom I'd been hanging out with for a few weeks, asked if I wanted to go for a joy ride on the nearby country roads, one of the few pastimes open to teenagers in Plano. A too-loud rendition of Bon Jovi's "Runaway" and a tight turn taken too fast ended with us getting stuck in a ditch along one of the narrow, ill-kept gravel roads. With no cell phones, we had to walk a distance to a nearby house to call his parents to come pick us up.

By the time I got home, the sun had already set. "Who is this boy?" my father demanded. I could smell the scotch on his breath from across the room and I knew I was in for it. "What were you doing with him?" He didn't even ask if I was okay after wrecking in a ditch. He wanted to know if I had been fooling around. *Does he see me at all?*

My dad and I never talked about boys—that was my mother's job. He used to call boys who looked at me "hairy-legged SOBs," and that was the extent of his sex education. He never told me outright the boys were the problem, not me. He never acted like he was afraid *for* me. Instead, he acted like he was afraid *of* me. Of what I might do to tarnish myself and the family's good name.

Standing just inside the doorway of our house in Plano in my soiled pink miniskirt, his words assumed the worst of me. Like I'd bought a miniskirt and turned into Jezebel. A sour taste made its way up the back of my tightened throat. I think it was a combination of betrayal and heartbreak.

"Don't listen to him," my mother said as she tucked me into bed that night, soothing the sting of my father's criticism. "You are beautiful both inside and out, and I know that you didn't do anything wrong." My mother saw the real me and gave me unconditional love. It would be enough to get me through the hard times with my father.

The only time my mother ever raised her voice to my father was when she was defending me or my brother. She would go into full-fledged Mama Bear mode to protect her cubs. Her only other streak of independence came from her home-based business selling fabric to other women. She'd get shipments of swatches and women would come to the house to look them over. This was still the era when many women made clothing for themselves and their children. If they liked what they saw, they'd order full bolts through my mother. It was the textile version of the Tupperware and Mary Kay parties that would become popular among suburban housewives in the '80s and '90s. My mother was good at sales because she genuinely cared about her clients' happiness. She excelled at management because she loved seeing her protégés advance. She became a kind of regional manager in a cottage industry of women entrepreneurs. But her ambitions produced a noticeable tension between her and my father.

"Where the hell do you want to go?" My father's voice boomed from the kitchen one evening. My brother and I were sitting at the top of the stairs. We had been trained that the first hour my father was home was "adult time" and children were to be rarely seen and never heard. I tiptoed down the stairs until I was close enough to hear my parents' conversation in the kitchen. Peeking around the wall, careful that I wasn't in anyone's line of sight, I could see my father's highball of gin, mostly empty on the counter.

"It's the Women Leaders in Business dinner," murmured my mother. Whenever my father's tone rose, my mother's would fall, as if she could balance his higher volume and not alert the children upstairs to their argument.

"So it's a bunch of women getting together to eat, drink, gossip, and neglect their families?" he said, going on the attack.

"No, but—"

"I work hard six days a week. The last thing I need is to come home at the end of a long day and pay for you to hang out with your friends at a social event disguised as business," he raged. I jumped as I heard a loud clatter. He'd dumped more ice cubes in his glass and was filling it up again.

"I have my own money," she said, a thread of confidence in her voice. "Besides, it's only ten dollars." She was trying her best to be conciliatory, hoping he would stand down. "Honey, I'm good at this job. I think I can really grow this business. I can make some important connections at this dinner."

He must have sensed her growing strength because he was quick to bat it down again. He gathered his tall frame and loomed over her. "So, I'll be responsible for feeding the kids while you're cavorting around town?" he sneered. "This pastime of yours is turning out to be more trouble than it's worth." Despite her soothing tone, his voice was getting louder and more hostile by the minute. She practically whispered her next words.

"Dinner's made and the kids have been fed," she said calmly. "I'll be home to put the children to bed. You won't have to do anything." She had planned everything perfectly to allay any objection.

"You're not going and that's final!" my father roared.

I heard the first floor bathroom door open and slam shut. Thirty seconds later, I could hear my mother's business heels clicking on the linoleum as she took the food she'd prepped earlier that day out of the refrigerator to start dinner.

My seven-year-old heart filled with an intense anger toward my father. The resentment built every time he belittled her abilities or used money against her. That night, my wrath left me clenching my fists, the nails biting into the flesh of my palm so the pain would distract me from doing something righteous that, even as a child, I knew was stupid. Let's face it, I had even less power than my mother. A conviction started to take hold of me. *No man would ever control me that way…never ever.*

I silently slipped to my bedroom, opening and shutting the door as quietly as I could. I turned the knob slowly—right to open, left to close—so no click would sound when it shut. Alone, I sat on my bed as angry tears started to slide down my cheeks and I buried my sobs in my pillow.

It seemed like a lifetime, but it was probably only minutes before I heard my door open and close, just as softly as I'd done it a few minutes before. The bed dipped as my mother sat down next to me. "Don't cry, Cheri," she said, her voice still miraculously calm. She tucked the lavender and white floral afghan she'd made for me around my shaking body and laid a warm hand on my shoulder. "Everything will be okay."

I took a deep breath and smelled the faint scent of Shalimar, her favorite perfume. The "Mommy smell," as I called it. I started to relax. "I love you, Mommy," I said. "You are the best mommy in the whole world."

"I love you, too, Sunshine," she said. "You deserve the very best."

Throughout the years of my childhood, my mother gave me a sense of safety to balance out my father's volatility. I'm not entirely sure where her serenity came from, but it might have had something to do with her religious beliefs. My mother had an abiding faith, which made me curious. Mom would take us to church while my father stayed at home to watch golf. Since he worked six days a week, Sunday was his only day of rest. There was no way he was going to spend it sitting silently in a church wearing a coat and tie.

My early experience of church was mixed. While I had fun doing youth activities with my friends, I didn't see many examples of spiritual growth or virtue. People gossiped. People had affairs. People judged and rejected each other. So what was different about church than any other place? I did my duty and fulfilled my responsibilities as a youth leader but was happy to cast all that aside when I went off to college. I figured, if my heavenly Father was anything like my earthly father, I'd take a pass.

These were the messages of my childhood. In simplistic terms, I learned that women were nurturing, selfless, and loving; men were domineering, selfish, and scary. I wasn't even sure I could trust God based on what I'd seen in His church.

One lesson stood out above them all. I would never let another man have power over me again. I now knew their secret. Their power was a double-barred cage made from muscle and money.

I couldn't get the muscle, but I'd be damned if I wouldn't get the money.

CHAPTER 3

MARRIED TO MY CAREER

"WOULD YOU CARE FOR ANOTHER CABERNET, MS. Bergeron?"

I glanced up from the latest *People* magazine I was thumbing through to see Desiree, the flight attendant, smiling down at me. Her perfect white teeth peeked from behind her mauve lipstick just enough to teeter on the line between pretty and sexy. She looked sharp in her tailored American Airlines uniform, dressed in a dark navy blazer, white shirt, and tight navy skirt with a red scarf tied at her neck. Her long blond hair was pulled up neatly in a bun. Everything about Desiree exuded the feeling of elegance—the kind of elegance that you'd expect in business class on an international flight to Paris.

"Yes, thank you, Desiree," I responded, raising my glass to make it easier for her to pour. It was all a bit surreal. Here I was at the age of twenty-six, headed to Paris on my first European business trip. The flight was over six hours from O'Hare to Charles de Gaulle, so my employer let me fly in business class.

It was my first job. I'd only graduated college with my BA in marketing six months earlier. It was a dream come true, getting a marketing specialist position in an established tech company that made hardware and software for data centers around the world. My salary of $28,000 a year was barely enough to get by on Northern California's soul-crushing cost of living, but to me it felt like a fortune. Now, I was on my way to visit customers with our international distributors to introduce our new product line in Europe.

In the pre-9/11 era, international travel was simpler, less stressful, and far more luxurious. I marveled at the comfort of the leather seats that almost fully reclined. I felt like a kid in a candy store when Desiree presented me with my own personal movie player and noise-canceling headphones. I know it's commonplace now, but keep in mind this was before search engines and cell phones. In 1995, data was stored on floppy drives and the industry was buzzing about this new thing called the World Wide Web. One of the trappings of the high-tech mogul I aspired to be was a shiny new Palm Pilot—one of the first personal digital assistant devices on the market—with a whopping 512 kb memory that was charged using three AAA batteries. Having the ability to watch movies on demand from my own seat felt like something straight out of *Lifestyles of the Rich and Famous*.

It felt surreal when Desiree presented me with my own leather toiletry bag containing toothbrush and toothpaste, socks, earplugs, and a sleep mask. I tried to play it cool as I gazed at the printed menu detailing the dinner and breakfast offerings. There were snacks to be enjoyed in between meals, and, delight of delights, adult beverage options I could order throughout the flight. Unlimited food, fine wine, and spirits. *What more could a working girl want?* I tried hard to maintain my professional composure and not let on to the other business-class passengers that this was all new to me and I was giddy as a schoolgirl. This was a level of glamour I'd never experienced in my modest middle-class Midwestern upbringing.

I could get used to this.

I went back to my magazine as the second glass of Cabernet kicked in. Meryl Streep, it turned out, just gave birth to her third child at forty-two. "Wow," I thought, "she figured out a way to have it all!" I recalled recent news that Susan Sarandon delivered her son at forty-five. "I've got time," I told myself, studying my smooth manicured hand holding the pages. "I can build my career before building a family."

We landed at Charles de Gaulle airport early on Sunday morning. I had the rest of the day to recuperate before my meetings started on Monday, so I decided to take a walk and absorb the sights. I was now a world traveler, so I should see and enjoy that world. It was a sunny day in April and Paris overflowed with life. The linden trees burst with delicate blooms and the meticulously landscaped gardens competed to show the most shades of green. Everywhere I felt the weight of history, of millions of lives having walked the same cobblestone paths I now walked. How fortunate was I that someone was paying me to see all this beauty? That I was lucky enough to have a job that gave me these life-changing opportunities?

I decided to rest and have coffee at a quaint little café. Cafés are classically French—English even stole the word *café* from the French language—and my trip to Paris wouldn't be complete without indulging in that cultural whimsy. Sitting alone at my tiny wrought iron bistro table, I noticed a couple beside me, about my age, with a three-year-old girl flouncing around their table. The little girl was striking. Blue eyes laughed from her round, porcelain face and curly brown hair haloed her head.

The mother attempted to keep this angel amused so the parents could enjoy their coffee and croissants before the girl's curiosity irritated the adults at surrounding tables. She was at the age where everyone was just a friend she hadn't met yet.

"Bonjour, Mademoiselle!" she squealed at me, tottering over, hands outstretched, jam smeared on her left cheek. "Etes-vous Americain?"

"Bonjour, aussi," I laughed, holding out my hand to catch her if she fell. "Oui, je suis Americain," I said, impressed by my miraculous recall of seventh-grade French class. I guess my white tennis shoes and blue jeans had given me away as a non-Parisian.

"Pardonne-moi, mademoiselle!" the mother gasped, scooping up the toddler just before her buttery fingers made contact with my silk blouse. She grinned ruefully at me, woman to woman, and took the cherub back to their table to bounce on her lap. It had only been a moment, but I somehow felt bereft.

Occasionally, during my years of travel, a glimpse of a different life would seep into my present reality. This was one of the first. Sitting next to this harried but happy couple, I wondered what life would be like if I had a family of my own. I didn't entertain the thought for long because it filled me with anxiety, so much so that I quickly got up and left, my coffee cup still half full.

I had work to do, anyway, to prepare for tomorrow.

In French, the name *Cheri* translates as a term of endearment, something like "honey," "baby," or "darling." Suffice it to say, when you are the youngest person in the boardroom, the only person who doesn't speak French, the only woman, and your name is the equivalent of Boom Boom L'Roux, playing hardball with a bunch of chauvinistic, fortysomething Frenchmen poses a challenge. "Make sure you wear a short skirt to the meeting," my French distributor told me. So, of course, I wore pants.

We were negotiating pricing and I'd thrown our final number out. I laid my hands, palms flat, on the gleaming black onyx conference table and slowly made eye contact with all of them. These middle-aged men clad in gray pinstriped suits smelling of cigarettes and a cacophony of expensive cologne didn't hold my gaze for long. Instead, they turned to the distributor standing to my right and started talking back and forth with him in French. Essentially, they were talking behind my back right in front of me.

Their boyish games did not impress me. "Gentlemen." My tone sharp, I paused, straightening all of my five-foot-nine-inch frame, until the room quieted and all eyes were on me. "If we're going to have this meeting, we *will all* converse in English. This is our best offer, and I advise you to take it." On the inside, I felt like I was about to pee my pants, but I didn't flinch. I had the power, and I wasn't going to hand it over to these French jerks. I was the voice of the company coming all the way from the US, and we were going to do this my way.

And we did.

The Paris trip was ultimately successful, in no small part because I threw my proverbial dick on the table at just the right moment. That kind of power is heady stuff, especially for a girl who'd spent her childhood getting an education in how women were kept powerless. The little girl I'd seen at the café faded from my consciousness as I reveled in my ability to outthink, outperform, and out-negotiate a room full of men with decades more business experience than me.

My win was cause to celebrate. I felt like a hero returning from battle as I gleefully purchased a Hermès scarf and Gucci purse in the best stores on the Champs Elysees. They were my spoils of war. From that day forward, I would use my skill and determination to claim the power and prestige that I deserved. I would be in the position to call the shots and never allow myself to be controlled. It was a potent drug. And I wanted more.

Perhaps a small part of me felt it was my responsibility to go as far as my intellect and drive would take me. Growing up in the 1980s, the feminists who came before me had paved the way for me to become whatever I wanted. There was an unspoken obligation to fulfill the destiny they had fought for. Many of the women that I worked with reinforced that idea, too. The mentor at my first job, a woman named Merida, was vice president of sales and marketing. Most of the company worked for her in one way or another. And though she reported to a male CEO, the product and service people all knew Merida was in charge. I looked up to her. She had traveled far and wide, made her mark in a man's world, and enjoyed tremendous financial success. In her late thirties, she decided she wanted a child. Just like that, it seemed, she was pregnant. She kept her position but decided to take a break from traveling. It was a golden opportunity and I took it, earning my stripes as her apprentice, starting with the pivotal negotiation in Paris.

The years flew by quickly. Focused on my career and the goal of being independent, I always seemed to find another hill to climb. Unlike the world of personal relationships, there was no stigma attached to changing it up every two or three years. In fact, it was expected. Each job move rewarded me with a more prestigious title and better pay as I climbed up each rung on the corporate ladder.

Ten years into my career, I joined a sexy software company that was the darling of Silicon Valley. Their stock was rising rapidly, which meant the money, fun, and alcohol flowed freely.

Our products were cutting edge and our customers loved us. Every day felt like another victory celebration, another notch on our belt. I was responsible for managing some of the company's largest technology partnerships.

"I want you to go to Austin," Jack, my boss, told me one day. Most of the people on Jack's team were young, attractive women, and he liked it that way. The #MeToo generation would consider him a bit too handsy—for instance, he had a habit of massaging his team's shoulders in stressful situations—but overall, he was a good guy who made sure we had the support and opportunities necessary to excel in our jobs. "Teverone is having their annual user conference next week. I need you there to press the flesh and show our support."

I was very familiar with Teverone. Their products integrated with ours. My job was to work with them to drive large deals for our joint solution. Teverone was another hot commodity in our industry. The next week I was on a plane to their headquarters in Austin.

Going back to Texas brought mixed feelings. I'd gotten out of Plano, the land of stick trees, big cows, and even bigger hair, during my college years. My parents still lived in Houston, which to me wasn't much of an improvement from Plano. I thought Houston was nothing more than a flat hillbilly sprawl full of antiquated ideas and an endless maze of highways that flooded with each Texas rainstorm. It got so hot and muggy in the summer that some buildings advertised underground tunnels between the front door and the parking garage to entice high-end tenants. Look, you won't sweat on your Armani walking from your car! No way in hell I would live there.

I wasn't sure how I would feel going back to the Lone Star State. *Would it be the same even though I had changed?* I was in for a shock.

Austin wasn't anything like the small Central Texas city I remembered from my youth. Unlike much of Texas that's oppressively dry and flat, Austin had an abundance of rolling hills and lakes. It sat on the edge of the Balcones, an area that had been cracked open by the restless earth long ago, lifting up white limestone slabs of ancient seabeds littered with prehistoric shells from the time of the dinosaurs. During the taxi ride on the way to the hotel, I was struck by how the town had changed—it had grown up and become more cosmopolitan. It had skyscrapers, designer boutiques, and an undeniable cool factor. *How had I been so wrong about this place?*

The conference was held at an upscale hotel in the Arboretum, which was known as the high-end shopping area. The event was quite a production—lights, video, studio-quality sound, and a professional stage. Impressive. The day was filled with talks from Teverone's executives, who attempted to channel Steve Jobs to put the audience under their spell of optimism and prosperity. Even though I was wise to their tactics, I felt myself being drawn into their orbit.

The day ended with a huge gala. The hotel ballroom had been transformed into a Vegas-like casino. The room flowed with sequined gowns and tuxedos juxtaposed with groups of people in jeans and T-shirts with an antiestablishment "developers rule the world" vibe written all over them. Phil Collins and his band played "In the Air Tonight" on the main stage and were putting on one hell of a show. Food stations featuring delicacies from five-star restaurants were everywhere, including the best sushi, steak, seafood, pasta, and desserts that money could buy—a virtual world tour of culinary delights. It was a scene that embodied the trappings of success and excess that dominated the 1990s high-tech industry.

I scanned the room until I saw a familiar face. Peter was at a craps table with an open fifth of vodka stationed by his right hand. He was a vice president at Teverone and one of their earliest employees. Power flowed from him like water, much like his money, and all the hot twentysomething females at the company fawned over him. My company skirted propriety from time to time when it came to workplace relationships. Teverone had long since buried propriety under a mountain of lacy thongs.

Per usual, Peter was flanked by two beautiful women with necklines down-to-there and short skirts up to their jing jangs. While the money being gambled was fake, the sexual energy among the three was very real. He'd probably be taking both women back to his hotel room that night, never mind that Peter was married. What happened at a Teverone party, stayed at a Teverone party. I must admit, I wasn't completely turned off by this flavor of opulent, debauched freedom. I felt like I was in a Martin Scorsese movie, and I was all about playing the confident heroine in my black velvet off-the-shoulder Oscar de la Renta dress and messy updo.

"Looks like you're winning," I said to Peter as I glided up to the craps table on ridiculously high Jimmy Choo heels.

"Damn right, I am!" crowed Peter. "I'm on a roll. Keep me company, would ya?"

It looked like Peter didn't need any more company, but I smelled an opportunity that had nothing to do with plunging necklines and short skirts. "Sure," I said, carefully positioning myself to watch while still maintaining an arm's length between us.

Peter commanded the table and made one winning roll after another. After twenty minutes of racking in a copious amount of chips, he turned to me and said, "Let's go get a drink." I agreed and Peter whispered in the ear of one of his companions and patted the other one on her backside. "I'll catch up with you ladies later," he assured them. "I need to talk some business with Cheri."

Peter walked up to the bar and grabbed two shot glasses and guided me to an empty table in the midst of all the madness. Thankfully, there were no chairs for the high cocktail tables, so I didn't have to take the chance of embarrassing myself by trying to slide onto a stool in a dress with a side slit up to the thigh. "So, Cheri, how are you liking the conference?" he asked slowly, glancing at me as he poured two shots of Ciroc vodka from the bottle he'd snagged from the craps table as we left.

"It's incredible, Peter," I said. "You've really got something special here. I loved it when your customers got on the main stage singing the company's praises. Really powerful stuff. Seems like Teverone is setting the pace for the entire industry."

Peter leaned closer to me and paused for what felt like forever. I wondered for a moment if he was too drunk to compose a coherent thought. "Cheri, let me be frank," he started. I smelled the alcohol on his breath, stronger somehow than the smell of the liquor in my glass. The air left my lungs. "I like your style. We need someone like you to manage our partnerships. What would it take to get you to come work for me? Any chance you would move to Austin?"

That…wasn't what I thought he was going to say. *Thank God, he wasn't making a play to get me into bed.* Relief gave way to surprise—and interest. I never envisioned myself moving back to Texas, but Austin had opened my eyes to a side of the state that I never knew existed. These people were cultured, savvy, and liberal-minded. Most tempting of all, they were talented and successful.

Still, I hesitated. "Peter, I'm flattered. Let me think on it for a bit. I've never considered leaving Silicon Valley. I just bought my condo a year ago."

"Oh, come on, Cheri," he said, his Brooklyn accent coming out stronger the more he drank. "I know Austin's not California, but I'll make it worth your while." Peter wasn't going to take no for an answer. As I well knew, he was used to getting what he wanted. "Let me get an offer to you. We'll handle all your move preparations. You won't have to lift a finger. Give me a week, and then let's talk. In the meantime, let's drink to a successful future together." He tilted his glass toward me in a toast, as if to seal the deal.

I don't do hard liquor and definitely not shots, but I knew better than to refuse Peter. I downed the Ciroc like a pro. I'd learned in Paris long ago to never back down from a challenge, especially from a man in a position of authority. Not if I wanted to maintain respect.

Peter wasn't kidding. Five days later, I had an offer I couldn't refuse in hand—a senior director title that came with benefits and perks galore, plus an obscene amount of money. They would sell my condo (at no expense to me), pack up all my belongings, arrange for my car to be transported from California, and pay a sizable signing bonus. Six weeks later, I was an Austinite.

CHAPTER 4

HOMECOMING

MY DECISION TO MOVE TO AUSTIN WASN'T JUST ABOUT the job.

I'd longed for the stability of friends, family, and a reasonable cost of living for quite some time. But if I was really honest with myself, the hole I was looking to fill was much bigger. For all the success achieved in my career, it felt like something was missing. Something with meaning. Something substantive in a way my job could never give me. I'd caught a glimpse of it when I dated men who had kids. None of them felt right, but a vague, distant message resonated in my soul. *You are meant to be a mother.* I'm not sure I believed it, but the voice was definitely there and growing louder with every passing week. Month. Year.

Moving back to Texas would be a mixed bag. My brother lived in the Houston area along with my parents. He was on his third child. "When are you going to settle down and have kids?" he asked me at almost every holiday gathering. My brother met his wife, a devout Catholic and kindergarten teacher, when he was twenty-one and married her a couple years later. He converted to Catholicism and their first child arrived around their first wedding anniversary. They had a modest new-build house in a remote suburb about an hour south of downtown. Theirs was the old school, traditional type of marriage similar to my parents'. In my eyes, they lived on a completely different planet than me. I didn't know how to relate to someone my age who was often covered in baby vomit.

I was more drawn to talking to my dad and brother about business rather than entertaining an infant rolling around on the floor. My business exploits finally gave us something in common to talk about. Despite my career success, I still sought their approval and validation. I wanted them to see me for the savvy businesswoman I had become. I wanted them to tell me I was doing a good job. And my dad did notice. He marveled at how fast I was ascending in the business world and lived vicariously through all my professional adventures. I could tell he was proud of me.

But my brother hadn't changed his stripes. "I think Mom and Victoria could use some help in the kitchen," he said one February weekend as I tried to strike up a conversation about his career. "Hey, Dad, let's go outside and get some fresh air. March Madness is coming up and we need to put together our brackets." The message was clear as they got up and headed out to the back patio. I would never be welcomed into their boy's club, no matter how hard I tried. To them, there was only one mold in which women could fit and I refused to be put into it.

I bought my first house shortly after moving to Austin. Eighteen-hundred square feet with a yard and a beautiful view of Hill Country greenbelt that was all mine! Slowly, I got settled into the city and continued my personal pursuits, which included travel, socializing, and an old love of mine from college, country western dancing. All in all, I was at the top of my game and thought I'd made the right decision. I was living life on my own terms.

Tickling the back of my mind, though, was something else. An impulse that had nothing to do with advancing my career or the glamor that came with it. I'd been racing for success for over a decade by this point. I was only in my early thirties, but I felt tired. A subtle ache that I could ignore when the day-to-day demands of work were inundating me but couldn't be silenced in the quiet moments that came in the middle of the night. The feeling ate away at my heart. Subconsciously, I was putting pieces in place that would make a home for the family that would make all my efforts worthwhile. How that family would look was still just echoes of a dream.

Sunlight blinded my eyes as I twirled around, my hand reflexively reaching up to restore my vision. The air was filled with loud music, indistinct chatter, and the delighted shrieks of children. I smiled as a person dressed in a mouse costume waved at me as I walked by. My mouth watered as the aroma of French fries and hot dogs floated on a breeze tinged with salty air and sunscreen. I could hear the unmistakable rumble of a vintage wooden roller coaster, the sound growing louder, then softer as it chugged up steep inclines before plunging over the brinks with a roar. Suddenly, I realized that I was on the Santa Cruz boardwalk, a place I had visited many times before. I searched through the throng of sun-kissed faces, hoping to find one familiar to me. *Who am I looking for?*

"Mommy!" a child yelled for his mother near me.

The realization bloomed in my breast like the faint hum of

my mother's singing. I was looking for my child. *My child.* She had to be somewhere nearby.

I began to walk forward, looking for her in every little face I came across. At first, I wasn't worried and my search was slow and casual. Soon, however, it struck me that I was in a heaving swell of people and she was nowhere in sight. There were teenagers huddled in groups, families going from ride to ride, and children running everywhere. As my eyes darted through the crowd, my panic began to rise.

"Where are you?" I murmured to myself, threading through the crush of strollers and strangers. My legs were beginning to ache but before I could give in and sink to the ground, I heard a giggle. I knew that sound.

A little girl with fair skin, light brown curly hair, and blue eyes stood a dozen feet away from me. She looked straight at me and then smiled, big and wide and joyful. A smile that would make buds want to blossom and butterflies dance. My panic ran out of me into the pavement below my feet. I grinned back at the little girl and waved, then held out my hand for her to take it.

"Mommy!" she squealed, reaching. But suddenly, she twirled around and began running in the opposite direction, her frilly dress bobbing across the ocean of humanity.

"Wait for me! Sweet girl, come back!" I called out. I wanted to call her name but I was lost for words—why couldn't I think of her name?

My heart raced. I started to run even though I couldn't feel my legs. She was getting farther and farther away. Tears streamed down my face as I dodged colorfully dressed fairgoers, carnies hawking cheap stuffed animals as game prizes, and food vendors tempting passers-by with every state-fair-grade junk food you could think of. None of it looked fun anymore.

I ran as fast as I could, but my little girl always kept just out of reach.

I was losing her.

"Please, stop!" I sobbed, as I dropped to the litter-strewn ground in exhaustion, the sun beating down on me mercilessly. I couldn't catch my breath. It felt like I was drowning.

Perhaps I am...

I woke up with a start. The fantasy aroma of French fries gave way to the strong scent of coffee. The air was cool and profoundly silent. My body shuddered, catching the attention of others. I avoided eye contact and smoothed my hair to regain my composure. The dream felt so real.

The room was filled with men, which was no surprise. As an executive at my company, I was often the only woman in the room. It was lonely and isolating, but I'd long since learned to deal with it. In a few short years after moving to Austin, I had risen through the ranks and was now the vice president of marketing at a billion-dollar company.

A well-dressed man that I didn't know stood at the front of the room. He looked fiftyish with salt-and-pepper hair and silver-rimmed glasses. Never a good omen to see a stranger at a leadership meeting on short notice. A pit immediately formed in my stomach. The sunny day of my dream was replaced by gloom and doom, which was a feat given the bright fluorescent lights that pervaded our modern office space. I was anxious, waiting for everything to start. The second I stepped into the office we were called into the executive boardroom for an emergency meeting. It was the last thing I expected on a Monday morning.

Like most of those in the room, I didn't know what the meeting was about. It wasn't until the well-dressed man started to speak that we learned everything was about to change.

"Alright, everyone, thank you for joining this meeting on short notice," the man said. "For those of you who don't know me, my name is Douglas Pennymaker, and I sit on the board of directors." He paused for dramatic effect, looking around the room. "As you are aware, the company has faced a number of challenges in repositioning our solutions." He received collective nods. "And because of that, we are going to be doing some restructuring."

I bit my tongue. I knew "restructuring" meant that heads were going to roll.

"The company needs to go in a different direction. Today, we announce Justin Farethewell, chief executive officer, and Ernest Whisperwind, chief marketing officer, are leaving the company. Effective immediately, Frederick Powerlust will be assuming the role of interim CEO. I'll turn the floor over to Frederick."

A shiver went down my spine. Frederick was known for being smart, arrogant, and ruthless. He was a win-at-any-cost kind of guy who was feared by many and liked by very few. Everything for him began and ended at the bottom line. I got an uneasy feeling when I was around him and sensed deep down he couldn't be trusted.

Dressed in a meticulously tailored sharkskin Italian suit, Frederick slunk to the front of the room. His raven hair was slicked back from his deeply receding hairline. His dark beady eyes penetrated every gaze that dared meet his. He reminded me of a weasel. Being around him made me remember never to let my guard down. In my view, Frederick was as vicious, bloodthirsty, and greedy as they came.

"I know this announcement comes as a surprise, but it's the right decision for the company," Frederick said somberly. "I want to thank Justin and Ernest for all their hard work and contributions. I'll be working with our board to make sure a swift action plan is put in place that will take us to the next level." His demeanor was cold and impersonal, completely void of compassion or empathy. It felt like the company was now being run by a Wall Street robot.

I let out a sigh, the weight of my dream still heavy on my mind. *No time for introspection*, I thought, shaking it off, *I need to focus on the job at hand.*

"We've got a lot of work ahead of us," Frederick went on. "I'm going to need your full focus and dedication. We need to step up the effort and get some real results. Let's make it happen, people!" Frederick finished, rubbing his hands together.

Ugh! Prepare for long hours ahead, Cheri.

It was horrible timing. I'd been thinking for a while that I needed to take a step back from my career if I really wanted to become a mother. I needed time for myself and the baby. Time to love each other. *But how could I do that now?*

Frederick was true to his word. We hit the ground running with another meeting that same week to set up our new company agenda. "If we are to be a great leadership team, we need to get to know each other," Frederick said. Well, this seemed to be getting off on the right foot.

We went around the room, sharing the hopes and dreams of our personal lives. One person was building their dream house. Another was taking his wife to Greece for their twenty-fifth wedding anniversary. Bart had a dream to finish his master's degree and fix up that classic Corvette. When Felix's turn came, you could almost see him puff out his chest underneath his Oxford suit. "My partner and I are looking forward to starting a family! We're in the process of having a child using a surrogate." He couldn't contain his huge grin. Felix was gay and had married the love of his life soon after it became legal.

"That's great, Felix!"

"You'll make a fine dad!"

"Congratulations, man!"

Everyone was quick to slap Felix on the back for stepping into the role of father. I knew that half of the guys in the room were homophobes, but they sure didn't let it show. Even if it was disingenuous, it was nice to see the other execs outwardly giving him support.

"You know what," I said, after everyone settled and my turn came, "I can relate to you, Felix, because I'm looking forward to starting a family, too. Gaston and I are trying to get pregnant! We've waited quite a while, and it feels like the time is finally right." I paused for the joyous reaction, but there was nothing but crickets. No excitement, just polite smiles and then everyone moved on. The awkward silence and lack of enthusiasm was palpable, and I suddenly felt naked and exposed. Were they concerned about my ability to both work and parent? No one seemed concerned about *Felix's* work-life balance. But Felix was also a man. I guess the expectation was that he wouldn't need to give up any time to be a parent. Or maybe it was fine because Felix wouldn't need maternity leave.

What's their deal? I thought, now distracted as the serious business of the meeting got underway. Plenty of women make career and family work. Ursula Burns made it work at Xerox, except it sounded like she had her kids earlier in her career. Mary Dillon, CEO of US Cellular, was able to manage younger kids and still do the top job. They proved that it could be done.

I wanted to have a career like my idols. Like my father. But I wanted to be a mother, too. If a woman wanted to be successful in business, did she need to sacrifice family? Couldn't those two things coexist? Couldn't the feminist image of Career Woman mesh with the traditional image of Loving Mother? Couldn't I have it all?

"Can I see you in my office?" Frederick said, pulling me aside after the meeting ended.

The unease from my peers haunted my steps as I followed Frederick. Now that I knew what I wanted to hold onto, I wouldn't let it go.

Frederick didn't waste time once he closed his office door behind us. "What the hell are you doing?" he asked bluntly.

"What do you mean?" I said. I feared I knew where he was going with this, but I needed him to spell it out for me.

"Did you really announce in a room full of executives that you have some kind of mommy complex? What do you think that does for your credibility?" he said accusingly. I felt my temperature rise and my face start to turn red.

"Are you suggesting that I'm not entitled to pursue a family the same way as Felix?"

"I'm saying you have now put everyone on notice that you're going to bail the second that you become barefoot and pregnant," he said bluntly.

"That's not fair, Frederick. I'm just starting to explore my options with fertility. Who knows how fast this will go, but I'm sure I'll have at least a year before I'd need to take some time off."

It was obvious that he wasn't happy for me.

"I didn't think you were the type to jump on the baby train," he commented, looking pointedly at me. I was speechless. I felt my mouth gape open like a fish. "I thought you would do more in life than settle for being a soccer mom," he continued, refusing to pull any punches.

"I beg your pardon?" I said, outraged, trying to digest his words without kicking him in the groin.

"Look, I get that your biological clock is ticking, but we're at a critical point in the company right now and I need everyone on my team giving a hundred and twenty percent. Family is going to have to take a back seat while we work to turn this ship around. You're not going to be much use to me if you are so hopped up on hormones that you lose your focus and objectivity."

There were a bajillion things wrong with his sexist rant, but I focused on the double standard. All of my male counterparts had families. *But I couldn't?*

"Frederick, this is really important to me. I'm sure we can figure this out. You have Veronica and your two kids. All the other guys have families, too. I just want what all of you have."

Frederick's harsh voice broke into my plea. "Cheri, enough. You made your choice when you set your sights on the executive boardroom. You're forty, right? Too late to turn back now."

Stunned, I looked around Frederick's office. A photo framed in gold sat at the front of his desk, a boy of about seven grinned as he knelt beside a soccer ball. Then there was his twelve-year-old beaming in her middle school cheerleader's outfit. I brought my eyes back to Frederick, his arms crossed and leaning on his desk. I wouldn't lose my little girl. *Not this time.*

"Fuck you, Frederick, I quit."

"You're going to regret this," he said in a thunderous tone.

"I doubt it," I quipped as I pivoted for the door.

I walked out of the room with zero regrets. I glanced at my slim Rolex. I'd be home in time for an early dinner with Gaston. My heels dug into the commercial grade carpet as I made my way back to my desk to clean it out. On second thought, maybe I'd go out to that new sushi spot alone. To decompress, of course. My brain still spun on what I had just done.

They had all lied to me. Every last one of them. My father was right. My male co-workers were all hairy-legged SOBs, but they didn't hide that fact. But all those women had lied, too. Streep, Sarandon, and all the others. I should have paid more attention when Merida stepped back to have her kid. With all my intelligence, I should have figured out the truth: I could have it all as a woman, I just couldn't have it all at the same time. Clearly, there weren't enough hours in the day to serve two masters, career and family, simultaneously.

Carrying a copy paper box filled with my belongings, I strode out the double glass doors of the building. It was late February once again, one of the bleakest months in Texas, when what little winter we got was in full force. The air was crisp and the trees were barren. I felt barren, too. *Had I just made a huge mistake?*

No, I reassured myself. I had done the right thing. In a couple weeks, my employer and colleagues would forget I was ever there. But motherhood would last. That's what I wanted more than anything. When presented with the final choice between high-powered career woman or high-touch mom, it was simple. I wanted to have the time and energy to hold my babies and sing "You Are My Sunshine" whenever they needed it.

I am coming, my sweet girl.

I needed to get myself to the fertility clinic with my husband, Gaston, and fast.

It didn't occur to me that, while I had just shaken off one fairy tale, I was still stuck in the throes of another.

CHAPTER 5

LOOKING FOR LOVE (IN ALL THE WRONG PLACES)

IT WAS A TYPICAL TUESDAY NIGHT, BUT I WAS EXCITED. IT was a beautiful Texas evening. The temperature was just right—warm enough you didn't need to wear a jacket but cool enough you didn't start sweating getting out of your car. For those acclimated to the Texas climate, that's a balmy seventy-eight degrees for most of America. It felt pleasantly like walking through warm milk. Baby-pink tinged the sky toward the Hill Country to the west and a light breeze carried the subtle scent of limestone and cedar. It was a gorgeous evening, and I wondered if Ruth had gotten us a good table.

We were meeting up for happy hour at Roaring Fork. I parked my car and placed my sunglasses on top of my head, looking at the restaurant with a smile. Austin is known for trendy eateries, and this was one of my favorites. Hip but classy, with local artists featured on the walls and the wine served in big-bellied Riedel glasses perfect for big red wines.

I pushed the heavy door open and paused to fill my lungs with the aroma of medium-rare tenderloin, grilled salmon, and old wood. I glanced across the dimly lit hall, looking for Ruth. Long rectangular cherrywood tables accompanied by bar-height red leather upholstered chairs graced the room. A wall of windows across the back revealed a large deck overlooking a man-made lake. Chatter from the growing mass of patrons drifted on the air accompanied by discernable strains from Austin singer Toni Price. *God, I love this place.*

Locating my friend Ruth, I waved and she grinned, then I wove my way to where she sat at the bar. Ruth and I had worked together at several tech companies over the years, and our collegial relationship quickly turned into a ride-or-die friendship. It wasn't long before I had a full glass of Jordan Cabernet in one hand, green chili pork in the other, and laughter on my lips.

Suddenly, a voice I almost recognized cut in from my left. "Tito's on the rocks." Before I could turn, the voice said, "Cheri, is that you?" I pursed my lips and turned my head to see who was interrupting our coveted girl time.

My irritation turned into a smile as I recognized the voice. "Shade, hi!" I said with a grin. It was Gaston's old classmate from college. We had met briefly at Gaston's birthday party about a year ago. "It's great to see you!"

"Mind if I pull up a chair with you, ladies?" he asked, snagging his tumbler from the bar as he handed his card over to start a tab.

I glanced at Ruth. In the space of ten seconds, our faces held a silent conversation. *Are you good with him staying?* Yeah, but only if you want to talk to him. *I'm okay if you're okay.* Then let's make this a party of three, but if you give me the high sign, I'll run interference so we can send him packing.

"Of course, Shade, pull up a stool."

We did the customary I-kinda-know-you cautious chitchat before we got into the topic of our families and what we were up to.

"How's Gaston?" Shade asked. *Was I imagining things, or was there a slight distaste in his voice?*

"He's doing well," I lied.

"Is he? I'm glad." Shade smiled, but the distaste had now turned to interest. Like a shark, he sensed blood in the water. "A while back it appeared to me like he was in a tough financial spot. I was worried he might end up bankrupt."

Even with all my boardroom experience, I couldn't help dropping my jaw for a moment at Shade's casually lobbed bombshell. I closed it quickly. I had no idea what Shade was talking about, but I wasn't going to let my ignorance show. And who knew if Shade was credible anyway? I barely knew him. I wasn't going to believe just anything. Gaston was my husband of four years. But I was going to figure out what he knew.

"No, he's doing fine," I insisted. Shade shrugged. I tried changing the subject. "We've been doing some work on the house. I'm hoping to make VP at my company soon, and we're talking about starting a family." I blathered on for ten minutes about any topic I could think of, hoping Shade would move on to a different subject.

"Wow, that's incredible, Cheri," he said when I finished. I felt my cheeks grow warm. It could have been the wine—or it could have been my perennial need to impress the men around me. *Stop that!* I told myself. Shade paused for a moment to motion the bartender to pour him another. "You know, I feel Gaston has always been lucky. He landed two beautiful, accomplished women when us poor schmucks can barely attract one. I wish I could get that kind of loyalty when I screw up."

"Screw up?" I asked casually. Now I was the one smelling blood.

"Yeah, didn't he tell you?" Shade said slowly, realizing he might be going out of bounds. "Honestly, I'm surprised Belle stayed with him so long. From my perspective, I was afraid he was headed for trouble with the IRS."

"Go on," I said calmly, twitching my fingers at Shade like I was some sitcom witch casting a truth-seeking spell. Hopefully, I didn't sound *too* calm. Extracting sensitive information from another savvy party was always a balancing act. I had no idea where the conversation was going, but I wanted it to get there. Meanwhile, Ruth was overly involved in sipping her drink. I think she just downed her second espresso cosmopolitan in twenty minutes. My heart was beating faster, and my senses heightened, burning through the alcohol I was drinking. I caught the subtle notes of Steve Miller Band's, "Take the Money and Run."

Shade swirled the ice cubes in his second glass of vodka on the rocks before he took a sip. "So, Gaston never mentioned why Belle left?" I silently shook my head in denial, feeling a little light-headed. Good thing the restaurant was dark and he wouldn't see my pale face.

"In my opinion, she figured out he wasn't the mover and shaker he'd made himself out to be. It seemed to me he played the role of a real estate hotshot, but there were rumors he got into some hot water with a few bogus write-offs." Shade hunched his shoulders slightly and visibly leaned toward me. He was on a roll now and seemed to relish the chance to gossip. "From what I could tell, Gaston came close to losing everything. Didn't he tell you about it?"

I gnawed at my lip. My lipstick was a hopeless cause at this point, but I didn't care. Gaston had only told me tales of glory from his time in Chicagoland.

"Wait." I raised my index finger in the air. "I'm sure that's not what happened." I tried to smile, missing lipstick and all.

"I'm sorry, Cheri. I thought Gaston must have told you this stuff. Jeez, I feel like a jerk dredging all of this ancient history up," he said in a tipsy slur. "He always seemed like such a nice guy. I guess all the high-stakes drama caught us a bit off guard." Shade's voice was low, but I sensed he was telling the truth. He had no reason to lie to me. "Please don't tell Gaston that we spoke about this. Frankly, the person I felt sorry for was Belle. In my view, she tried to save the relationship by moving with him to Texas, but I guess she took off soon after that for Seattle. Maybe she wanted a clean break."

Sweat started to form on my upper lip as I tried to find something to say that wouldn't make me look like a complete idiot. Several of the points that Shade made coincided with things Gaston had told me. Enough that I had a pretty good idea they were true. What I couldn't figure out is why he hadn't been up front with me about his past.

"So, how 'bout them Longhorns?" Ruth chimed in, coming to my rescue. God bless her, she knew when I needed backup.

I tuned out of Shade and Ruth's football conversation after that. My mind was numb as it flipped through all the heart-to-hearts I'd ever had with Gaston, searching for the red flags I'd missed.

But all my brain could do was run in circles. *Oh shit, had I married the wrong guy?*

Again?

I started dating Ari in my sophomore year at the Texas A&M business school, where I had big dreams of becoming a high-powered marketing executive. We knew each other from high school but hadn't spent much time together. Ari, short for Aristotle, was good-looking and extremely intelligent. He was ambitious and on the fast track to success. The package was very attractive.

At the end of my sophomore year, I came home to stay with my parents for summer break. After getting a taste of self-determination at college, I found it intolerable to be back in the dysfunction of my family home. The chronic drinking, unpredictable and explosive arguments, and my father's controlling nature were too much. I wanted to go back to campus early so I could be free of everything, but my parents wouldn't pay for summer housing if I wasn't taking any classes. Before summer was over, I told them I was moving in with a girlfriend from school when, in fact, I moved in with Ari. In my mind, he was the ticket out of my hellish existence. He would solve all my problems—be the safe place I had longed for all my life.

Ari was about to graduate from A&M with a free ride to Stanford for graduate school. He invited me to go with him. *He needs me!* I thought, feeling warm and fuzzy. This was the adventure I had been waiting for! It would mean putting my own college pursuits on pause, but I really didn't care. A voice inside of me was screaming, "I've got to get out of here!" and I was inclined to listen.

My parents disapproved. They were products of the 1950s, which meant single people didn't have sex prior to marriage, much less cohabitate (it always seemed to me that the rule was stricter for women than men). It went completely against their values and ethics. My father was the most vocal about it. With my father, there was no compromise.

"I'm moving to California with Ari," I told my parents over the phone.

My father was furious. Even over the land line I could feel the heat coming off him. "Where in hell did you get that kind of crazy idea?" he puffed. "What about your education?"

"I'll finish my junior year then take a break for a while. I'll go back once I get in-state residency in California. This opportunity for Ari to get his PhD from Stanford is too good to pass up," I said, trying to sound confident and rational while also slipping in Ari's credentials.

My father wasn't impressed. "Take a break? Take a *break*?!" he roared. "Use your head, Cheri. You don't need to be running after every boy who gives you the time of day. And you're going to shack up with him too? Your mother and I didn't raise you to be that kind of girl!" he continued, as if his words could pound me into submission. "I forbid it! If you defy our wishes, you're on your own financially."

There was only one thing I could do to secure my parents' approval. It was clear that I had to make a choice between what I wanted and what my parents would accept. Ari knew the realities of the situation without me having to explain it. We made the only decision that would get us both what we wanted.

Ari and I decided to get married.

I wasn't terribly excited about the idea of getting married, but I did love throwing a good party! My mother and I got busy with wedding preparations. That part was fun. But behind the scenes, Ari and I fought over how we were going to combine our lives. Our biggest dispute? I didn't want to take his last name of Smith. It had too bland a mouthfeel compared to Bergeron. And I couldn't help feeling like I would lose part of myself by giving up that foundational part of my identity.

Ari would have none of it. "I want my wife to have my last name," he would say. We must have had that fight a dozen times. His reaction baffled me. After all, his mother had already defied the conventional norms of her time. As a single mom, she made her own money and raised her son in a manner that was fiercely independent and unapologetic. Given this upbringing, I had every reason to believe he would value a strong, educated woman. I would put aside our petty differences in crystal and china patterns and forgive him for liking red velvet cake when Italian cream was so much better.

Ari and I were married that summer in a small country church surrounded by one hundred of our friends and family. I wore a princess dress with puffy sleeves and a long train. A veil studded with pearls graced my forehead. We had dated for one year.

Shortly thereafter, we made our way cross-country in a U-Haul containing all our belongings. *Good riddance, Texas. Let the adventure begin!*

When we got to the Bay Area, we found one of the few apartments we could afford—in a rundown complex in a sketchy part of Mountain View just off the El Camino Real—and furnished it with the finest garage sale décor. Not long after that, the honeymoon came to an abrupt halt as it felt like Ari abandoned me to immerse himself in his graduate studies. I hardly saw him, even though it seemed I was expected to keep house and cook for him when he got home. I buried myself in the role of supportive wife, helping pave the way for her man's success.

I began working at his university as a secretary in the Engineering Department. It was the best I could do without a degree and only one car between us. It was a job that supported our meager lifestyle, and I could do it with my eyes closed. I hated being in a supporting role to a bunch of men. Everything about it felt demeaning. I was at the bottom of the totem pole with no upward mobility. A "Girl Friday" surrounded by a veritable fraternity of elite intellectuals in a male-dominated field.

Life sped by while I stood still. I watched my friends graduate and land great jobs. They got hold of their future and wrestled it to the ground, while I wallowed in a sea of mediocrity, playing a supporting role in my own life.

It's funny how people don't notice the fairy tale that is marriage until they are in it. Deep down, Ari and I had very different beliefs and expectations when it came to a lifetime partner that we didn't discuss with each other. I theorized Ari was drawn to me because I reminded him of his mother. So predictably Oedipal. But underneath, it seemed Ari longed to have a nice, traditional wife. The kind of agreeable, compliant woman that his father chose as his second wife when his parents divorced and he settled down in Kentucky.

I had my fair share of ingrained marital beliefs, too. I was terrified Ari would try to control me as my father controlled and marginalized my mother. I feared I would disappear into nothingness like a ghost if my identity was taken away from me. Little did I know, I'd run screaming from one haunted house only to trip in the woods because I didn't look where I was going, like some dumb blond in a low-budget slasher flick.

The one bright spot in my life was dance. It was a skill that started on my high school drill team and deepened in country dance classes and social gatherings at A&M. I must have danced twenty-five hours a week (how I maintained my grades, I'll never know). Once in California, I joined the Stanford Ballroom Dance Club and met up with them at various locations (not bars, more like gymnasiums). I learned to waltz, foxtrot, samba, jive, rumba, and two-step with the best of them. I loved the push-pull interaction and artistic expression between two people on the dance floor.

To me, dance is the perfect conversation between partners and a way to let my desire for power rest for a while. I lost myself in movement and music. The old dance adage, "Women are always right," which reminds partners that the follower position starts a dance pattern with the right foot, is the ruling metaphor on a dance floor. The woman is the star. She equals her partner's strength, tuning in to the subtle muscle shifts of a shoulder or a hand that will guide her through the athletic and beautiful patterns she'll draw with her body. You may be a "follower," but you are not weak—"No spaghetti arms!" as Johnny Castle says in *Dirty Dancing*—nor are you unthinking as you create flourishes and flashy footwork that extend from your fingertips to your toes. As a lead, the man frames and supports his partner, suggesting and guiding instead of controlling or overpowering. A good lead will get you to do things you never thought you were capable of without you even realizing what you've accomplished until you're on the other side of the dance hall, breathless and ecstatic. It *does* take two to tango—otherwise you both fall.

Ari had no interest in dancing. He was far more cerebral than athletic and professed to have two left feet. We would fight every time I had plans to go out dancing, or as he would call it, "cavort with other men." We were seeing a marriage counselor at this point, but all those sessions didn't seem to help. One night, Ari and I had the biggest fight yet. "No wife of mine is going to go out on the town and flirt with men all night. Am I supposed to stand by while they put their paws all over my wife? They touch your ass, for Christ's sake!"

"Actually, they touch my hip," I snarked back.

Ari didn't seem amused. "You walk out that door and we're through!"

His words were alarmingly similar to the ones I'd heard hiding on a long-ago staircase in my parents' house. Had I made a terrible mistake? *Had I married my father?*

"You don't own me!" I said, trying not to scream as my past

pressed in on me. "I've given up everything to be with you, and this is the one thing that brings me happiness. I'm not doing anything wrong. It's harmless. It's great exercise. And, in case you care, I'm good at it. I'd think you would support me the way I have supported you. Either way, I'm going!" I declared defiantly. I wasn't some caged bird. I wouldn't let him steal my light and thunder. That wasn't going to be my story.

"If you go, don't bother coming back," he said, his eyes deadpan. I knew he meant it.

"Go to hell," I snarled, choosing myself—my identity, my values, my dreams. I slammed the door on my way out and called a girlfriend to pick me up since I wouldn't be taking the one car Ari and I shared. I moved out the next day.

After just eleven months of marriage, we were through. I was divorced at twenty-three.

I had to face a harsh reality when my marriage crashed and burned. I was on my own and very far from home. I had two choices: go back to Texas with my tail between my legs or hold my head high and make a life for myself in the competitive, fast-paced world of the Bay Area. My parents desperately wanted me to come back to A&M and pretend it was all a bad dream. But there was no way I was going to go backward.

After the breakup, my father came out to visit me. He was on a business trip, so my mother wasn't with him. In the years of my adulthood, it was rare that I would be in his company one-on-one. I can't say I was looking forward to it. Like the little girl who struggled to find something to say to her father in the car, I wasn't sure what we would find to talk about once the surface conversation about our business lives was exhausted.

"I think you should move back to Texas, Cher Bear," he said, using my childhood nickname as we drove from the airport to his hotel when I picked him up. *Not one to waste time, was he?*

"Dad, I'm not the same person that I was when I left Texas," I said, trying to explain. "I'm not that fledgling girl that I was in college. I'm a woman trying to make her way in this world. I know I have made my share of mistakes, but I love California, and I think this is where I'm meant to be."

My father paused and looked down at the floorboards. "That's just it, Cheri. I'm afraid that if you stay out here, I'm not going to like you anymore."

And there it was. In that moment, I realized my father's brand of love meant that I had to have the same beliefs that he had. That I had to make decisions in the way that he would make them. That I had to share his political beliefs. He wanted (dare I say, needed) me to be a mirror of himself.

I didn't know what to say, but his words cut me deep. *Sorry Dad*, I thought to myself, *that's not in the cards*.

Two months later, I enrolled at San Jose State University to complete my college degree. I got a promotion, supporting the Dean of Engineering, but it still wasn't enough to make ends meet. One of my dance friends introduced me to the owner of the Arthur Murray Dance Studio, where I became an instructor. That's where I met Cash.

Yeowch!

My left instep was on fire, and I tried not to look down at the damage from my partner's big Rockport shoe. I sucked up the pain as I wrangled my new student back into the starting position.

"No, start the box with your left foot, Cash. One, two, three. One, two, three."

"Sorry, Cheri," he said sheepishly, "I feel like I'm dancing in cement shoes."

"No problem, Cash, you're still learning," I said as I stepped in a tight square around the studio's wood floor, trying to add some grace to Cash's clunky waltz movements. The waltz was meant to be elegant and flowing. This felt more like a wrestling match between two alley cats. "Be sure to hold those shoulders back, tuck in your stomach, and firm up those arms. Keeping a nice frame will help prevent stepping on your partner's toes."

He grinned boyishly. "Thanks for the tip, Cheri, I'd hate to think I was the reason your pretty toes got banged up. Blame it on me being an uncoordinated tech nerd."

I laughed. "Oh, Cash, you're doing fine," I lied. "We'll have you twinkling around the dance floor in no time." My words reassured the slightly portly, thirty-seven-year-old man who came dressed in a full suit and tie, hair stiff with Paul Mitchell gel, for every ballroom dance lesson. He may have dressed to impress, but he kept a beat like Mr. Roboto and I couldn't quite take him seriously. We moved on to the East Coast swing. *It would be easier to dance with an elephant.* I blinked and chuckled at the thought. Now *that* was an image! Cash must have thought I was fluttering my eyelashes at him because he gave my hand a warm squeeze.

God help me, I squeezed back.

The truth was I wasn't a very good teacher, so part of Cash's lack of progress could be chalked up to my impatience. I rushed him. I couldn't help it. I liked strong partners in the ballroom. But in the romance department, I'd settle for someone safe.

Cash was not the half-baked college boy I'd divorced six months ago. He was well-established as a design engineer at a Japanese-owned semiconductor company and earned good money. He traveled. He owned more than one tailored suit. I think part of me longed for a taste of that life, the life I'd started my business degree for and taunted me as I did my secretarial duties. By this time, I was excelling at my marketing classes at San Jose State University, and I was confident that my career aspirations were back on track.

Despite his business success, Cash's greatest appeal was his family. He was born and raised in the Bay Area and was close to his two brothers. He had lunch with his mother once a week. He helped one of his brothers and sisters-in-law move. He had a cat. He had the type of family dynamic I wished I had. He seemed to genuinely care about others. And, most importantly, he didn't try to control me.

Was this the man who'd be just right?

Cash put his best foot forward when it came to wooing me. Fine dinners. Fancy jewelry. Weekend getaways to the Camellia Inn in Healdsburg. We'd go through the antique shops and boutiques in quaint little coastal towns, and I'd run my hand across the oiled mahogany curves of an heirloom Chesterfield chair and think of my shabby green garage sale couch that smelled faintly of cigarettes and potato chips that I bought for twenty bucks. *Never again!* I reassured myself. We spent a lot of those getaways driving around Napa Valley in Cash's silver Lexus with a built-in cell phone that felt like a ten-pound brick, stopping for wine tastings at upstart boutique vintners like Cakebread Cellars. That's when I fell in love with the big, bold California Cabernet Sauvignon.

Before long, Cash dropped the dance lessons. I'm pretty sure it was just a ploy to meet women anyway. Six months later, Cash and I were engaged. Six months after that, we were married in a small garden ceremony in Carmel, California, in front of forty friends and family. The sky was blue, the sun was shining, the temperature a perfect seventy-three degrees with a breeze and no humidity. In California, every day is a good hair day, and mine was stunning, even with the wind tugging locks of it askew. I again wore white although I didn't quite feel pure (Cash was the marital virgin, not me). The dress was an off-the-shoulder number with beautiful roses gracing the romantic sweetheart neckline. Our vows were simple and benign. No "thou shall obey your husband." My parents renewed their vows at the same time to add a bit of nostalgia along with their seal of approval. We managed to make our way through an overly rehearsed nightclub two-step for our first dance. *This time would be different*, I promised myself.

Under pressure from Cash, I reluctantly took his last name and hated every moment of it. Here I was, compromising my identity and conceding to be "Mrs. Him." I reasoned this must be a deal killer for most men since he was the second husband-to-be who was willing to fight for it. Perhaps I was being unrealistic. Unrealistic or not, it felt like I was selling myself out.

After an extravagant two-week honeymoon in Hawaii and we got settled into married life, I came to believe that Cash's life wasn't as put together as he pretended. From my point of view, he'd lived extravagantly for a decade before we met, buying a house in Colorado that he couldn't afford, furnishing it with new furniture and decorations, buying jewelry on a whim for the girlfriend du jour, and going on lavish vacations. His parents had given him a chunk of change that looked suspiciously like a bailout. I'd just gotten my first real job at a tech company after graduating with honors, and I felt compelled to spend chunks of my income paying off the tab for what appeared to be his bad financial choices.

From my viewpoint, Cash was quick to show a lot of flash on the outside, but that was a cover for his lack of vitality on the inside. He seemed...passionless. Weak. His desire to not cause friction tainted our interactions. We quickly settled into an uninspired, platonic existence. *Was this what marriage was supposed to be like?* I mean, I didn't feel threatened as I had with Ari. Frankly, I didn't feel much of anything at all.

Cash's personal saving grace was Midnight, his black cat. Now, I'm not a cat person, but Midnight was pretty cool. She'd come and sit with you in the morning while you ate breakfast, staring at you from her perch across the table, and yammer at you with a series of meows and yowls that sounded for all the world like a girlfriend spilling the tea about her nightly escapades. Midnight was sweet, but make no mistake, she was also the boss of the neighborhood. I could respect that vinegar in a fellow female.

One Sunday night, we returned home from one of our weekend road trips. It added more debt, but those trips were one of the few things we both liked doing with each other, and I was desperate to kindle any kind of spark between us. On this trip, I realized I could sooner start a bonfire under water.

I was tired and frustrated as I put my purse on the entry console table. Midnight walked into the room to say hello, but I could tell right away that her mannerisms were off. With growing horror, I saw the oozing grape-sized abscess on her throat. A sticker burr had gotten lodged in her throat, probably picked up while she was crawling through unkempt parts of the yard. What would normally be a minor injury had developed into a serious infection. Midnight looked weak and felt feverish. This was serious.

I sprang into action. "Cash, Midnight's hurt. We need to call her vet. What's their name? Crap, it's Sunday. Do they have emergency hours? Where's the closest emergency vet hospital?" I rifled off every question that came into my head as I went to find her cat carrier and a clean towel.

When I got back into the living room, Cash still stood by the door, stunned and silent.

"Cash, are you alright?" I asked, waving my hand in front of his face. "We need to get help for Midnight."

"Yeah, I'm fine," he replied. "I'm just trying to remember if I've gotten everything out of the car," he said glibly. *Who gives a shit about our luggage?* Cash turned away from me and disappeared into the other room while I frantically looked for an emergency vet clinic in the six-inch-thick Yellow Pages book. I located an open clinic and pulled out the page.

"Cash?" I called, not seeing him in the room. Midnight was now lying motionless on the carpet. I tucked the towel around her, and she meowed faintly as I touched her neck. "Shhhh, it's going to be okay," I soothed. "I'm going to get you some help." I went looking for Cash.

I found him in our bedroom, unpacking his bag from the weekend.

"What are you doing?!" I asked, incredulous. I felt like I was in an episode of the *Twilight Zone.*

"I'm unpacking," he said quietly.

Midnight wasn't my cat. We were only roomies. I wasn't responsible for her daily care and feeding. But something about his slow movements made my hair stand on end. Furiously, I ground out, "Cash, we need to take Midnight to an animal hospital RIGHT NOW! Her infection is very bad and she's clearly in a lot of pain. I'm afraid we could lose her."

"Okay," he said. His voice was flat, as if he was in a trance.

"I'll drive." Obviously, he was in shock. "You go get Midnight and put her into the car."

"I can't," he mumbled. I could barely hear him.

"What do you mean, you can't?" I exclaimed in utter disbelief. "She's your cat!"

"I can't pick her up. Not like that." He was almost panting now.

"Screw it," I huffed. "Just get in the car." I went back to the living room, grabbed the keys and my purse, scooped up Midnight, towel and all, so she wouldn't scratch me in her pain, and placed her in Cash's lap in the passenger seat as we sped off to the vet clinic.

The vet on duty admitted Midnight. He told us that if Midnight had gone another couple of hours without treatment, she would likely have died. Thankfully, because we'd gotten her in when we did, she'd recover.

Midnight's health crisis was a wake-up call. My gut was telling me he would check out and leave me to handle future crises on my own. Abandon me. I couldn't take the risk he'd do the same if the situation involved our child.

That night when we got home from the vet, I told Cash I thought we should separate. He didn't object. By the age of twenty-seven, I was divorced for the second time.

My second divorce made me question many things, most of all myself. Ari and Cash weren't bad people. They were far from perfect, but they weren't bad. I refused to think I was that blind when it came to choosing a mate. And yet, a quiet voice inside me asked a question I was afraid to answer.

Was I the problem?

After Cash, I entered a period of serial monogamy. I could either slow down a little and be more careful about who I brought permanently into my life, or I could try to break Elizabeth Taylor's record of eight marriages. But the idea of "slowing it down" was relative. I spent eight years dating. No boyfriend lasted more than a year. I was usually the one who pulled the plug. I felt like a dark-haired version of Goldilocks trying out men—

this one was too hot, this one too cold, too short, too tall, too controlling, too passive, too ambitious, too lackadaisical, too aggressive. None were just right.

And some were downright wrong. In one memorable incident, I fled my own house and called the police while hiding behind my front bushes after being thrown to the ground and sat on.

The only good thing to come out of this hot-and-cold relationship seesaw was a renewed interest in my faith, brought about by a devout boyfriend who took me to church every week. I began to wonder if my stagnant faith had something to do with the misery my love life had become. For the first time, I sat down and read the Bible. The New Testament, mostly. I read of God's unconditional love for me. *Unconditional?* That was a kind of love that I had never experienced from the men in my life. I started having conversations with God. I started attending church regularly and joined a weekly women's Bible study group. Maybe God was a key ingredient that had been missing in my search for the right partner and father to my future children. God and I were in the early stages of our relationship, but I resolved that I would see where it led.

With each romantic relationship, it seemed that the flaws and negative consequences were getting worse. I was getting more experienced but somehow no wiser. My view of intimacy, filtered through my dysfunctional relationships with my father and brother, had grown into something confused and distorted.

This level of disorientation is hard to describe, but I feel it's important to try. Simone Biles, world-renowned gold medalist, had to bow out of the 2020 Olympics because she lost her sense of orientation when she was in the air doing her routines. Gymnasts call it "the twisties." It's dangerous. Extremely dangerous to lose your bearings in a situation where you're rapidly moving forward and tumbling a broken neck's distance from the ground. Pilots experience a similar phenomenon if they fly without instruments and lose awareness of the horizon and what constitutes up and down. Such was the case in the crash of John F. Kennedy Jr., when his plane went down in the Atlantic Ocean off Martha's Vineyard in 1999.

I had the twisties when it came to men. I couldn't orient myself to a healthy relationship because I couldn't see one. Men represented some gain: this one will get me out of Texas, this one will get me familial acceptance, this one will get me a child. I never really fell in love to meet my true match—all my relationships just seemed like jobs. A means to an end, as opposed to a lifetime partnership.

In retrospect, I think I chose all my relationships in those eight years *knowing*, deep down, that they wouldn't go anywhere. That I wouldn't marry them. I wanted companionship and someone to fill my bed, but I didn't want to commit and risk making another mistake. And no commitment meant no kids. I still believed the fairy tale that I needed a good husband before I was ready for that last step of motherhood.

I was single and thirty-five with no good prospects on the horizon, and the clock was ticking.

CHAPTER 6

TICKING CLOCKS

THE MUSIC CARESSED MY EARS, AND I CLOSED MY EYES AS it seeped into the pounding of my pulse deep inside me. The hair on the back of my neck rose and a bunch of butterflies fluttered in the pit of my stomach. My smile grew broader as I opened my eyes, only to find a pair of green eyes gazing back at me, reading what I felt. If this felt good. A hard bicep under dampened cotton tightened under my left hand and I responded willingly with my whole body, gliding like silk in the direction it commanded me to go. Flynn, his red hair mussed with effort and sweat, mirrored my smile, so big it hurt his cheeks. As "Save a Horse (Ride a Cowboy)" by Big and Rich swelled, his smile gave way to something else I couldn't quite read. It looked like passion, either for the dance, the music, or for his partner.

Our eyes locked as our bodies found the rhythm together and I put extra energy into the way I swayed my hips. The way I pointed my toes in the soft-soled strappy heels. The way

I strained to touch-not-touch my thumb to my middle finger when I unfolded my right arm out into the darkness for a flourish during a turn, with only a whisper of distance between our skin. A slight shudder chased a droplet of perspiration down my spine. Flynn and I raced to the finish, rousing each other's bodies to new feats of athleticism and elegance, intent on getting there together. We didn't need to speak to know we looked good doing it.

As the duo's voices soared for the final chorus, I lost myself—to the music, to him, to myself. I always felt like this moment was the closest I'd ever get to one of those epic dance scenes in a romantic movie (think *The Mask of Zorro* or *Mr. and Mrs. Smith*) where the two leads owned the room with their undeniable chemistry and skill.

Too bad the only time I felt in sync with a partner was on the dance floor. Flynn was an excellent dancer, and all the women flocked to him when we went out as a group for social dance nights at local bars, but I knew he wanted a homemaker for a wife. I didn't want to go down that road again.

Both of us needed a break after that energetic two-step and we went outside to the patio to get any kind of breeze to cool off. Party lights were strung everywhere, between poles, the side of the barn-like building, and ever-present limbs of live oaks, their shine blocking out the darkened Texas sky. I guess no stars tonight, big *or* bright.

"Thanks for the dance, Cheri," Flynn said, as we sat down at a wooden picnic table, bleached almost white by the summer sun. "Dancing with you never gets old. You are amazing at following my lead."

Tired but sated, I glanced at Flynn. He could be considered handsome in a Ron Howard kind of way with his thinning ginger hair and freckles covered by a cowboy hat, but he was a head shorter than me and a tech support guy. Not my type. Once our bodies stopped moving in unison, his Rico Suave allure vaporized, and we landed solidly in the friend zone. But as steady dance partners, we had formed a comfortable bond.

Over the years, we had both shared aspirations for our romantic lives. He had his sights set on a subservient mail order bride from the Philippines. His search was still a work in progress. Flynn knew about a few of my relationship misfires and was a good shoulder to lean on (literally and figuratively).

"Sorry to hear about your boyfriend," he said as we got settled in.

"Yeah, that was an interesting one," I said, resigned. "Why is it that the ones who are the best lovers are also batshit crazy?"

"No idea, but I can relate," said Flynn. "That's why I'm getting someone from overseas with traditional values. No more crazy American chicks!"

"Good luck with that, Flynn," I said, only half-sarcastic, knowing that the risk of crazy was a global phenomenon not exclusive to the United States. *Poor misguided boy.* "At least you have a plan. I wonder if I'll ever create the family that I want."

"I didn't know you wanted to settle down," Flynn remarked sincerely as he took a sip of his beer. "I've often wondered why you weren't married by now. I mean, you're a great catch."

Up to this point, I hadn't felt the need to unpack all my relationship baggage in front of Flynn. I guess it was time. "I'm thirty-five, Flynn. I've got two failed marriages under my belt and a string of boyfriends, but no relationship ever seems to work out. I'm worried I bolt from every relationship because I'm afraid of failure. I don't know if the right guy exists for me."

"Well, marriage isn't for everyone. Maybe it's not in the cards for you."

I started to tear up as Flynn's comment reached my ears.

"Flynn, you don't understand. It's not the guy that means so much to me. I want to be a mother, and I need a man to get me there."

"Ah," Flynn uttered, finally understanding my dilemma. "I'm sorry, Cheri. I didn't mean to sound callous. I had no idea that you wanted to have a baby." He put his arm around my shoulder to ease the sting of his words.

"It's okay. I know I don't always give off that warm and fuzzy maternal vibe," I said, trying to ease his guilt. I sighed and sipped my drink. "I can't fully explain it. I mean, it's something I've wanted for a long time. I keep having these dreams…" An involuntary smile spread on my face, thinking about my little curly-haired girl. "This desire is getting stronger in me as time goes on, Flynn. Every time I lay my eyes on a baby with its little hands and feet, or I hear a child's giggle, my heart warms. I almost start crying." I could feel the tears welling up in me again, but I took some long, deep breaths to keep them at bay. I didn't want to show him too much of my tender underbelly. We weren't *that* close. "Children are the world's hope. They're *my* hope. It hurts, sometimes, somewhere in the core of me, to think that I will miss out on what I believe will be the most meaningful experience of my life. If I let motherhood pass me by, I'll regret it for the rest of my life." Flynn's eyes followed my hand as I twisted a lock of my long dark hair with my fingers. I knew that was something *I* did when deep in thought. I wondered if Flynn had picked up on my tell.

Flynn stared at me intently for a moment and picked up his drink. "If children are what you want, Cheri, then you better move past your fear and find yourself a good man. Stop wasting time."

One of Flynn's other dance partners found us outside and beckoned him back inside to join her in a jitterbug. But his words lingered in the air and resonated in my soul. Was I sabotaging my own life? Was I the one preventing myself from moving forward? If I wanted to be a mother, I decided, I would have to get over myself.

The conversation with Flynn flavored my thoughts the next time I went dancing. It was a typical Sunday evening at the Dallas Niteclub, a popular venue for country and western dance enthusiasts. On Sundays, the traditional honky-tonk took on a more tame, family-friendly vibe. When I went dancing, the drink of choice was ice water straight up, and the agenda was a large dose of much-needed physical and social exercise.

My skin felt prickly as I gently ran my right hand over my left arm and glanced around the room. The entire place was filled with human chatter and music. An old piano sat over by the door, unused as the DJ played. Vintage neon beer signs lined the walls above dark red leather upholstered booths. The head of a longhorn steer, the badge of honor for self-respecting Texas speakeasies, lorded over a smattering of pool tables and dart boards toward the back of the hall. A few feet out from the seating along the walls, a wooden railing drew a rectangle of empty wood floor around the center of the big room, designating the dance floor, its oak boards stained and scarred with time and patina. It was my happy place.

That night, a man caught my eye. If you pursue dance as a serious hobby, you get to know everyone in the scene, but I hadn't noticed him before now. *Was he new?* He appeared to be someone from the South, all debonair gentility in his crisp, tailored button-up and well-fitting, faded blue jeans. He seemed confident, relaxed, and laughing with his companions.

Curious, I asked him to dance. He thought for a moment and took my hand. The song was "Brokenheartsville" by Joe Nichols. My new partner, Gaston, was okay. Not particularly a strong dancer. He had a somewhat awkward way about him, which made him appear cute in the moment but didn't distinguish him on the dance floor. It was very different from the electric dance chemistry I had with Flynn and my other favorite partners.

When the song ended, I politely said, "Thank you," and walked to the other side of the dance floor to the space I and a few dance friends had carved out as a waystation between dances. Gaston followed me.

"Hey." His voice made me stop and turn to look at him. I frowned a little because it was still awkward to make eye contact with him.

"Yes?" I said.

"You dance really well." He smiled. I just nodded, smiling back politely.

"Where do you work?" His question was straightforward, but I paused before I replied.

I told him that I was working in high-tech, and he told me that he was in the same industry, taking a job in finance after getting his graduate degree. The room didn't feel as cold as it had when Gaston followed me back to my side of the dance floor. It was evident that Gaston wanted to keep talking but I didn't, so I quickly accepted the invitation for a waltz with one of my regular dance partners. I figured he would take the hint and move on by the time I got back.

To my surprise, Gaston was waiting for me after I finished my third dance. One part of me was annoyed. The other part, intrigued. Gaston was attractive and polite. He carried himself well. He had a golden retriever. *What villain has a golden retriever?* I reasoned. He seemed safe enough.

But still...

"Um, I have to go. It's getting late," I told him, trying to be as polite as possible.

"May I walk you to your car?" he said, even more politely than me. So, a true Southern gentleman, then.

"Sure." I smiled.

"After you," he said, making a gesture with his hand toward the door. I laughed and began walking.

Once at my car, in the darkness with the stars shining down, his low voice rumbled in my ear as he held my driver-side door open for me. "I'd like to see you again."

Do I really want to do this, or should I think of an excuse? I asked myself. My heart gave me a nudge and I decided to give it a go. "Sure," I agreed. We can't confine ourselves in the tower forever. Can we?

It was Memorial Day weekend, so Monday was a holiday. "I need to buy a new mattress and I wondered if you would go with me," Gaston proposed. It was one of the strangest pick-up lines that had ever been tried on me. I couldn't figure out if it was a come on or whether he didn't want to undertake the chore alone.

But it seemed harmless enough. How much trouble could you get up to in a mattress store having a holiday blowout sale? "Okay, I'll meet you there."

At first glance, there was nothing outwardly objectionable about Gaston. He seemed like he had it all together. Past relationships were serious but not too serious. A small family that included a sister who lived out of state and a mother he visited every six weeks. An MBA from a prestigious business school. He had a sensible Toyota Camry, nice looks, and a dog. He was thrifty with a dollar (he'd even save his vacation time and birthday money for a rainy day). He was good-natured, polite, and laid back. Perhaps a little too laid back, but I could work with it. His dog, Samson, proved he could at least go to the vet when needed. Most importantly, he wanted a family. That was a lot of common ground and checked a lot of the boxes I'd added to my wish list after my string of failed romances. With all the hot and cold of my last relationships, would Gaston prove to be just right? Was this the kind of guy I could have kids with?

We saw each other almost every day for the next nine months. I, too, had a dog. Carley was an artful mix of boxer and German shepherd. She was a brilliant, badass dog. Beautiful, athletic, smart, and fiercely loyal. Samson and Carley became fast friends. *Was it a sign?*

Gaston made me feel optimistic about the future. He seemed to check a lot of my boxes. Educated, stable, trustworthy, Christian. Addiction free. It felt like the pieces were finally falling into place. Like our lackluster first dance, he didn't exactly light my world on fire, but at least he was a dancer. You can't have everything, right?

For the first time in a long time, I didn't nitpick the relationship. I regularly replayed Flynn's words in my head, and I thought meeting Gaston when I did must have happened for a reason. I believed Gaston was a good man, just like the fairy tale of love and marriage dictated. He had all the major earmarks and the quirks I could live with. Weren't small imperfections what couples learned to love most about each other? I dreamed of building a family, and with my ticking biological clock, Gaston was my hope. I'd asked myself the all-important question: *Could I have kids with this man?* And my answer had been, *Sure.* Most importantly, he didn't seem the type to ever hurt me.

Nine years after my second marriage ended, ten months after Gaston and I started dating, I once again walked down the aisle.

My third wedding was a small affair. Just immediate family in the chapel of a little church. I wore an elegant, fitted white sequin dress. I figured nine years of being single entitled me to wipe my tarnished marital slate clean. Our reception was a dinner at an Italian restaurant out by Lake Travis. I wanted to avoid the grandiose gesture of a big event or destination wedding. Maybe the fairy-tale wedding was compensation for a relationship that didn't match the fairy tale at all. So, I ditched the elaborate party to concentrate on the partnership Gaston and I were building. I was sure this time was going to be different. I had more experience with men. I was more evolved. I could make better choices. I would keep my name this time, too. No more Mrs. Him. In this marriage, we would stand by each other's side as equal partners.

Turns out, I was spinning more straw attempting to make gold.

Fast forward four years, and Gaston and I were having the same argument we'd had so many times before. Only this time it was flavored by the conversation I'd had the day before at happy hour with Shade and Ruth.

"Why is it so hard for you to get a better job, Gaston? You have an MBA and good work experience," I muttered, looking pointedly at him.

"I don't know!" Gaston exclaimed, running his hands through his hair. I could tell he did not want to be having this conversation. "It's not something I have control over!"

I wasn't buying that. "That makes no sense, Gaston. All your co-workers are getting better jobs. I saw on LinkedIn that Jake from your group got a director job. Weren't you guys in the same position? And last month, Ben went to Dell. Earlier this year, Charlie got a great job at Adobe. He's making almost twice what he was before. How can this be out of your control?"

Per usual, Gaston had no response. We sat there in silence for what felt like an eternity. "Okay," I recall him saying, "I'll brush up my résumé tonight and reach out to my headhunter in the morning."

This is the way our arguments would always end. I felt like I was stuck in the movie *Groundhog Day* and Gaston was Bill Murray's character, reliving the same day over and over again and never making any progress. I'd even jumped in to make Gaston's advance as smooth as possible. I had worked on his résumé a dozen times. I introduced him to his headhunter. I got him networked with many of my contacts. Still nothing happened. From where I sat, he didn't even try. For all his talk of ambition and his complaints about his job, it appeared Gaston was content to stay where he was. As far as I was concerned, Gaston was stuck in the village where I found him and would be there until he died.

"I'm paying the biggest share of our household bills, Gaston. Our anniversary trip to the Caribbean was on me, too. And the trip to Europe before that. If we want to maintain this lifestyle, one of us has to be the breadwinner, and it's time for me to be a mother. How can I step back in my career so I can take care of our children if you won't step up?" I asked.

"Well," he said glibly, "maybe we just won't have kids."

I felt the blood drain from my face as he threatened to take away the one thing I still needed from him. "You always said you wanted kids, Gaston," I growled. "I can't believe you would sacrifice our future family because you're afraid to man up and take on your fair share of the financial responsibility."

We avoided each other for the rest of the night. As I lay in bed with my back facing the bathroom, I imagined Gaston shirtless, admiring himself in the master bathroom mirror and flexing his gym-sculpted muscles for an adoring collection of self-tanning potions and age-defying elixirs.

Everything Gaston did and said felt to me like plastic shallowness. In my mind, he was like a Ken doll, freeloading in Barbie's dream house, an accessory to Barbie as she went out in her career to conquer the world. And now, hearing what Shade had to say made me question everything that Gaston had told me about his past. *Was it all a lie?* The knot in the pit of my stomach revealed my belief that I had been duped by a congenial, unassuming con man.

Had I picked the wrong person for a third time?

"Gaston?" I called for the umpteenth time. "Close the bathroom door, please, if you are not coming in here to talk."

"Ah aah," he mumbled, starting up his electric toothbrush.

I covered my eyes with the pillow and shifted farther to the edge on my side of the king bed. "Good night!" I yelled, knowing he couldn't hear me over the hum of the rotating bristles.

Our relationship was stagnant and growing progressively worse. We had no intimacy, emotionally or physically. Gaston's toothbrush got more action than I did. *It's going to be impossible to get pregnant this way.* Was this really my life now?

"No time for a divorce," I told myself out loud. "I've made my bed and now I'm lying in it. If I want to be a mother, I'll have to do it on my own."

I kept trying to find my white knight while maintaining my power as an independent businesswoman in a conventional marriage with traditional gender roles. It took me a long time to realize those things aren't always compatible. Often, I would end up with a traditional man who wanted the control he thought was part of that type of masculinity. Or, I'd go for a guy that liked a strong woman who took control, but so much so I'd have to carry him (and carrying both your husband and children is hard work). Control of me was a deal killer, but so was me controlling every important aspect of my husband's life.

I was trying to come to terms with my parents' relationship and figure out how I could alter it to fit me, but I was never able to find that right fit. Find someone who would let me be me and want to take steps forward side by side, as a partner.

But now my biological time was up, and I was out of options.

PART 2

THE ROADS TO MOTHERHOOD

When the fairy tale of love reveals itself to be a fantasy for less fortunate Cinderellas, then a mother on a mission can get down to the business of exploring less conventional, but more realistic, ways of building a family. Prepare yourself: the road is fraught with obstacles and failure stalks the shadows.

CHAPTER 7

BECOMING A FOSTER PARENT

THE AROMA OF HOMEMADE CORNBREAD HIT ME AS SOON as I entered Jack Allen's Kitchen. The first time I visited this restaurant, I fell in love with its fresh, down-home recipes, the pepitas in their smashed guacamole, and the deconstructed chicken enchiladas to die for—all things indicative of exceptional Southwestern cuisine. You also knew it was good because tech people hung out there in droves from open to close. Today was no exception. The place was bustling with quick-footed servers and raucous groups in business casual attire gathered around the bar and adjacent patio.

"Hi, there!" I waved to my friend in a navy blazer, crisp white shirt, and dark jeans in a side booth as she stood up to greet me and we went in for a hug. "I need to drown my sorrows in a stiff margarita and some shrimp tostada bites."

"Sounds bad," said Ruth, sliding back into the booth and picking up a strawberry daiquiri the size of a small pony. "What's up?"

Before I could get a word out, tears streamed down my face. I put my head into my hands so as not to create a scene. As I fumbled for a napkin to blot the dampness on my cheeks, I looked up to see a look of concern and empathy in her eyes.

"What has he done now?" she asked, brandishing a tortilla chip dripping in habanero salsa like a crusader. Ruth liked things spicy. "Should I start sharpening my knives?"

"It's the same old stuff," I sighed. "Gaston won't lift a finger to help create a better life for the family we've always talked about. I just don't get it. It seems like he'd rather stay in his comfort zone than go out and make something of himself. Now he's saying he'd rather remain in his dead-end job than have kids."

"What a weasel," Ruth paused significantly, "but we kind of knew that already. That conversation with Shade just cinched it." I winced. Her words were true, but that didn't mean I liked admitting I'd married the wrong guy for the third time.

I took a prolonged sip of the margarita our server had just set down in front of me. This next part would be hard to say. "We've been trying to get pregnant for four years, Ruth, ever since we got married. Sex is just mechanical now. I've learned to indulge in orgasms on my own time. But I've begun to wonder, if there's no love in your lovemaking, is it really going to create a life? Do I really want my children born out of some emotionless chore?"

Ruth didn't say anything, just sat with her listening face on sipping her massive drink as I stared at the happy duo of guacamole and salsa in the middle of the table. Even the side dishes had better success at lifetime partnership than I did.

"I want to have kids more than anything," I murmured, as if speaking the words aloud might jinx it. "I don't have time to placate Gaston's petty hangups and immaturity. I just turned thirty-nine. I'm starting to think motherhood is never going to happen for me."

I waited for Ruth to console me and order us another drink. Instead, she dropped a bombshell. "Have you ever considered adoption or fostering?"

"I'm sorry, what?" I stared at her, dumbfounded for a long minute, next drink forgotten.

Ruth plowed ahead. "A friend of mine named Larkin and her husband, Klaus, became foster parents a couple years ago. Like you, they'd been trying for years to have kids of their own, but nothing came of it. They ended up adopting two adorable boys from a placement agency. Presbyterian Home for Children was the name, I think. Lark and Klaus aren't religious, so I don't think you need to be Christian to get on their list. The agency works with Child Protective Services to rehome kids in bad situations, and they have a foster-to-adopt program. It was really life changing for all of them." Ruth stopped to take a breath. This was a long speech for her, but her eyes glinted with excitement at the possibility of this being the answer to my motherhood quest.

I didn't know what to say. Fostering had never crossed my mind.

Ruth pursed her lips and her eyes softened. "I know you dreamed of making babies the old-fashioned way, but this is an option, too." She reached over the table, parting the salsa and guacamole, to give my hand a squeeze. All I could do was squeeze back.

"Here, look," she said, withdrawing her hand and replacing it with her phone. "I have their picture."

I looked down at an outdoor shot of two little Hispanic boys with dark hair and complexions, about three and five. They had brand-new swim trunks paired with matching swim shirts—Mickey Mouse for the younger brother and Buzz Lightyear for the older—set against a background of a wide waterfall cascading into a shallow, mirror-like pool. It looked like the swimming hole below the lower falls at McKinney Falls State Park in South Austin. The older boy was grinning from ear to ear, but the younger one couldn't be bothered to look at the camera. He was too busy dribbling pebbles into the water around his feet.

I couldn't speak as I looked at the picture, my vision blurred as I felt the tears again push at the backs of my eyes.

Suddenly, I was seeing the road to motherhood in a whole new way. I knew instantly that my heart would be open to welcome a child in need, especially if I could give them the security they deserved in difficult times. And if chances were good that I would be able to adopt at the end of it? Perhaps this was the way that God wanted me to become a mother. Maybe He'd finally answered my prayers!

When I got home, I started researching everything I could about becoming a foster parent. I read all about the preparation and selection process. I pored over information about the agencies that contracted with the state-run CPS department to find good homes for foster children. The more I read, the more excited I became. This could be a way for me to become a mother, but equally as important, it would give a needy child a safe and loving home. That night I couldn't sleep, and I was up bright and early the next morning to get the process started and figure out what Gaston and I would need to do to become foster parents.

I don't want to get into a tremendous amount of detail, but let's just say becoming a certified foster parent is no cakewalk. People only hear about the cases of bad foster parents who are just in it for the money, or who abuse kids themselves, but that's not the norm. The irony is that it is harder to become a foster parent than it is to become a regular parent. Gaston and

I had to prove, in advance, that we would be worthy of having a child in our home.

There are two kinds of caseworkers that candidate foster parents work with. The Child Protective Services (CPS) caseworkers prepare and advocate for the children, and the placement agency caseworkers prepare and advocate for the foster parents. Our agency caseworker, Elizabeth, walked us through the whole certification process, while our CPS caseworker, Carla, made sure we met standards and communicated with us about children placed in our care. We had to get a background check. We had to do a home study with our agency caseworker to prove our house and family were safe and secure and submit to monthly inspections to make sure it all stayed that way. We had to sign a firearms agreement that said we wouldn't bring guns into the house. We had to do drug tests. We had to get our new car seat inspected. We had to lock all medications in a safe. And that was just for home set up.

Then there's a gauntlet of training. We needed to complete six weeks of education on a range of topics: autism spectrum disorder, psychotropic medications, trauma, sexual abuse and harassment, child growth and development milestones, nutrition, time management, and get our child and infant CPR and first aid certifications. Then there are training extras. The STAR Program comes with additional training and resources. SMART training prepares caregivers for appropriate behavioral interventions, plus a host of continuing education in parenting. I swear, some college degrees are easier to get than foster parent status.

Finally, we had to make a Family Book to introduce our household to potential foster kids. Here is who we are, where we live, and what our home is like. This part made me feel like a bit of a fraud. With my marketing background, I could do a promotional Family Book with my eyes closed, but I felt my relationship with Gaston did not match the close, loving family I made us out to be on paper.

To my surprise, Gaston hadn't objected to the idea of becoming a foster parent, and he followed along and did what we needed to do to become certified in a foster-to-adopt program with the stated intention of being placed with children that we might be able to adopt. But I never quite trusted his level of commitment, especially when I ended up doing most of the work. I sometimes wondered if he even wanted to become a father like we'd talked about so many times in the early days of our relationship.

I have to admit, I may have swept Gaston up in my tidal wave of energy. I applied everything I knew about business to my special life project, pursuing it with the same rigor and determination I'd poured into my career. I could follow a clear set of steps and jump through prescribed hoops to advance toward the goal. In some ways, I felt more in control of this kind of motherhood than I'd felt when my fate was left up to a chance meeting of sperm and egg.

So I laid the groundwork for the child that would come. *Had* to come if I manifested a future for him or her. I would create my dream family like I'd created my dream career. *This is going to work*, I thought. Failure was not an option.

I was ready.

In the foster-to-adopt program exists a curious term: *legally free*. Or *nearly free*, as the case may be. These are children who are available (or close to being available) to be adopted because their birth parents had legally given up their parental rights or had their parental rights terminated by the court system. These kids had already progressed through multiple phases of the foster program over many months, and it was very likely they were in need of permanent, adoptive parents. It took about twelve months from when CPS picked them up for a child to become legally free.

Once you are an approved foster parent and prospective adoptive parent, you are added to an email list that gets periodic bulletins of legally free children who need a new family. This part of the process always made me squirm a little. To me, the bulletins looked like sales catalogs, and unlike the Family Book I'd put together, I suspected the kids had no part in how they were depicted. All you have to go on to make your initial pick is a photo, their age, a bit about their personality, any health conditions, and if they have siblings. If you are lucky, you'll find out about their favorite toy. And from these brief snippets, you as a prospective parent must envision yourself as the long-term caretaker of this little human. Would we get along? Would they be happy in my home? Would they want to call me Mommy?

A couple of short weeks after Gaston and I got our foster parent certification, I received an email about two little girls who were legally free to adopt. Their names were Destiny and Serenity, ages one and three, and I thought they were the most beautiful African American girls I had ever seen. They needed a home. They needed me. And I was going to make sure that I gave them everything that would make their lives better.

"What?" Gaston flushed red, then purple, then red again when I told him I wanted to submit our home study for consideration for adoption. If we were picked, we'd have to wait to see if we were in the top three, then do interviews before meeting the children and a final selection, but I was ready to take in these two girls.

"What's the problem?" I asked, surprised by Gaston's reaction. "We trained for this. These girls have been through so much and they need a good home. We can give them that home," I argued.

"How are we supposed to raise Black children?" he blurted.

My jaw dropped and I opened and closed it a few times before I could get it working again. Was this conversation really starting out this way? I thought he'd be excited! This was the culmination of two months' worth of work for us.

Cautiously, I continued my case. "I'm not sure what you mean, Gaston. These girls are innocent children. They will be our children. Their skin color doesn't matter. All kids need the same stuff: food, a home, family, love..."

"What I mean is," Gaston cut me off, getting more agitated, "what will it be like raising Black children when we're White? They won't look like us. They probably won't act like us. It'll be obvious to other people they aren't ours, uh, biologically speaking," he said.

He was digging his hole deeper. "I don't care about any of that, Gaston. Did you think we were going to find only White children in the foster care system? Maybe you missed this fact in all the training: most foster kids are non-White. But they need a family and deserve love just like White kids," I insisted, angered I'd even need to speak these words.

"What if my family doesn't accept them?" said Gaston, relentless on this topic. "You know they are from Alabama and things are, um, different there."

Different? Oh, no. It occurred to me that this might not be about whether or not Gaston's *family* would love and accept these two little girls. I believe Gaston was worried that *he* would be unable to love and accept them. It felt like a dagger of prejudice to me, another one to join the others now lodged in my heart over this parenting journey. Through this new hurt, I pitied Gaston. I pitied that he didn't think he could love a child that didn't look like him—that he couldn't love a child of color.

"Sorry, this can't happen," he said, as firm as Gaston ever got, and walked out of the room.

Outwardly, we spent the evening in stone-cold silence. Inside, I was in turmoil. I wanted these two girls so badly, but I knew I could not move forward unless he and I were on the same page.

The next morning, when Gaston returned from one of his early morning workouts at the gym, he made an announcement that shocked me. "I've changed my mind. Let's move forward and put our name in as potential adoptive parents for Destiny and Serenity."

Putting my makeup on in the bathroom, I couldn't believe my ears. "Are you sure?" I said in disbelief, my hand still holding a blush brush.

"Yes, I think it will be great," he said firmly, as if to convince himself.

I ignored the slight hitch in his voice and leapt for joy, giving him a giant hug and accidentally dusting his T-shirt with rouge. We both smiled.

Makeup half-done, I immediately reached out to let the agency know. My excitement intensified later that day when I learned we'd been chosen as one of the three finalist families.

I couldn't wait to tell Gaston when he came home from work. But he didn't return at his normal 6:00 p.m. He walked in at 9:00 p.m., and he didn't look good.

"Where have you been?" I asked, worried as he came into the living room. I wrinkled my nose as the smell of liquor hit me.

"What?" he mumbled.

"I've been trying to reach you for three hours. We were

picked as one of three finalist families," I informed him, my worry giving way rapidly to anger.

"Oh, well, I was meaning to talk with you about that," he said. *Was it just me, or does his voice sound slurred?* I thought. A knot started to form in the pit in my stomach. "Yeah, I just think there'll be too many ob-skulls, uh, ob-sta-cles. I just can't get my head around it."

I saw red. "How could you do this to me?" I managed to get out around the lump in my throat. "Do you enjoy toying with my emotions? With the futures of two little girls? How could you get my hopes up only to shoot them down once again?" I knew yelling at him was futile, but I was so *angry*.

Frankly, there was nothing that he could say to me that would repair what felt like another betrayal. I was filled with disgust. I went upstairs to regain my composure. Was he sabotaging my efforts to become a mother again? I had made it as easy for him as I possibly could, and now he vetoes these two beautiful little girls on what looked like the color of their skin? Gaston had always been shallow, in my opinion, but this was a new low. It made me sick. It felt like a hard kick right in the uterus. The voice in my gut was clear. *I've got to get out of here.*

I hurriedly threw a few things in a bag and walked downstairs. I went to find Gaston and discovered him slumped over on the living room sofa half-asleep. "I'm leaving, Gaston," I said. "I can't even look at you right now. I'll let you know where I land." I knew if I stayed, I would say something that I would regret. I walked toward the front door, grabbed my purse, and walked out. I had no desire to look back.

I got in my car and started driving. It was getting late, but I was now wide-awake with rage, and I needed to be anywhere but here. I pulled out a map and stared at it. My eyes went to Santa Fe, New Mexico. I'd always wanted to visit.

The drive was eleven hours from Austin, which gave me lots of time to think—probably too much.

How could I have missed what so clearly seemed to me like racist beliefs?

Why did I get married to him so quickly?

How could I have trusted him?

What am I supposed to do now?

Mostly, I was numb. I don't even know what CDs I loaded into the car's player as I drove into the night.

Will I ever become a mother?

CHAPTER 8

A BETTER LIFE FOR AURORA

I GOT TO SANTA FE AS THE SUN WAS COMING UP. HOURS ago, driving up Highway 84, I'd left the flat deadness of East Texas, baked brown by the sun and dotted with cacti and the distant view of gigantic solar-powered windmills. The trees had grown steadily taller and fuller as I approached the New Mexico border and the bleached siding of Texas houses gave way to box-shaped adobe structures with rounded edges in an array of brown, taupe, peach, and rust.

My eyes feasted on a panorama of towering red cliffs painted on a canvas of crimson and orange by the rising sun. Fluffy white clouds floated on a crystal blue sky that played peek-a-boo with the most majestic mountains that I have ever seen. I felt like I was driving through the song "America the Beautiful." My lingering rage gave way to awe, washed away by the warm rays of sun on my skin filtering through the car windows. Life couldn't be all bad if there was such beauty in it, and I humbly sent up a quick prayer thanking God for reminding me of His bigger world and purpose.

It isn't hard to believe God exists in Santa Fe. The town, surrounded by natural grandeur and cooler temperatures created by the mountains, is a mystical, magical oasis in the desert. A city of blended cultures and histories outside of time. For three days, I wandered the historic plaza and side streets with their small art galleries, delicious local restaurants, and eclectic boutiques filled with a brilliant pageantry of color and wondered what my future would hold. It was a beautiful backdrop as I contemplated what to do next.

I should divorce him, I told myself, trying the idea on for size. *He isn't the type of person you want as the father of your children.* But even as the idea formed, I knew I wouldn't go through with it. Not this time. I was too old to start again from scratch. If I wanted children, I'd have to come back and patch this hole in our family somehow. I'd made my bed, and I would have to lie in it.

Ring ring! Ring ring! Annoyed at the interruption to my reverie, I reached in my pocket to grab my phone, but my crossness turned to heart-pounding anticipation as I noticed the number was from the foster placement agency.

"Hello? Hello!" I said into the line, hoping I'd get reception.

"Hi, Cheri," Elizabeth, our caseworker, chirped from the other end of the line, "I've got some exciting news! I have an emergency placement for you. It's a twelve-month-old little girl. Her name is Aurora. Are you available to take her today?" she asked.

I froze in disbelief. A little girl? Could this be *my* little girl?

The fog that had settled on my mind the past few days cleared, blown away by the Sante Fe breeze. "I'm currently out of town, but Gaston is in Austin, and I'll be home tomorrow morning. Yes, we would be happy to provide a home for Aurora."

Unlike with the children in the bulletins, who are in relatively stable placements until a permanent home could be found, Aurora, as an emergency placement, needed a home *right now*. Most often emergency placements are kids who have been urgently taken away from their birth parents by CPS because there was a serious concern for the child's safety. The child's legal status is still up in the air, but they need a safe foster situation, pronto.

Immediately after I hung up with Elizabeth, I called Gaston and told him that we were receiving an emergency placement that evening and I'd drive home through the night to meet them in the morning. Nothing was mentioned about the fight or our lack of contact over the last three days. Aurora was all that mattered now.

I called Ruth to see if she could go to my house and be there when the agency brought Aurora home. Gaston didn't know the first thing about babies, so he was going to need some backup until I got there. Ruth was happy to help. She dropped everything and flew over to the house like a fairy godmother, complete with some toddler essentials: baby shampoo, diapers, a pacifier, and a long-eared stuffed bunny for her to cuddle. A short time later, still driving across the endless expanse of the Texas panhandle, I received a text from Ruth. "Cheri, meet Aurora," it read. Then up popped a photo. I had to pull the car over to stare at it.

Before me was an adorable little girl with fair skin, blue eyes, and light brown hair. *She looks a bit like Gaston*, I thought curiously. I felt like I knew her already. *No, not quite like Gaston*, I amended. *She looks like the girl from my dreams.*

It was all I could do not to break all of Texas's already generous speed limits. The eleven hours that it took for me to get home were some of the longest I had known.

Dawn was breaking when I pulled into the driveway. It felt appropriate, somehow, that I'd arrive back where I started at sunrise. Gaston was there, but I didn't want to talk. "Where's Aurora?" I said with singular focus as I burst through the door.

"She's upstairs sleeping," Gaston said from his position on the couch, watching golf. I knew Ruth had left the night before after Aurora had gone to sleep. Thankfully, Aurora had slept through the night. I was afraid she would wake before I got there. I wanted to be the first face she saw on this first morning in her new home.

Most new parents strive to get a crib up before the baby's due date, but one of the certification requirements for fostering was to prepare an entire baby's room and have it ready because any minute you may get the call. I didn't know if we'd get a boy or girl, so I kept the theme neutral. It was vintage Winnie the Pooh, with pale yellow walls, an oversized light green Pottery Barn upholstered rocking chair, and a simple natural wood crib with a soft baby-sized quilt my mother had made in pale green, yellow, and white draped over the railing. I painted Pooh and Piglet walking hand in hand on the back wall, a quote from A. A. Milne written in book script underneath them: "Sometimes the smallest things take up the most room in your heart." Creating this space had been my favorite part of the whole foster parent certification process.

I opened the nursery door slowly so as not to wake the baby and the smell hit me. Where before the room had smelled slightly of paint and new furniture, now the intoxicating scent of baby filled the space, a concoction made from baby shampoo, milk, and fresh, pure life. I noticed a stuffed bunny with long, floppy ears sat in the corner of the crib. It was the softest brown fur that I had ever felt with white accents on its ears, belly and feet. The silky insides of its ears turned out ever so slightly as if the rabbit could hear a child calling. *Thank you, Ruth.* It was the perfect choice.

Aurora was deep asleep, wearing a Little Mermaid top and tiny denim shorts, the only clothing she owned. She had one pink sock on, the other lost somewhere under my mom's quilt, now half-draped around her sleeping form. I stood over the crib and let my eyes trace her sweet little body, marveling at the pudgy limbs, the wisps of brown hair, the cupid's bow mouth pouting in easy sleep. Her tiny fingers touched the foot of the stuffed bunny, tethering it to herself for security and well-being. I listened to the sound of her soft breathing, and the world moved under me as I fell in love. "You poor thing," I whispered quietly. I could only imagine what this sweet little girl had been through the day before.

At least for this moment, for this child, I was her caretaker. Her security. Her family. A hollowness inside me I'd grown to tolerate almost hurt as it filled to bursting. *I am a mother.*

The next few days were a whirlwind of activity. The first thing I had to do was find a suitable daycare for Aurora. I hadn't seriously envisioned the idea that I would get an emergency placement and my life would change overnight. But that's what happened. I went to all the daycare centers on the agency's list and found the Rainbow Center. It was the best one available that would accept the government stipend.

There were several appointments required when a foster parent gets a new placement. The most important one was with CPS. I'd faced down countless high-powered male executives in the boardroom, but I was nervous when Carla, our CPS caseworker, came through our door. Since Aurora was my first placement, I knew she'd be sizing me up. I had to be at my best.

When everything looked to be in order, Carla sat down with me to provide a bit of background on our new charge. "Aurora has had a really tough first year," Carla told us. "Her mother, Dolora, was in and out of foster homes as a teenager and aged out of the system without a stable family support system. She had Aurora at seventeen as a single mother, fell into a drug habit, and got a job as an exotic dancer to make ends meet. It's not a healthy situation." Carla told of times when Dolora would leave Aurora at a babysitter's house, saying she'd pick her up that night, and then disappear for days. CPS had finally taken Aurora out of her care on grounds of abandonment.

My heart broke to hear what Aurora, and her mother, had been through. The whole situation sucked, though I knew this story was all too common. All I knew was that it made me want to hug Aurora closer to me, to make up for her troubled life so far.

"Aurora was removed from her mother's care at the age of six months and was placed with her mother's half-sister," Carla continued. "Unfortunately, on a routine drop-in visit, we discovered that the half-sister and her boyfriend were doing drugs as well. That's why we needed to remove her from their custody and do an emergency placement."

"How terrible," I said, shaking my head in disbelief. The level of trauma foster kids go through was staggering. Thankfully, I was in a position to right the balance. I squared my shoulders. "Gaston and I will do everything we can to make her feel safe and secure. She's been through so much already."

"Yes, she has," Carla agreed, nodding in approval. "Are you and your husband open to the idea of adoption? Aurora has already been in the system for six months. She'll become eligible for a permanent home in another six."

I just about jumped out of my skin. *Down, Cheri!* I commanded under my breath. I didn't want to come off as desperate or overeager. Deliberately, slowly, I said, "Well, yes, we would certainly consider that."

Carla looked at me and smiled. An experienced caseworker, she knew when she had a fish on the hook. But I was happy to be caught. I escorted her to the door and shut it gently behind her. *Is this really happening?* Euphoria spread through me, the kind that's even more addictive than the drugs that Aurora's mother had fallen prey to. It was surreal. I tried to contain myself. The whole story was sad. But I couldn't help the hope that flowered through the dust that was Aurora's life.

Would this be my chance at motherhood? Is this the purpose God meant for me?

The next six months were pure bliss. Aurora spent her second ever Halloween with us. She was dressed as Tinker Bell, the little pink pom-poms on her spring-green felt elf shoes tinkling as she walked. I sewed bells on the pom-poms so we could keep track of her now that she was walking. We visited the Lady Bird Johnson botanical gardens and chased a rainbow assortment of dragonflies over man-made streams and koi ponds. We went to a friend's Christmas party and took a family picture under their nine-foot tree, done up in gold and silver. We were a regular family.

Truth be told, these were some of the best times that Gaston and I had ever spent together. All of our effort was focused on Aurora, and I had never felt more fulfilled. *She's our missing piece*, I thought. *We now have our fairy tale.*

Each day with Aurora filled my life with a level of happiness that I had never experienced before. The world seemed brighter. I reveled in meeting her every need and skipping out of my part-time consultant gig early so I could pick her up from daycare at three o'clock sharp. I loved buying clothes for her, teaching her how to swim, and seeing her delight when Santa left presents under the tree. It was her first taste of normal, and I'd helped give it to her.

One day, when I went to pick Aurora up from daycare, she squealed and ran to me on chubby legs. "Mama!" she called out in a high, clear voice. My heart skipped a beat as I gathered her giggling body in my arms and let the tears flow. I did not feel the need to hide my joy. The daycare teachers covered their mouths with their hands, their eyes also shiny with tears. They knew enough of Aurora's story to know what this moment meant to me and for her.

I am a mother. I am HER *mother.*

Despite our growing attachment, I knew the adoption process was far from over. All those months, I counted down the days like I was opening doors on the world's most nerve-racking advent calendar. Carla had told us parental rights are typically terminated after a year in the system. Aurora was almost twelve months in.

It was a cold January day when Carla arrived for one of our routine home visits. But Carla's normally open face looked pinched and strange.

"Cheri, there have been some developments regarding Aurora," she said, her tone distant when before she'd been so friendly and encouraging.

"What developments?" I had a bad feeling about this.

She said, "The state of Texas has a new pilot program that seeks to reunite foster children with their families. If their parents aren't able to get on track to regain custody of the child, and their close relatives also fall through, then the state looks more broadly at all possible blood-related family members."

No no no! This couldn't be happening. "It was my understanding that Aurora's mother didn't have much family, and that the family members that were identified were not deemed suitable. Is that correct?" My language was getting just as businesslike and stilted as Carla's.

"Well, yes, but some distant family members have been identified in the Texas panhandle. They are potential candidates."

"Has Aurora had any contact with these people?" I asked, trying to negotiate my way out of this.

"No, I don't think they've ever met Aurora." Carla looked like she'd just swallowed a frog. I got the impression she didn't like the situation any more than I did.

My knees began to buckle, so I sat down to compose myself. Aurora had already been displaced from two different homes within her first twelve months of life. And now they were going to rip her away from a good home where she was safe and happy? To live with some hicks she'd never met in Nowhere, Texas? I knew I was being uncharitable, but I couldn't help it. Every day it felt like our caseworkers were pushing us toward adoption, and now it was, "Sorry! Better luck next time!"

"But, we are in a foster-to-adopt program...," I trailed off, still struggling to understand what was happening.

Carla stiffened her spine. As a government worker, she'd do what she was told to do. "That's irrelevant, Cheri. Placing children with blood relatives is our top priority."

Ever the executive, I couldn't accept my raw deal. "This makes no sense to me, Carla. Aurora is thriving here. We're repairing the trauma that was done in her first year. She's… she's started calling me Mommy." My voice rose and I tried to keep it together. "Moving her again would be really damaging for Aurora." I searched Carla's eyes, but all I could see was blankness.

"I'm sorry, Cheri," she said, her voice devoid of emotion, "but CPS believes that biological family members should get custody over nonrelatives regardless of whether there is an established relationship or not. It's best that you not get too attached."

Not get too attached? *Not get too attached?!* Aurora was a

human being, not a kitten! She had feelings. *We* had feelings. They told me that there was a good chance that I could adopt this little girl, and I'd trusted the system. Given my heart to it. How in the world could I not get attached?

She called me Mama.

I don't remember Carla leaving the house. But I remember looking at the calendar. It was Aurora's eighteen-month birthday. She'd been in foster care for one year. She'd been my daughter for six months. This was supposed to be the day we'd be together forever.

But now everything was ashes.

It took CPS a month to track down and make arrangements with Aurora's distant family. CPS held a court hearing without telling me about it. Instead, I got a call at 8:00 a.m. on a Tuesday after I'd just sat down to work in my home office. I hadn't even taken a sip of my coffee yet. It was Elizabeth, our placement agency caseworker. "CPS is coming to pick Aurora up in four hours," Elizabeth said, sounding as miserable as I felt. "You need to pick her up from daycare and gather her things."

I knew I was not dreaming this time. I ran to the hall bathroom as soon as the line was disconnected and threw up.

Why? Oh, God, why is this happening? I thought You meant her for me. How could they take my little girl away? She loves me.

As much as I love her.

I tried wiping the tears away from my face, but they flowed uncontrollably, leaking from the place in my heart that Aurora had filled a short seven months ago. I did not give birth to her. I did not share her blood. But we were family. As much as any two people could be family. How could she possibly be better off with someone she didn't know? Were a few strands of matching DNA really that important?

As luck would have it, Gaston was away on a guy's trip

around Europe and couldn't get home. Deep down, I knew he would be of no comfort to me anyway. Ruth was great in a pinch, but she was in California on a business trip. *Who can I call?* I thought desperately. I needed calm. I needed grounding. I needed someone to help triage the hole in my bleeding heart from the landmine I'd just stepped on. I called Serena, a social worker friend I knew from church and my weekly Bible study group. She'd heard about Aurora for months and had seen us together every Sunday.

"Serena, they are taking Aurora away!" I sobbed into the phone. "I'm having a panic attack, and I'm not sure I can survive this."

"I'll be right there," she said. It was the middle of the afternoon, but she told her bosses at All Saints Hospital she needed to leave for an emergency. Within thirty minutes, she was by my side.

When Serena swept through the door, flushed and windswept in her white sweater, denim jeans, and knee-high black boots, I felt a guardian angel had arrived. "Breathe, Cheri," she said calmly, touching my hand lightly to anchor me. "Close your eyes. Focus on my voice. Now listen to the air as it goes in and out of your lungs. Feel my hand on your hand. That's it," she encouraged, as I gulped air in choppy gasps. "That's it. I'm right here. I know this won't be easy, but I'll be with you every step of the way."

Serena drove me to the daycare center and said she'd wait for us. As I stepped out of the car, I vomited again. Emotionally wrecked, I entered the door code and walked in to collect Aurora from her room. All the staff had been alerted. The atmosphere had the solemn feel of a funeral. I walked past faces touched with disbelief and sadness. They'd seen us every day. They knew my plans. My dedication. My love.

They knew it wasn't right.

I sucked in a breath before opening Aurora's classroom door. I had to be brave and strong for her. She might be young, but she could read emotions just like any toddler. I didn't want to add to her trauma. "Mama?" she said when she saw me, knowing it was early to pick her up. They were right in the middle of story time, reading Robert Munsch's *Love You Forever*. My gorge rose again but I swallowed it back down.

"Everything is going to be alright, sweetheart," I said, not believing a word of it. "You're going to go meet some of your family." I couldn't look at the daycare teachers slowly gathering Aurora's things, their eyes shiny and wet.

When we got home, I walked around like a zombie collecting Aurora's belongings as Serena occupied Aurora in the playroom. Most of the toys wouldn't be going with her—there was no time, and there were too many. My stomach in knots, I packed up her personal things. Toiletries and medicine. A pink baby spoon and cup. The beautiful clothes that I had bought for her. I slowly folded the Little Mermaid T-shirt she wore when CPS first brought her to the house, now too small. I hugged the stuffed brown bunny she'd dubbed Bugs that was her prized possession. I put him on the top of the luggage, so she'd have him close at hand. Then I sat on the edge of the couch, dreading the moment the clock struck twelve and my princess carriage turned back into a pumpkin.

Serena was a trouper with kids and very gentle, but Aurora's little face, normally so animated, was still and silent. She'd had one too many bad experiences in her life and knew something awful was about to happen, despite my brave face.

At noon on the dot, someone from CPS arrived, but it wasn't Carla. *How cowardly of her not to show up*, I thought dully.

The modest government sedan was loaded quickly. One trip,

and all Aurora's things were stowed away in the trunk. As the nameless CPS worker picked her up to carry her away, Aurora called out, "Mama!" and stretched her small arms toward me, frightened by this stranger and the emotions in the room. For a moment, I thought I smelled beach sand and heard the sound of a thundering roller coaster.

"Everything's going to be okay, sweet girl," I said, rogue tears slipping down my cheeks as I gave her Bugs to hold. "Will you take care of Bugs for me?" I asked, in an attempt to give her a mission to focus on. Aurora nodded with her whole head. "Everything's going to be okay because I'll love you forever. Promise me that you'll be a good girl."

Aurora's big blue eyes stared at me as the caseworker hurried her toward the front door. Hugging Bugs as if her life depended on it, Aurora said, "Bye, Mommy." Under the harsh midday Texas sun, I watched as she was bundled into the car and they drove away.

I never saw her again.

I'm not sure exactly when Serena left. I think she slipped out as I retreated to the solace of my bedroom. I don't know how I would have gotten through that ordeal without her.

I hid under my bedcovers for days afterward. My faith was rocked. How could God lead me down the path to believe that this would be my chance at motherhood, only to rip my daughter from my arms?

Losing Aurora felt like a death.

It took me a long time to climb out from under those covers. When I did, I was met with another kind of loss.

Shortly before Aurora was taken from our home, my father

was diagnosed with an aggressive form of prostate cancer. By the time they found it, the cancer had already spread to other parts of his body. The cancer treatment required him to be on a very restrictive diet that wouldn't feed the growth of the disease. He also stopped drinking and smoking immediately. It was the first time my father had been free from the influence of substances that had ruled him for his entire adult life. Being clean for the first time in decades gave him a clarity about his life that I hadn't seen before.

I still remember my last conversation with him.

"I'm sorry to hear about Aurora," he said to me as I sat by his bedside. We had created a makeshift hospital room at home where he could spend his final days in comfort. "I didn't want to be right about that. I was trying to protect you from getting hurt."

"I know, Dad," I said, as I put my hand on his. "I just wanted to be a mother so badly and I thought this was my chance," I managed as tears stung my eyes.

Then my father gave me a look I'd never seen before. It was a mix of love, sadness, and clarity. The kind people get when they are near death.

"I have a feeling this motherhood thing is going to work out for you, Cher Bear," he said, as he, too, started to cry. "I'm just sad that I'm going to miss it."

As difficult as my father was, I knew at that moment he loved me. And I knew he would have loved my children. I sat there until the evening sun peeked through his bedroom window, bathing his face in a soft glow.

My father lost his battle three months after he turned seventy years old. My parents were married for forty-six years. My mother and I were by his side when he drew his last breath.

My dad and I hadn't agreed on much over the years, but I prayed his motherhood prophecy was right.

CHAPTER 9

THE ROAD TO FERTILITY

HOW THE HELL DID I GET HERE?

The thought repeated in my head as I looked down at the chart Dr. Babymaker laid out on his dark mahogany desk. The sun was still shining outside, but inside the office I didn't feel those warm rays, and now I was cold and numb after the initial panic had worn off.

Nothing good happens when a bunch of numbers are pushed on you right after the bad news that you may be infertile. What I saw on Dr. Babymaker's chart, with its neat organization of data points, numbers, and lines shocked me. Shocked me so much I wanted to include it in this book so other hopeful mothers wouldn't get blindsided.

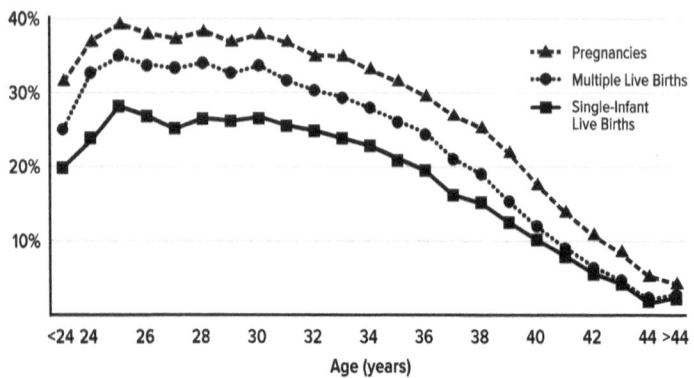

Percentages of ART Cycles Using Fresh Embryos from Fresh Nondonor Eggs That Resulted in Pregnancies, Live Births, and Single-Infant Live Births, by Age of Woman,* 2016

* For consistency, all percentages are based on cycles started.
Source: *National Center for Chronic Disease Prevention and Health Promotion, Division of Reproductive Health*

Fertility prospects are bleak for women over age thirty-eight

I don't want to bore you with all the specific science, but here's the story of conception and its relation to fertility in a nutshell.

Women are born with all the eggs they will ever use in their lifetime. After puberty, each month, one egg is released and makes its way out of an ovary (the ovaries often take turns each month, but not always) to embark on its journey down the fallopian tube to the uterus. If the egg is fertilized in the brief time it travels through the fallopian tube, it develops into an embryo that can implant once it reaches the uterus. Baby growing happens from there.

A woman is born with a finite supply of eggs (unlike men's sperm, which gets made in new batches daily). Once entering adolescence, her egg quality deteriorates over time, just like the rest of our bodies. Old eggs, like any old thing, can have problems. The DNA itself starts to fall apart, which can cause genetic defects. If the body doesn't naturally abort in a miscarriage, the fetus may be nonviable, which means it can't survive outside the mother and dies at birth. Then there's a whole host of genetic issues that can affect an infant who does live, including Down syndrome, autism spectrum disorder (ASD), and a bunch of rare conditions caused by chromosomal abnormalities that no one except doctors have even heard of. Some conditions are so rare that many doctors have only read about them in medical journals.

Overall, a woman's eggs are considered high quality until the time a woman hits thirty. At age thirty, her fertility starts to decline with each passing year. Between thirty-five and forty, the curve goes into freefall with eggs rapidly losing both quality and number until their viability bottoms out around age forty-four when the majority of a woman's eggs have died off.

Fertility complications aren't always the result of low-quality eggs, or the lack of eggs. Sometimes, it's caused by misfires in the machinery—fallopian tubes or uteruses or placentas or cervixes that don't work right and can't support a baby to full term. The low numbers depicted in the chart aren't just about genetic defects and abnormal development of the fetus. Pregnancy complications, miscarriages, and stillbirths for other reasons also skyrocket. Considering everything that can go wrong, it's a wonder women have babies at all. This is why doctors break out the kid gloves for pregnant women over thirty-five and give these mothers lovely descriptors like "advanced maternal age" and "geriatric."

But as much as modern women want to throw around a few curse words at ageist or sexist language, our biology doesn't care about our feelings. Here's the brutal statistical truth—at thirty-five, the average woman has a 25 percent chance of having a normal, healthy baby in a normal, uncomplicated pregnancy.

At forty, her chances drop to 10 percent. After forty—well, let's just not look at the numbers after forty.

"I'm such an idiot. Why didn't I freeze my eggs when I had the chance?" I said under my breath.

I guess I was louder than I thought. "Cheri, don't beat yourself up," Dr. Babymaker said. "While egg freezing first started in the mid-1980s, it was considered experimental until 2012. I don't recommend that women freeze their eggs after age thirty-two, due to the egg quality issues we've discussed, which for you would have been in 2000. Unfortunately, egg freezing wasn't a realistic option for women of your generation."

His words took my self-loathing down a notch. "Is it already too late for me, Dr. Babymaker?" I was amazed I got the full question out and didn't turn into a complete puddle on the floor.

"I know it looks bleak, Cheri," he said, his tone soothing, "but we have options. I've been doing this for a long time, and there are several steps that we need to take to get a true picture of your fertility. It's premature to be fatalistic. I'm showing you these numbers so you know we have a long road ahead, but I wouldn't be in this business if I wasn't good at defeating those odds."

Time to put my big girl panties on. I took a deep breath to compose myself. "Okay, tell me what I need to do to get pregnant."

"The first thing we're going to do is order blood work to check your hormone levels. And there's an AMH test, which stands for anti-mullerian hormone test, that is an indicator of how many eggs you have remaining and whether y our body is in perimenopause."

"Menopause?" I yelped in disbelief. I wasn't even thinking about menopause! This was getting worse and worse.

"Yes," he nodded, "your body may be entering the early stages of menopause."

I felt like a WWF fighter getting pummeled by one body blow after another. How much more could I take before I surrendered?

It's not impossible for me to get pregnant, I gritted my teeth and tried to reassure myself, *this will just be a little more complicated.* "So what's next, Dr. Babymaker?"

Dr. Babymaker smiled encouragingly. "Try to stay positive. We need to be optimistic while we figure out what's going on with your body. Your mindset is just as important as your physical journey, so don't lose hope yet."

Then he laid out the sequence of events that would be my world for the next few months.

I'd do a hysterosalpingogram (his-ter-oh-sal-PING-o gram), or HSG test, to X-ray my uterus and fallopian tubes by inserting a dye into my reproductive tract to locate any physical obstructions that would prevent conception or carrying a fetus to term.

Blood work would include an FSH (follicle-stimulating hormone) test, which measures levels of the hormone that stimulates ovary follicles to mature and make an egg, and an LH test, or luteinizing hormone test, which measures the hormone that takes care of the ovaries and can determine how many eggs I might be able to produce during a cycle.

"All of this will help us understand what's preventing you from getting pregnant naturally," he reassured me. "Once we identify the issues, we'll figure out what's needed to get around them. Of course," Dr. Babymaker continued, "we'll also do a Fertilome test, which is used to identify forty-nine genetic variants in the mother's DNA that cause various disorders and diseases that could impact fetal viability and quality of life." Beneath his medical jargon, I translated: they needed to make sure I didn't possess genetic defects that could cause my baby to develop severe abnormalities or even die.

I was overwhelmed by this point and so disappointed in my body I almost missed asking, "What tests does Gaston need to take?"

"Actually, not many," said Dr. Babymaker. "We will check to make sure he has viable sperm. Since he doesn't do drugs or drink heavily, I don't anticipate a big problem there. We'll be prepping the sperm and using medical intervention to inseminate you, so we don't need to worry too much about overall volume, quality, or motility, meaning how well the sperm swim. We'll pick the best specimens to introduce into your uterus."

"Oh, how sweet," I said, perhaps a little too brightly, "you're going to introduce the sperm and egg. Sounds like a good old-fashioned courtship to me." I couldn't help it—I needed to lighten the mood.

"Oh, and one more thing. You and your husband will take STD tests."

I almost laughed. Gaston and I barely had sex anymore.

"It's standard procedure," Dr. Babymaker said, for once almost sounding embarrassed, or like he was trying to give me an argument to get my husband on board. "We need to make sure we aren't putting you or your partner at risk of contracting any sexually transmitted diseases while we undertake fertility."

"I can follow the plan, Dr. Babymaker," I said, the absurdity of the STD test requirement reviving the corporate executive in me. I was pretty sure this requirement came from their lawyers to reduce their legal liability. "All these hoops are similar to what I've already had to go through getting foster parent certification."

I'd need all my determination for the task ahead. This first gauntlet of tests was just to figure out exactly where I was in my own fertility lifespan. Some women mature (a nice word for *get old*) faster than others, which means their fertility drops off at earlier ages.

Two weeks later, I was back in Dr. Babymaker's office for my test results.

"I have good news and bad news," he started.

Of course he does, I thought. "What's the good news?" I needed some good news.

"The good news is there's no obstructions or structural issues with your fallopian tubes or uterus. You should be able to carry a child just fine, which is great, because that means you won't need a gestational surrogate to carry the fetus for you."

I blinked. *At least there's that.* "So what's the bad news?"

Dr. Babymaker watched me closely. "The bad news is your body is approaching menopause at a faster pace than average for your chronological age. Your internal clock ticks a little faster than other women's. This means your egg count isn't where we'd like it to be for a natural conception." *Oh, great. Yet another strike against me.*

Each setback on this road of medically assisted fertility brought a new wave of despair, desperation, and loss. So much so that it caused me to envy (dare I say, resent) seeing how effortlessly motherhood came to just about everyone else. I'm sure it was a false perception and oversimplification, but it felt very real. I'd worked for so long and so hard to make the perfect fairy-tale castle for my future children and ended up with no one to live in it. *Why is it so easy for those women and so hard for me?* Why did I have to go to such extreme measures simply to get what other people were given so easily?

When would I have to stop proving that I was worthy to be a mother?

"Is my body too far gone to have a child?" I asked, breaking from my self-pity and forcing my attention back to Dr. Babymaker's words.

"Don't worry," Dr. Babymaker said, giving me a grin. "We

have ways to stimulate production of your eggs. But we'll have to take over your body to get it to conceive."

I flinched. Giving up control was my nightmare, but I would do it for my little girl.

That nightmare turned out to be more vivid than I wanted it to be. Out of all the things I'd done to become a mother to date, this was the most difficult. I'd have to give up the control that had become so important to me in adulthood. I was also giving up control of the most intimate parts of my body. I felt like I was in that old 1970s sci-fi movie *Invasion of the Body Snatchers*, but instead of the movie being done after two hours, I was in it for months on end.

Every aspect of my body's functions were monitored and regulated by outsiders I didn't know. I took weekly blood tests (did I mention I have trypanophobia, an extreme fear of needles, and had avoided them most of my life?) and did physical exams to tell how many follicles were producing eggs and how those eggs were maturing. I was on a bajillion drugs and hormones—Clomid to help stimulate the production and development of eggs, estrogen to grow and maintain endometrial lining, and progesterone to stimulate egg release and the thickening of the uterine lining. Some were injected into my belly daily with needles, and others came in the form of pills and vaginal suppositories. Between the suppositories and a host of medical instruments to check the effect of the suppositories, I had everything but the kitchen sink shoved up my hoo-ha.

All the poking and prodding and the cocktail of hormones wreaked havoc on me physically, emotionally, and mentally. Every negative feeling was magnified. I yelled at the mailman. I cried at diaper commercials. For month after month, the world was in a perpetual state of coming to an end.

All of this done with the single goal of getting my body to make a good egg that would accept Gaston's pampered sperm.

The first and least invasive fertility method Dr. Babymaker wanted to try was intrauterine insemination, IUI for short. This is the "turkey baster" approach that most people think about when they hear the words "fertility treatment." As the path of least resistance, it's also the least expensive method, at only $2,000 to $3,000 per cycle.

In IUI, the mother goes through a similar process to make a healthy egg, but a combination of medications are administered in a high enough dosage to stimulate the production of multiple eggs instead of just one. Then, doctors use human chorionic gonadotropin (hCG) to trigger the release of mature eggs as candidates for insemination. The sperm are collected from the father (yes, it's what you're thinking, using the tried and true "watch some porn and ejaculate in a cup" method), then prepared in a special wash, concentrated, and placed directly into the uterus at the best moment to be fertilized—when the mother's eggs first drop into the fallopian tube. In essence, the doctors are making it easier for the sperm to reach their target.

When Dr. Babymaker explained it to me, I couldn't help thinking of what I viewed as Gaston's inherent laziness and our lack of sex life. Here I was, going through a battery of tests and procedures to the point where I felt like a Muppet with one too many hands up my snatch telling me what to do, and Gaston's sperm got a layup?

The whole thing was both ridiculous and exhausting, and when you're always on the verge of either laughing or crying during your path to fertility, it's best to share with a friend.

"I mean, how many strangers *really* need to see your vagina?" I said to Cindy, as we enjoyed pastries and chai lattes at Lola

Savannah's coffee house after church one day and I fanned myself through another hot flash, a side effect of the medications.

"I know, right? And I can't stop watching baby animal videos!" Cindy lamented, sipping her latte. If Ruth was my wine friend, Cindy was my coffee friend, a trend in my outings that had grown as I prepped my body for pregnancy. We both needed a sympathetic ear to survive the fertility process.

I met Cindy in the same Bible study group as Serena. She was a fellow high-tech colleague in a similar fertility boat as me, and like me, she had kissed more than her fair share of frogs before finally meeting her prince. She was married now and determined to knock down any roadblocks hindering her from becoming a mother. "We'll take this path together," we'd vowed, relieved to find a kindred spirit that knew the struggle of measuring her life in thirty-day cycles, the time it took to go from the start of a new menstrual cycle to pregnancy. Both of us lived for the three-to-five-day window in which an egg could be fertilized. I was happy not to have to go on this difficult journey alone.

The first month after I started my IUI treatments, my ovaries didn't make enough follicles that would produce eggs, so we had to abort the cycle.

The second month there were enough follicles, but they didn't mature properly, so no eggs were viable. Another failure.

With each cycle, the arrival of my dreaded period devastated my world and dashed my hopes on jagged rocks. It meant I wasn't pregnant and would have to start the process all over again.

The third month, there were enough follicles, and they were maturing well.

"This could be the one!" I said to Gaston as the doctors happily informed us that we could do the insemination procedure on Friday, three days later.

On the day of the procedure, my fickle hormone-induced emotions soared. "Third time's the charm!" I chirped joyfully to Dr. Babymaker in the exam room as I finished tying my hospital gown.

"Um, Cheri, we have a problem," Dr. Babymaker started, looking at the notes his nurse handed him. "We don't have an STD test on file for Gaston."

My face drained of color as I glanced over at Gaston, who now looked like a puffer fish as he studiously avoided eye contact with me. "So, that means we can't do the procedure?" I asked, aghast. *This could NOT be happening!*

Not one to dwell on failure (or perhaps, he didn't want to get thrust into the middle of a heated fight between husband and wife), Dr. Babymaker gave me a long look. "I want you to do one thing," he said. "Go home and have sex with your husband."

I don't think there's a name for the level of fury I felt at that moment. "You're supposed to be my partner in this, Gaston!" I yelled, once we were in the car heading home. "I'm going through hell and all you had to do was jack off in a cup and take a fucking STD test! You had months to do that test, *months*. Where were you when I needed you? When our future child needed you?"

"It just slipped my mind!" Gaston groused. "I think I misplaced the lab slip but didn't want to tell you. I can't be expected to remember everything in all this complicated fertility stuff."

Speechless, I hugged my middle as I rode in the passenger seat, cradling my precious eggs. *This was supposed to be our chance! My* chance to finally become a mother.

The sex was the most awkward chore I'd ever experienced. Mechanical, but somehow worse than the robotic procedures of the fertility clinic since our coupling came with an undercurrent of resentment and rage. I found myself envying insects like the praying mantis, where the female of the species eats the male after sex. A girl's gotta get that baby-making protein somehow! Not surprisingly, the mother mantis only cannibalizes weaker males. As a bonus, if I ripped off Gaston's head mantis-style, I wouldn't have to look at his pathetic face. I wondered if Gaston had taken Viagra to get and sustain an erection, as there certainly was no tender foreplay. It felt like the torturous act would never end. Ultimately, it was an aborted mission.

I was actually relieved I didn't get pregnant this time because I didn't want my child's conception story to be tainted by the memory of that loveless act. But I also felt completely demoralized after another failed attempt at becoming a mother.

Despite all the false starts, I wasn't prepared when my fertility prospects went off the cliff.

The fourth month, my ovaries stopped responding to the treatments. "Your eggs aren't maturing the way they need to," Dr. Babymaker said solemnly. "Based on what I'm seeing, I'm concerned about the quality we'll get, too." We'd been trying to get my body's beleaguered egg-making machine to go interstellar, and it felt like Scotty from *Star Trek* was frantically saying to Captain Kirk, "I'm giving it all she's got, Captain!" but nothing was happening. At some point, we had to acknowledge my jalopy of a starship was done.

It felt like no matter what I did, it was doomed for failure. I'd been trying and trying, doing everything I was supposed to no matter how uncomfortable or inconvenient or painful, and now I was done? My curly-haired girl was disappearing from my sight, and it seemed the harder I tried to catch her, the faster she ran away—just like my dream in that boardroom so long ago.

After all this time, all these years of waiting, hopelessness crushed me, and I wasn't sure I could get up again. I was tired of getting my hopes up only to have them dashed again. Now,

I was even more bitter and angry at Gaston than before. From my perspective, he had wrecked our last chance with his selfishness and stupidity.

I needed a break. I went home and downed a bottle of Stag's Leap Cabernet. At least this was one stag that would deliver.

After a week of licking my wounds, I got a call from Dr. Babymaker's nurse. He wanted to see me.

I went into his office the next day and Dr. Babymaker got right to the point. "I think you should consider using an egg donor, Cheri," he said suddenly, seemingly oblivious to my despair.

My emotions reeled, refocusing on the life preserver he'd thrown me. I'd heard of sperm donors but not egg donors. "Is that a thing?" I asked.

"Yes, it's extremely useful to use an egg donor. It can dramatically increase your chances of having a healthy baby. We know your uterus is healthy. If you use eggs from a twenty-five-year-old donor, your odds of carrying a healthy child to term will be that of a twenty-five-year-old."

Recalling the stats on the Chart of Doom, my eyes widened. This was like finding the Fountain of Youth!

"So you know, using an egg donor in an IVF procedure costs $30,000 to $50,000 per cycle."

Hmmm, the Fountain of Youth is an expensive bitch, I thought cynically. But what was all my hard-earned money for, if not for this? I knew fertility wasn't cheap, and I was thankful that my good tech company insurance would cover at least a portion of it.

Dr. Babymaker was quick to get through the rest of his pitch. "You've got a couple options if you're looking for an egg donor. One option is to use a donor agency. There are several of them across the United States, especially in California. Using an agency is more expensive, but there's a lot more donors to choose from and you find out more about each donor. You can see pictures of them from childhood through to adulthood. Our office works with egg donors, too, but your selection of donors will be more limited. Either way you go, the donors have undergone all the genetic and medical testing in advance. If they've donated before, you can get a sense of how well their cycle went, including how many eggs were retrieved and how they mature."

Well, I'd done a kind of online dating while in the foster parent system. Why not for an egg donor?

But I did feel a twinge in my soul. Could I sacrifice the dream of having a child that shared my genetics? A petty part of me thought it was unfair that Gaston would get to use his genetics when he'd hardly done any of the work. Our child would still look like him and inherit his strengths, weaknesses, and quirks. It was a double standard I didn't even know could exist in the most feminine space of fertility and birth. Would Gaston somehow be more of a daddy to our child than I was a mommy?

I waved my hands in the air to shake off the image. *Get ahold of yourself, Cheri, you know from your experience with Aurora that blood doesn't make a parent.*

After getting home, Dr. Babymaker's words still echoing in my ears, I hit the internet to do my research and fell down the rabbit hole of epigenetics. Turns out, a child's genetic heritage comes from a combination of sperm and egg, but the actual expression of those genes is modified by the gestational mother who carries the fetus. Brain function and development, metabolism, stress tolerance—so many things that influence how a human approaches life can be profoundly impacted by the environment of the womb. This gave me a measure of peace.

My child might not have my DNA, but through carrying her, having my body nurture her through the first nine months of life, she would have my stamp. I would still be considered the birth mother. It would be a bond that no one could break.

Then I did some serious soul searching. Morally and ethically, I had to consider the unavoidable fact that an egg donor was my best chance to have a healthy baby. Did I really want to force something to happen that could put my child in danger or cause him or her to suffer? The more I thought about it, I decided it would be horribly selfish for me to use my own tired eggs, knowing I might cause my child unnecessary pain and hardship through birth defects or a life-limiting genetic condition. So yes, I would sacrifice my own DNA, if it would produce a healthy, happy baby with the best chance at a healthy, happy life.

This was my first true step toward motherhood—because motherhood, I'd come to realize, requires the willingness to sacrifice my needs for those of my child.

Maybe it wasn't all bad to get a fresh start on the genetics front. Hopefully, my child would be spared some of the wounds and character flaws that my blood relatives had inflicted on me.

So I started preparing for the biggest creative project of my life.

IVF, or in vitro fertilization, is when an embryo is made outside of the mother's body, either with the mother's eggs or donor eggs. The donor would be going through her own hormone treatments, exactly like I did during my IUI cycles, to stimulate her ovaries to produce multiple mature eggs that would then be retrieved in a surgical procedure where they suck them out through a tiny tube. Then, the doctors don't just give the sperm a layup, they serve the eggs to them on a literal tiny platter by putting them in a petri dish full of freshly washed swimmers.

Once the eggs are fertilized, the doctors watch the eggs for three days to see if the cells divide properly and develop into a healthy embryo. Hopefully, the process produces multiple embryos that are then monitored for growth. Multiple embryos enable parents to go multiple rounds of IVF if needed. Just because the embryo is healthy doesn't mean it will implant in the uterus. An embryo can only survive about five days after fertilization if it doesn't implant, the time it would take to travel down the fallopian tube after a natural fertilization. In IVF, on the sixth day after fertilization, the best-looking embryo is introduced into a hormone-prepped womb ready for implantation. Unused embryos are then frozen for future use. Eggs and sperm can also be frozen separately, in the case of younger adults wanting to hedge their bets when they get older, or who have fertility-compromising medical conditions like endometriosis or cancer, or who are transitioning to another gender. In most cases, freezing fertilized embryos is preferred by doctors because they are known to weather the freezing and thawing process better than eggs and sperm do.

When it came to selecting where I would look for my donor, I decided to go with a third-party agency. I reasoned I was going to be spending a shit-ton of money on IVF anyway. What's $10,000 more? Now wasn't the time to cheap out, especially if a donor agency would provide a broader selection of qualified donors to choose from.

Once I selected an agency, I went into work mode, tirelessly combing through donor profiles. I scrutinized the donors' photos, imagining what they were like growing up. I studied their medical histories and demographics, including things like appearance, height, weight, and ethnic origin—the things that make the selection process feel a bit superficial and reminiscent of the foster child bulletins I'd read only a year before.

But unlike the foster kids, the donors wrote their own stories. I pored through their interests and educational pursuits, their philosophies on family, what mattered to them, and why they'd become a donor in the first place.

It was the stories that drew me in the most. I wanted to know why these young, attractive, potential-filled women wanted to go through a rigorous and risky fertility process to enable a woman like me to have a child, a venture that most wouldn't do even with the hefty paycheck. I wanted to find a donor that fit, that felt just right.

Once I chose a donor, I'd effectively hire (go under contract) with them. Then the donor, expecting this call since she signed up for the program, would start her regimen of hormones, drugs, and check-ups. Since they are young and healthy to start, one or two cycles is the norm, but that's still a multiweek process compared with the two-minute commitment when a man donates *his* genetic material. The time and invasiveness of the treatments, check-ups, and retrieval process are why egg donors get paid upward of $15,000. Some donors who match the Barbie profile of genius Miss America with blue eyes, blond hair, and a Harvard PhD can get up to $100,000 on the private market.

Ultimately, I picked a donor who had coloring similar to the little girl I had seen in my dreams. She had a fair complexion and light brown wavy locks. The pictures from her childhood looked strikingly like the child I had envisioned. Her beautiful blue eyes pierced right through me. She was a nursing student who worked in a fertility clinic. She spoke about the way she had watched women like me struggle and she thought it would be gratifying to help a couple achieve the family they desperately wanted. She was the one; I just knew it.

The paperwork went quickly, and we were off to the races. Well, sort of. There's a lot of waiting at first. While you wait, you get updates on the donor's status as you go through your own treatments. My donor and I raced along parallel reproductive paths—she to produce healthy eggs, me to produce a healthy environment for those eggs once they were fertilized. It was a delicate handoff, a relay the doctors timed perfectly. There would be a three-to-five-day turnaround between when the donor went in for her procedure and when I went in for mine.

Twelve healthy, mature eggs were retrieved from the donor. Nine five-day embryos resulted from fertilization. A great outcome. We decided to implant one embryo and freeze the rest, not risking the complications that could come from multiple fetuses but wanting the chance to try again if my body didn't accept this first embryo.

The day I was to go in for the implantation procedure was gray and stormy, but I was unfazed by a little bit of thunder and lightning. Gaston and I still limped along in our relationship, so he came with me. I wished my mom was by my side for this moment instead of Gaston. She had supported me through the fostering process when my father warned it would only lead to heartache, and welcomed Aurora as her grandchild with open arms. She was also with me throughout the fertility process, experiencing the roller coaster of every triumph and disappointment as I got my hopes up only to land back on "Go" again and again. This was the backdrop for the most important journey of my life. But in this case, Gaston got first rights to be there for the embryo transfer, even though he didn't deserve it. Not wanting to encroach on our big parenthood moment, she stayed home.

There was little fanfare as I entered the room where the procedure would take place. I laid down and turned my head so I could see the embryologist, visible on camera in the lab, load my future child into the catheter that would be placed inside of me.

As I contemplated what was happening, my mind started to wander. The bright lights and sterile environment of modern medicine faded, and it was just me and the nameless donor as one woman, striving to bring life into the world with Dr. Babymaker and his team of nurses as our tribe. Admittedly, it wasn't the romantic picture I had envisioned, but it would have to do. Through the smells of antiseptic and latex mixed with the chill of the air and the instruments, I thought I heard the faint sound of the ocean waves and the wooden roller coaster again. *We will meet soon, little one.*

"We're done, Cheri!" Dr. Babymaker said, grinning. After all the anxiety and failures, the quickness of the procedure took my breath away. Did I feel any different? I wasn't sure. Dr. Babymaker patted my shoulder. "Now, we wait."

Yes, now we wait.

CHAPTER 10

RACHEL'S STORY

"CHERI, IT'S BARBARA, DR. BABYMAKER'S NURSE. I CALLED to give you this news personally."

It was two weeks after the embryo transfer and my blood tests had just been sent in. I held my breath and crossed my fingers and toes. It was unusual for the head nurse to make this call. I'd spent so much time at Dr. Babymaker's office over the last few months that I was on a first name basis with most of the staff. I instantly wondered if she was calling because the news was bad. She knew the tough road I'd had and perhaps she wanted to be the one to break the news to me. Or maybe it was a sign of good news. I was afraid to hope.

"Cheri, the test was positive. You're pregnant!" Barbara tried to stay composed, but her excitement jumped through the phone. After all the failed cycles, she'd become just as invested as I was in the outcome.

"Really?" I asked softly, wondering if I heard her wrong or whether this was a dream.

"I'm positive," she reassured me. "I checked the results twice." My own joy could hardly be contained. I wanted to share this news with everyone. "Oh my God, that's wonderful!" I got out. "Thank you so much for calling!" Immediately after I hung up, I called Gaston at work, then my mother, Cindy, Ruth, Serena…everyone I could think of that had played a pivotal role on my road to fertility. I knew couples often waited until after the first trimester was over to announce the news just to be on the safe side, but I'd already been waiting months—years!—and I couldn't wait any longer. I was pregnant at last and this child, THIS child, would be all mine.

A child no one could take away.

We had come so far to get to this point. I felt like I'd climbed to the top of a giant mountain, only to see a more massive edifice towering in front of me, making the mountain I'd just scaled look like a molehill. Sort of like the feeling Texans get doing a day climb of the rounded pink granite face of Enchanted Rock just outside Fredericksburg, only to realize its height didn't even come up to the big toe of Everest. I had reached a huge milestone, but my journey to becoming a mother was just beginning. I had nine months more to wait while my body nurtured and developed the child growing inside me.

Now that I was pregnant, I wondered if this could give Gaston and I a fresh start in our marriage. Aurora had brought us somewhat closer. Perhaps our own child would bond us even more. It was worth a shot, seeing that I wasn't going to divorce a third time, so we were stuck with each other. We'd start with some date nights to see where it went. What did we have to lose?

In the coming days and weeks, I maintained Dr. Babymaker's diligent routine of blood tests, oral medications, suppositories, and creams—all to ensure my hormone levels would continue to rise appropriately to sustain the pregnancy.

I found out I didn't need to worry about good hormone levels in an unexpected way.

On a Tuesday night, Gaston and I decided to go to The Oasis on Lake Travis. It was a popular Tex-Mex place with multiple tiers of decks and a spectacular view of the lake. In fact, it was the place where Gaston and I had one of our first dates, and we had enjoyed many birthday dinners and evenings with friends there. I loved their food—seafood enchiladas, sizzling fajitas, street tacos, and that staple of Texas restaurants, queso compuesto (for non-Texans, liquid cheese with seasoned ground beef on top). But as soon as our server brought out my favorite enchiladas and put them in front of me, I felt like I was going to puke. I put a hand over my mouth and barely made it to the ladies' room when I tossed my cookies.

I thought I might be coming down with something. The next day, I woke up feeling like a horse-drawn carriage had run over me. "I think I have a stomach bug," I told my friend Fiona on a call the next day. Fiona had been a friend of mine for over two decades. We met in middle school and carried our friendship through high school, college, and into adulthood. Now she was a frazzled mother of four boys, ages one, three, five, and eight. I had even stood in as her birth coach for her deliveries because her husband got queasy at the sight of blood.

"You've got morning sickness, silly!" she cajoled, amusement in her voice. "It's good that you feel like crap because it means your body's working to carry the baby. I had morning sickness constantly with all my kids. Saltine crackers were the only thing I could keep down for weeks!"

My wonder and relief at this new tangible sign of my advancing pregnancy was tempered by feeling absolutely miserable every single day for the next three weeks. No food appealed to me. Nothing except key lime pie. It tasted amazing—whether it was going down or coming up. I went to the store and bought five of them.

But other than the key lime pie, the continued nausea and onslaught of fatigue made me want to do something that would take my mind off my body's struggles. I called Fiona one night to commiserate.

"I'm thinking about going to Santa Fe again," I suggested. "I didn't get to see everything since my visit got cut short last time." So much had happened in the last nine months. I wondered what new luck the mystical city would bring me.

"Oh, I've always wanted to see Santa Fe," Fiona said wistfully. "It would be nice to sit and talk with other adults over a glass of wine without being interrupted," she continued, "or to consider a restaurant for the food and not worry about whether it has a playground. To sleep past seven o'clock in the morning and not have to change a diaper for three whole days. That would be heaven on earth."

Clearly, Fiona needed a break. She sounded desperate. "Do you want to come with me?" I asked, stepping into the obvious hole in the conversation that Fiona had left hanging open.

"Oh my God, really?" said Fiona, with more excitement than I'd heard from her in a long time. "I'm in! Let me sort some things out with my husband and my mom. This is going to be great. Thank you for letting me tag along!"

"Of course, it will be amazing to spend some time together," I said, feeling full-to-bursting with the good things in my life.

Just then, I heard a *bang!* and peals of laughter over the phone. Fiona paused as a more ominous *thud thud thud* drowned out her voice, followed by squeals and crying. "Brock, honey, get that baseball bat away from your little brother and untie him, please," she said, her voice raising. "Cheri, um, I'll have to call you later for the details, okay?" Fiona hung up so quickly I barely had time to say goodbye.

Boys, I thought. *God, please spare me from having boys!* I only half-jokingly prayed.

Then I called my mother. She didn't need any convincing to go. She'd been with me through thick and thin already and was up for a little R and R, plus, she knew Fiona well since we'd been childhood friends and she used to hang out at our house all the time, escaping her wicked stepmother. The trip would be a mini reunion of sorts.

The drive to New Mexico from Texas was starting to feel like a pilgrimage that was symbolic of my mission to become a mother. The last time, before I got the call about Aurora, the journey was tinged with dejection and betrayal. This time, I felt excited and triumphant, even with the persistent morning sickness, as the landscape transformed from flat barrenness to verdant trees and warm red cliffs that enveloped the car like an embrace. As my spirit got lighter the closer we got to our destination, I couldn't help noticing a few gray clouds to the west. I hoped we wouldn't be in for rain while we were there.

We got into town Saturday night, tired and stiff from our ten hours in the car. After a quick dinner we called it a night, planning to sleep as long as we wanted, followed by brunch and an afternoon of shopping on the Plaza.

At 2:00 a.m., I lurched out of sleep. The nightmare was still vivid. I was on the edge of Bridalveil Fall in Yosemite National Park. Awestruck as I took in the majesty of the scenery around me, I got distracted and lost my footing. I tried desperately to catch myself, but I began to plummet down into a canyon that was dark and deep. I gasped for my breath. A swell of panic overtook me. Instinctively, I reached down between my legs and felt a sticky wetness. I got up and went quietly to the bathroom, trying to avoid waking Fiona and my mother, who were sleeping in the adjacent queen bed. With all the suppositories and physical changes that I was going through, I didn't have any idea what this new feeling was.

When the harsh hotel bathroom light came on, it revealed a scene from a horror film. The hand I'd used to touch myself was stained red, and my blue cotton nightgown was covered in blood. This was not the usual first trimester spotting. I was bleeding. Bleeding *a lot*, I found as I quickly stripped and took stock of myself. Panic set in. Was I losing the baby?

I can't lose my baby!

I cleaned myself up the best I could and put on a menstrual pad I kept for emergencies in my luggage. It was the weekend, late at night, and we were far from Dr. Babymaker. I didn't know what to do. For an instant I thought about going to a hospital, but I couldn't make my legs work properly. I was frozen. I didn't want to believe it was real. I didn't want to give it life or energy. I told myself to banish that thought and hope it would all go away.

While I tried to stay positive, I couldn't escape the thought that I might be having a miscarriage, although I had no idea how a miscarriage would feel. I hated the term *miscarriage*. The very word *miscarriage* seems to blame the mother for a fetus that doesn't make it to term. An unfortunate stigma surrounds a mother who "miss carries" her baby, like she accidentally dropped it because of incompetence or some preventable mistake. But Mayo Clinic miscarriage statistics from 2023 estimate that 10 to 20 percent of pregnancies end in miscarriages before the twentieth week of gestation, a number that could be even higher because many pregnancies are lost even before the mother knows she's pregnant.

I stood upon the precipice of disaster in that Santa Fe hotel.

I lay motionless in my bed for the next three hours, willing the sun to come up faster, afraid to move or even breathe. I asked God to save my baby. I bargained every way I could. *I'll be a better Christian. I'll be a better daughter. A better friend. A better wife. I'm even sorry for all the bad things I've thought about Gaston lately. I'll do anything You want me to do. Just, please, God, save my baby.*

At 6:00 a.m. the light of dawn finally broke through a small gap in the hotel curtains heralding the start of Sunday, God's day of rest. *Please God*, I pleaded, *work a few more hours for me and my child!* I couldn't be patient any longer. I woke my mother in the bed next to me and told her what was happening. We agreed we should head back to Austin. Dr. Babymaker's office was closed, but one of the nurses was always on call. In the back seat of the car, where I could stretch out and take any kind of pressure off my middle, I scheduled an ultrasound appointment for Monday morning as soon as they had an opening.

"It's okay, Cheri," my mother tried to comfort me from the passenger seat. "Bleeding can happen. It doesn't mean the baby's in trouble." Her voice remained low and calm, almost a whisper—it was the I'm-scared-shitless-but-I-don't-want-you-to-know-it voice I remembered from childhood. My mom always wore her heart on her sleeve. When she's afraid she can say all the right things, but her face tells the real story: eyes wide, skin pale, cheeks deflating like a balloon when the hot air is turned off. It was a good thing she was in the passenger seat so I couldn't see her face. I knew my mother was also terrified of losing the baby, her grandchild, but she was trying to remain positive for my sake. Just like she'd always done.

There was a long pause as Fiona adjusted the driver's seat to her petite five-foot-four-inch frame and tried to find something appropriate on the radio, finally settling on a slightly fuzzy classical station in an attempt to ease all our nerves. Being a four-time mom, she knew a shadow of the fear I was going through. In fact, Fiona had been through her own crisis when birthing her second child. The doctors discovered meconium, the dark, thick, sticky first poop of a newborn baby that sometimes discharges while still in the womb, in her amniotic fluid while she was in labor. When a baby breathes in meconium in utero, it can cause severe illness and even death. That delivery was stressful and dicey to say the least, but fortunately her son made a full recovery.

"Maybe we should pray," my mother finally spoke, as she located a Christian station playing "How Great Is Our God" by Chris Tomlin, grasping at anything that could relieve the tension.

"You go ahead, Mom," I said. I had no words. I couldn't bring myself to care about anything outside my body. The praise and worship music brought me no comfort. *God, if I lose this baby, I will never forgive You.*

I lay in the back seat, not saying anything for the rest of the drive home, trying to breathe and stay calm. My mother and Fiona could say nothing to put me at ease, and they knew it, so they, too, fell silent as the car ate up an eternity of highway. Until I knew that my baby was alright, I was like a ghost, a shadow of myself, merely existing during the purgatory of the drive back to Austin.

We mercifully rolled into my driveway, and I gingerly hurried into the house to check myself in the master bathroom. I wanted privacy for this. My hands shaking, I saw a large clot in the toilet when I stood up. *Was that my precious baby?* At five weeks, he or she would be too small to discern with the naked eye, still only a small bundle of cells no bigger than a poppyseed. Not wanting to alarm Gaston or my mother any further, I flushed the dark red mass down the toilet and kept that information to myself.

The bleeding continued throughout the night. Sunday was another exercise in insomnia as powerlessness and worry gripped me and wouldn't let go. Gaston didn't know what to say, so he said nothing. We laid there sleepless and stressed on opposite sides of the bed. As the sun came up, I tried to prepare myself for the worst.

At 10:00 a.m. on Monday morning, Gaston and I went in for my ultrasound. I held my breath and squeezed Gaston's hand as Dr. Babymaker inserted the scope into my vagina. My baby was so small at this stage it would be undetectable with the normal probe-on-the-belly ultrasound. I didn't care. I'd long since lost all notions of modesty during my fertility treatments. I strained to make sense of the images on the monitor as Dr. Babymaker's practiced eyes darted around the screen, searching for signs of my baby.

During an ultrasound appointment, what you hear first is the ocean. The mother's living blood and organs make a low, continuous noise, like the crashing of waves on a distant shore. Out of this endless sea came the sweetest sound I'd ever heard.

Thump, thump, thump.

Could it be? That sounded a lot faster than my heartbeat.

Thump, thump, thump.

Dr. Babymaker smiled. "That's your baby's heartbeat, Cheri."

I burst into tears as gratitude and relief washed over me. I had convinced myself that my baby was gone. I didn't even think a heartbeat was discernable at five weeks, but there it was. I gave Gaston's hand a strong squeeze.

Thank you, God! My baby was okay. Everything in the world was okay.

"Be sure to schedule your first trimester sonogram with Dr.

Andersen," said Dr. Babymaker. "He's the ultrasound master." I could hear the smile behind his professionalism.

"I will," I said, elated.

After that frightful weekend, the pregnancy got much smoother. The regular blood tests and medications continued for the next two months. At three-months gestation, I would graduate from Dr. Babymaker to Dr. Ruby Heartsong, my regular OB-GYN. I was excited to move from the realm of fertility to the realm of everyday pregnancy. But first, I'd have to pass the next milestone: the first trimester ultrasound with Dr. Andersen.

Dr. Andersen had been doing ultrasound and prenatal diagnostics for over thirty-five years and, frankly, he was a legend. All he did all day was look at sonograms, or the pictures of a fetus generated during an ultrasound. Conservatively, the man was guardian to the health and welfare of over 100,000 healthy pregnancies throughout his career. Tall and thin, his gray hair gave him a stately air, but he still managed to be warm and caring, both with his staff and his patients. I felt confident that I was in incredibly good hands.

Traumatized by the scare at five weeks, I was on edge going into the ultrasound. I held my breath as Dr. Andersen sat back in his chair. "Your baby is fine, Ms. Bergeron," Dr. Andersen reassured me. "We'll see you at your twenty-week check-up."

When I arrived home, I glanced at my phone and saw that I had a message from Cindy. "Call me when you can," it said. I guess I was too preoccupied with worrying about the ultrasound to pay attention to my phone. When I reached Cindy, she broke some news of her own. "I'm pregnant, too!" she squealed. Cindy had started going to Dr. Babymaker soon after I selected him as my doctor. She was just a few months behind me in the fertility process.

"Oh, Cindy, that's wonderful! I couldn't be happier for you and Richard."

We got off the phone a few minutes later. Like me, she couldn't contain her excitement and had lots of people to call. This was the perfect end to a perfect day. Cindy and I would take this journey hand in hand. I envisioned taking pictures belly to belly with my friend. *Maybe we could purchase houses on the same block*, I thought dreamily. We'd both have girls. They'd play together. Go to school together. Graduate together. Could life get any better?

As I moved into my second trimester, the dreaded morning sickness subsided. Feeling physically better and with positive reports, I felt that I was hitting my stride.

This is really happening!

Now that I was past my first trimester, I started announcing the good news more broadly. After Aurora left, I had transitioned my multiclient consulting gig into a full-time role at a Fortune 50 company. It was nice to have a reliable income, paid vacation, and a steady stream of projects. I set about telling all my co-workers. I wanted everyone to share in my motherhood joy. To me, little else mattered.

I began making preparations for the baby, buying several big-ticket items—a high-end stroller, top-of-the-line breast pump, and the coveted multiposition cradle swing.

The one thing I couldn't bring myself to do was touch the nursery. From the day that Aurora left, that room had been sealed up like a tomb. It was a time capsule for the life I had with her. Even though I was elated about the new bundle of joy that had come into my life, the loss of Aurora still weighed heavily on my heart. I wasn't ready to let her go. In my desperation to become a mother, I really hadn't given myself time to grieve the loss of her. I told myself that I would deal with that later and busied myself with preparations for the child that was on its way.

As I occupied myself with binge-reading the What to Expect book series, starting with *What to Expect When You're Expecting*, and compulsively watching YouTube videos of childbirth and infant care, the weeks of my second trimester sped by. Before I knew it, my twenty-week ultrasound was at hand. I would finally find out whether I was having a boy or a girl! This was before the days of gender-reveal parties, so I'd had the standard early genetic tests at three months for a handful of chromosomal conditions, like trisomy 13 and Down's syndrome, that are more common for women of advanced maternal age. If the doctors had looked at whether the baby had an X or Y chromosome, they didn't tell me.

I was acutely aware that mothers were supposed to stay neutral and dispassionate regarding the sex of their baby, but after all my dreaming, my heart was set on having a girl. And, yes, I felt guilty about that. In fact, I had convinced myself that I would be the mother of two girls. I really had no logical explanation why I felt that way. I just had some innate sense. Whether this was true intuition or a reaction to my history with men, I wasn't sure.

On a Friday afternoon, almost two-thirds of the way through my pregnancy, Gaston and I waited with anticipation as I lay on the examination table. Jane, the ultrasound technician, squirted gel on the probe that would glide over my belly as it explored the health of my baby. *Goodbye, vaginal probes!* I thought with satisfaction.

"At least now we have a gel that warms up. No chilly goo for you!" Jane joked as she helped me tuck my shirt up. A quick swipe on my lower belly and she grinned. "There you are, baby!" Jane turned the probe right and left, then right again as I strained to make sense of the staticky images and blurry body parts on her screen. She ran the probe all down my belly and to my sides. Her grin faded and she sat expressionless, looking at her monitor. I fixated on her face for any scrap of information about my beautiful baby. I could see the monitor, too, but had no idea what I was looking at among all the light and dark fuzz on the screen.

Jane remained silent behind her monitor. After about five minutes, she turned to me, her face solemn. "Ms. Bergeron, I'm seeing some troubling things about your baby. Her spine looks curved, which might be spina bifida." Jane's eyes went wide when she realized she had spoken aloud, overstepping her bounds. "I'm, um, so sorry. I shouldn't have said that. I'll go get Dr. Andersen."

Shocked, I lay on the exam table, unable to move. A few traces of leftover gel grew cold on my belly.

Jane hesitated again, realizing she had missed an important step in the process. "Do you want to know the sex of the baby before I leave?" Jane asked softly, her humor forgotten as she wiped away the gel with a towel.

"Yes," I whispered.

"It's a girl." Then she hurried out of the exam room like she was running away from a crime scene.

My heart jumped into my throat and the world stood still. *What. Was. Happening?!* All I gathered was that my baby had a disease that didn't sound good. I had heard of spina bifida in passing, but I had no idea what it was. *Maybe she's wrong*, I thought to myself. *Jane's not the doctor.* Gaston and I sat in stunned silence until Dr. Andersen entered the room.

Serene and confident, Dr. Andersen came right up to where I still lay prone on the exam table, gathered his instruments, and angled the ultrasound monitor more toward us. "Let's see what's going on," he said, pulling a rolling chair up close to me so he could reapply the ultrasound probe to my belly. He worked in silence. Whatever he saw, he kept his face calm before he spoke again.

"Ms. Bergeron, from the looks of this sonogram, your child shows signs of spina bifida," said Dr. Andersen. He spoke so matter-of-factly about it, I wondered how many other mothers he'd given bad news to.

"I've heard of spina bifida, but I don't know much about it," I confessed. "What does this mean for my baby?"

Dr. Andersen sat back in his chair slightly so he could address both parents. "Spina bifida is a genetic condition where the baby's spinal cord fails to develop properly," Dr. Andersen said. "The causes of spina bifida are unknown, and it doesn't show up on standard chromosomal genetic screening," he continued. "It tends to develop later in gestation, which is one of the reasons we do a twenty-week ultrasound."

"Is she going to be okay?" I asked desperately. My voice trembled when I spoke. I wanted this information, needed it, but my vocal cords were seizing up, and I felt tears pressing at the back of my eyes.

For all his professionalism, Dr. Andersen hesitated. "From what I see, your daughter is very ill. It appears that her head is enlarged with fluid. Her spine is severely curved, and her spinal cord is protruding out of her body. You can see it here," Dr. Andersen said, hovering the probe over the grainy black-and-white image of my baby's back. "And her feet are twisted and misshapen, what we commonly call a club foot." Dr. Andersen sat back in his chair again. He seemed to take a long time cleaning the ultrasound probe and replacing it in its holder. "I'm very sorry, Ms. Bergeron. I know this is a shock for both of you. I'd like to have you come back on Monday so we can discuss this situation further."

"Okay, thank you, Doctor," was all I could say, the trauma striking me dumb. *Did I really just thank him?* If I wasn't already lying down, I think I would have fallen. Slowly, I got up from the exam table and wiped the last of the gel from my belly. So smooth, so pale an expanse of skin. It hinted at nothing of the tragedy it contained.

I walked out without making the appointment, being careful not to make eye contact with any of the other pregnant women in the waiting room. I felt like I had left my body, and my limbs were being manipulated by some other person who walked me like a marionette from the office, down the elevator, out to the parking lot, and into my car. I cradled my stomach as if there was something I could do to comfort my baby or ease her pain. As if I was trying to catch or save her. Gaston walked with me in silence. It seemed to me that he had gone inward, like he often did in times of trouble. Impenetrable. He hadn't spoken at all at the appointment after Dr. Andersen's diagnosis. We'd driven separate cars since he'd come to the doctor's office from work. He barely acknowledged me as we separated to go to opposite ends of the parking lot. Sitting alone in my quiet car, I called my mother.

"I'm having a little girl, Mom," I said, tears leaking down my cheeks, "but she's very sick." My voice stopped working. Her maternal instincts tingling, my mother remained silent and waited for me to finish. "Mom, she looked terrible. I'm…I'm not sure if she's going to live."

"I'm getting in the car right now. It'll only be a couple of hours before I get to Austin," she said, her voice giving me the strength I needed to make it home. "Cheri, I'll throw a few things in a bag, and I'll go as fast as I can. I promise."

My mother was coming. I didn't have to go through this alone.

As I drove, my mind whirled with shock, anger, grief, and despair. How was this possible? I had used a young egg donor. She'd been genetically screened for risk factors. I had sacrificed my own genetics to make sure my baby would be healthy. And now this? How could God do this to me? Didn't He realize how I had sacrificed everything to have this child? My money, my body, my control, my very existence?

I had given everything I had, and yet it wasn't enough. Worse yet, I couldn't escape one nagging thought. *Was this my fault?*

I sat in a stupor until my mother arrived. She did her best to try to distract me, but it was no use. The reality of my situation, and that of my child, was inescapable.

What was also inescapable was how useless Gaston's presence felt to me in my time of need. If ever there was a time that I needed my husband to be there for me, this was it. But to me, Gaston was completely missing-in-action emotionally. He sat motionless on the couch while my mother and I talked through every feeling and nuance of the situation. What could have gone wrong?

"I'm going to the gym," he said shortly after my mother got settled.

"To the gym?" I echoed in disbelief. "Gaston, I need you here. We have to make a plan!" I was incensed.

"I...I just need to be by myself for a while," he said, gathering up his car keys. It seemed like his only priority was self-protection, and that meant leaving me, the source of his emotional distress. It was like he was running away from a sickness, and I was that sickness.

"Gaston if you walk out that door, I swear, I'll, I'll...," I stumbled over my words as I hugged my belly tight.

He paused by the door and stared at me blankly. Through me. "I've gotta go." Then he left.

I grabbed a pillow from the couch and half-screamed, half-cried into it. I wanted, dare I say NEEDED, Gaston to be my comforter and my protector. I was carrying *his baby*, after all. He seemed like he couldn't care less. I still carried expectations that my husband would be a partner in our marriage, and he was failing miserably.

"You're being unfair to Gaston," my mother soothed. "He's grieving, too."

Yes, Gaston was grieving, too.

But I was the one who felt forsaken. I was the one who was carrying our doomed child inside me. I wasn't just losing my child, I was losing my faith that things would turn out alright. As far as I was concerned, Gaston resembled all the other men in my life who had betrayed and abandoned me.

God, where are you?

Truth is, I had told my mother very little about what I viewed as Gaston's many betrayals in our relationship, so she was blissfully ignorant of the man he truly was. I figured, if I'm not willing to divorce him, what good will it do to make my parents despise him, too?

The next few days were filled with brutal realities and difficult decisions. On Monday, I went back to Dr. Andersen's office with Gaston and my mother to learn more about my daughter's condition. Unlike the Friday before, Dr. Andersen was much more explicit about the life that awaited my daughter.

"Your baby's condition is very serious. I've been doing sonograms for over three decades, and from what I see on your daughter's, her spina bifida is very severe. In more specific terms, I would say it's likely that your daughter won't make it to term. If she does, it's probable that she will never be able to walk or talk. It's doubtful that she will be able to communicate, or even feed herself. You should prepare yourself. She will likely need to be institutionalized for the rest of her life, however long that is.

"Given all of this, it's my belief that your daughter's condition is incompatible with life, and it's my recommendation that the pregnancy be terminated. Of course, that's an extremely difficult and personal decision. I also recommend that you speak with our genetic counselor to get more information and understand the factors that contributed to your daughter's condition." Dr. Andersen paused after his speech, his eyes going soft. "I'm so sorry, Ms. Bergeron, I know this is not what any parent wants to hear."

"Okay, Dr. Andersen," I said. I didn't care if everyone saw my tears now.

We were ushered out of the clinic by a nurse through a back hallway and door. I wasn't sure if that was to spare me the view of the happy mothers with healthy babies in the waiting room by the front door, or to spare those mothers the sight of what it looks like when a dream becomes a nightmare.

I had worked so hard to become pregnant and suffered so much, and now the child I finally got to carry was going to die. Or worse. She'd survive birth and live out her brief life in a tortured existence, never able to walk and play and learn and live like other children.

Robyn, the genetic counselor, had as few answers for us as Dr. Andersen.

"The causes of spina bifida are unknown," she said, parroting what we'd already heard. "It's a very mysterious disease and we don't know much about it. Causes could originate in the egg, the sperm, or factors in utero," she finished, waving a few fingers in the air in a small gesture toward me.

"In utero?" I asked sharply. "Do you mean, like my body?"

Robyn gave an awkward smile. "We prefer to say *environmental*."

Robyn was way too blasé about all this for my taste, especially when I was sitting across from her carrying my sick child. I needed something firmer than "we don't know."

"Would it make sense for Gaston to get a genetic test? I was tested when we had first thought about using my eggs."

Robyn folded her hands on the desk. "It probably wouldn't make any difference."

"But my egg donor was healthy!" I said, trying to make sense of it all. "Don't the fathers contribute DNA, too?"

"Of course," she said soothingly, as if I was being unreasonable, "but there are no biomarkers we know of for spina bifida. It doesn't show up on genetic tests. It's actually a fairly common defect, occurring in one of every two thousand births," Robyn continued, as if I wasn't sitting in front of her as that unlucky statistic. "Once a child with a neural defect like spina bifida is born into a family, the chance of this problem recurring with another child increases to one in twenty-five. We suggest large doses of folic acid be taken by the mother in the first four to six weeks of pregnancy to help prevent it."

Prevent it? I thought. This was the first time I'd heard of that recommendation. It certainly didn't help me now.

For the next several days, my unborn child and I suffered together. She was still alive, but only because my body sustained her. I soon learned that terminating the pregnancy would be difficult because I was nearly at the end of my second trimester. For mothers like me, who got the awful news at their twenty-week ultrasound that something had gone horribly wrong in their cherished baby's development, this would constitute a "late-stage abortion."

Abortion? That's what I'm doing? It was the last thing I would ever want. In my mind, abortions were for sixteen-year-old girls who accidentally got pregnant, not forty-year-old women like me who had spent tens of thousands of dollars on fertility and had been trying desperately to get pregnant for four years.

I was told there were only a handful of doctors in Texas who would perform late-stage termination procedures. Outside of Planned Parenthood, there were none in Austin. I was warned that if I went to an Austin Planned Parenthood clinic, I would likely face altercations with pro-life protesters, which would only amplify my pain and anguish.

There were a couple doctors in Houston and a few in Dallas. If I waited more than a few days, I would likely have to go out-of-state to have the procedure done, as Texas law in 2011 cut off all abortions at twenty-four weeks. I had to make a decision quickly.

While I was dealing with the impending death of my child, it seemed like Gaston retreated further into his own shell. He kept going to the job he told me he hated without taking any personal time off. From my point of view, he checked out. He didn't speak to me when he got home. He would go to the gym, sit on the couch mindlessly watching TV, and then go to bed early. I felt abandoned on every front. First by God, then by my own husband.

In those two days of suffering, I made one request of Gaston before he went to work one day: think of possible names for our child. "Gaston, we're going to have to say goodbye to our little girl in a couple days. She needs to have a name. It's really hard for me to think straight right now. While you're at work today, please spend some time thinking about what we should name our baby."

Ten hours later, I met him at the door. "Gaston, have you thought of any names?"

The look on his face was blank. "I didn't have time to think about that," he told me. I was thunderstruck. *How could you think of anything else?* I know everybody deals with loss differently, but Gaston always seemed to be absent when loss came knocking on our door.

The jury in my head had come back, and its verdict determined Gaston had failed me as a husband.

I felt he'd misrepresented his character and his background to me early in our relationship.

He hadn't stepped up to get a better job so I could step back from my career to be the mother I wanted to be.

He'd pulled the rug from under me with the two foster sisters.

He hadn't been home when CPS came and took Aurora away.

I felt he'd emotionally abandoned me when we got the spina bifida diagnosis.

So, amidst all the other betrayals, I had to stomach what I viewed as Gaston's cowardice on this front, too. I would have to name our baby alone.

In light of the struggles I had with relinquishing and then reclaiming my last name, I knew names held significant meaning. I decided to name her Rachel Marie. It was the prettiest and most French-sounding name that came to mind. The name Rachel is associated with purity, beauty, and gentleness. Marie meant "wished-for-child." This was a name befitting my precious baby girl.

Dr. Andersen referred me to a specialist in Houston that did complex medical procedures. I guess it was a nice way of saying late-stage abortion doctor. Once again, I was in the back seat of my car. My mother was driving. Gaston was in the passenger seat. *Of course he was*, I thought bitterly.

I would have driven, but I had to write a letter. A letter to my little girl. I placed my right hand on my belly as if to connect with her by ESP. With my left hand, I began to write.

My Sweet Rachel,

I don't know where to start. Our relationship has just begun, but I'm told we have to say goodbye. I'm not sure I can do that.

The last six months have meant everything to me. I have dreamed so many dreams about who you would become, the adventures we would have, and the mother I wanted to be for you. But those dreams are being ripped away from us without warning. How could God give you to me and save you at five weeks, only to take you now? The cruelty is more than I can bear.

When we started this journey, I made a promise that I would protect you no matter what. The brutal truth I must face is that your life will never be what I want for you. You deserve a life filled with love, joy, and possibility. Fate has dealt us a hand where your physical body is irrevocably broken and your life on earth would be filled with immeasurable pain and struggle that no child should have to endure. As your mother, I must keep my promise and put your well-being above my own. I will not allow you to suffer. I have to make the heart-wrenching decision to let you go.

So, my precious girl, I entrust you to God for now, and I will carry you with me forever. Though our time together is cut short, your impact on my heart is eternal. I can only pray that you will be there to greet me when I get to heaven. I will be the one running toward you.

With a heavy heart and boundless love,

Mommy

CHAPTER 11

RIPPLE EFFECTS OF LOSS

IT'S A THREE-DAY PROCESS TO PERFORM A D&C, OR DILA-tion and curettage procedure—a.k.a., an abortion. The day I went into the clinic was day one.

"Do you want anyone in the room with you?" the doctor asked.

"No," I said. I'd had the long drive from Austin to Houston to think about this. I believed Gaston would be no comfort to me, and I didn't want my mother to carry the burden of witnessing what was about to happen.

The first part of the procedure stops the baby's heart.

The doctor and his nurses hooked us up to heart monitors. First for me.

Beep—beep—beep.

Then for Rachel.

Beep, beep, beep.

A fetus's heart always beats faster than an adult's.

Beep—beep—beep.

Beep, beep, beep.

A thin needle was placed through my abdomen into her heart.

Beep—beep—beep.

Beep, beep, beep.

Then medicine was administered through the needle to stop the heart.

Beep—beep—beep.

Beep, beep, beep.

I was awake for the whole fifteen-minute procedure.

Beep—beep—beep.

Beep, beep, beep.

For a while, the only sound in the room was the dual beeps of the heart monitors.

Beep—beep—beep.

Beep, beep, beep.

Beep—beep—beep.

Beep, beep, beep.

Beep—beep—beep.

Beep, beep, beep.

Beep—beep—beep.

———

Beep—beep—beep.

———

I cried out, "Is she gone?!"

Then I stopped breathing.

I woke to the doctor and his team crowded around me and my own heart monitor stabilizing back to a normal rhythm. They had revived me. I wished they hadn't.

"Is my baby gone?" I asked again.

"Yes, Ms. Bergeron. The procedure is over," said one of the nurses. "You should rest now. Do you want your mother and husband to come back to be with you?"

"No. I'm not ready to see anyone."

"Okay, no problem. Someone on the team will be back shortly to check on you."

Now there were no more monitors. Just silence. Silence and the realization my baby was dead.

"Goodbye, Rachel. I love you," I whispered, as tears streamed down my face.

God, how could you take my baby away? I felt empty.

But I wasn't empty. Not physically. The ordeal was far from over.

A late-stage abortion is a multiday ordeal. Part one was over. The second part of the procedure places an instrument that looks like a thin stick, called a laminaria, into the cervix to dilate it enough that doctors can then scrape out the uterine lining to remove the now-dead tissue. Essentially, it's a medical technique that simulates what a woman's body does instinctively when she is about to give birth. It was meant to pry my body open to take my baby out. When the doctor put the laminaria in, I tensed up and cried out in pain because it hurt so bad. Hearing a woman screaming in an abortion clinic is the last thing you want other patients to hear. One of the nurses injected me with something to silence me and keep me still. I'd endured emotional and spiritual torture for the past week, and now I added physical torture to that list.

When that part was over, the doctor said that I could go home. I'd have to wait for the laminaria to work fully. I felt heavy with the knowledge that I was carrying the lifeless body of my little girl with me. My mother, Gaston, and I drove to my mother's house, the one she still owned in Houston, in silence.

The next day, my brother came to my mother's house for a visit.

"It's already getting hot and we're not even out of April," he mentioned casually to Gaston, who had his feet propped up in my parents' well-worn burgundy leather La-Z-Boy recliner.

"Sure is," Gaston said, perhaps relieved that someone was talking to him about something easy and trivial.

Phillip paused and sipped the sweet tea my mother gave him before turning to me. "How's the new job going?"

I blinked as I sat on my mom's burgundy-and-blue plaid couch, trying to breathe through the pain in my middle and in my heart. *What is* wrong *with him?* I thought. *Doesn't he know what I just went through? Does he even care?*

But even as I felt my brother was acting strangely, I didn't have the energy to confront him about it.

"It's fine, Phillip, work is fine."

Work? Is that all he could talk to me about? Phillip went on for the next thirty minutes about his job, the fact that he won the Super Bowl pool at the office, and how my niece was about to go through confirmation in the Catholic church. I hoped he was there to comfort me, but it seemed to me he wasn't there to give love and support. His presence, compelled by a sense of obligation, felt hollow.

My life felt hollow, too.

It took three days for the laminaria to do its job. Three days of agony curled up on my mother's king-sized bed. Three days of carrying my dead daughter before I could go back to the clinic for the last part of the procedure, when the doctor would scrape the uterine lining to remove what was left of Rachel.

Once again, I was spread-eagle on an exam table. The doctor

used something that looked like a slim vacuum cleaner attached to a hose to go through my vagina and cervix to the uterus, where he sucked out the placenta and the uterine lining that three days before had provided sustenance to my baby. Thankfully, I couldn't see this part, but hearing it was almost as bad. I did not escape pain here, either.

I asked if there were any remains. Anything for me to bury or cremate.

"There's nothing to bury," the doctor said. "The endometrium tissue we collected looks like a mass of clotted blood. It's treated as biohazardous material, like the tissue left behind from a surgery. The clinic will dispose of it in an appropriate way."

There was nothing left of Rachel to grieve over.

She was gone.

After we returned from Houston, my relationship with Gaston unraveled. My opinion of him was clear—he had abandoned me when I needed him the most. I felt he wasn't trustworthy. And I couldn't forgive him for committing what I viewed as the ultimate betrayal—the abandonment of me and our child. Essentially, we stopped speaking to each other. There was nothing more to say.

I sought escape in my work. I volunteered for a special project, a new acquisition. I still had my other responsibilities, so I was essentially doing two full-time jobs. Interacting with my co-workers was strained. I had shared my pregnancy with everyone. They knew I had been out of work for several days with a medical emergency. I guess word had gotten around that I was no longer pregnant. Everyone tried to act like nothing had happened, but I could see the discomfort on their faces as they tiptoed around me. They were at a loss what to say, and I didn't blame them. People are comfortable consoling someone who has lost an older relative or a pet, but losing a child was a whole different ball game.

I worked myself from 8:00 a.m. until midnight, tucked away in my home office. I would start drinking at 5:00 p.m., averaging a bottle of wine a night. I would get about four hours of sleep and then start over again.

I was trying to keep myself numb, but nothing could block the pain for very long. As evening darkened, my house quieted, and the wine kicked in, so would my despair, nearly overcoming me.

Engulfed in my pain, I called Fiona.

"I don't think I can make it without Rachel," I said, sobbing. "I need to be with her."

"Cheri, don't talk like that," Fiona said in a panicked voice. "You're scaring me."

"There's nothing left for me here, Fiona. I don't think God wants me to be a mother. I believed it when the Bible said he wants to give me the desires of my heart. Well, I wanted a baby more than anything, and He took her away. First Aurora, now Rachel. I hate Him."

"I don't know what to say, Cheri. I agree—it's totally unfair. But I need you to stay around. I love you, and I need my friend."

When we hung up the phone, I continued my argument with God directly.

Why are You doing this to me? Was it my bad romantic choices? Was it my materialistic jet-setting lifestyle? Was I undeserving in Your eyes to become a mother?

Was everything a punishment for trying to play God?

I was convinced that God hated me as much as I hated Him. Fiona's love for me would have to be enough, at least for today.

I continued to bleed from the D&C in the days that followed. My doctors told me some residual bleeding was expected, but this looked like a lot. My womb seemed to want to do the weeping I was trying to hide from the outside world.

I isolated myself from my friends, from church, even from my mother. Maybe because I couldn't deal with how some people, though well-meaning, failed utterly at comforting me.

"My friend Margaret sent something for you," my mother said on one of her now-frequent visits. "It's a keepsake that means a lot to her family."

I took the careworn shoebox from her and popped the haphazardly applied scotch tape holding the lid on. Sifting through crumpled white tissue paper that had obviously been reused, I laid my hand on something cold and hard.

I pulled a ceramic figurine out of the box. It was a vintage Dresden porcelain angel from the 1950s. I'm sure it was rare and valuable. She was about six inches high, her hands joined in prayer beneath a face devoid of expression or features. The sheen on her curly hair and flowing robe had lost its brilliance with age. Then I noticed one of the wings was chipped off, lost in a past accident. I ran my finger along the rough edge, the shattered porcelain still sharp enough to cut. I felt the blood drain from my face as my temperature rose. The cold ceramic grew warm under my clenched fist.

"Why would your friend send me something like this?" I hissed, flinging the offending angel back in its box.

Shocked, my mother took a step back at my anger. "That angel is precious to Margaret. She's had it since she was a child. It was meant to make you feel better!" my mother said, raising her hands placatingly, unsure whether to defend her friend or console me.

I looked at my mother, who seemed so much smaller now that I was an adult. My eyes burned.

"My baby's not broken!" I shouted in my pain. Then I burst into tears and stormed out of the room.

I knew I was being irrational, but I couldn't help it. Logically, I knew my mother was dealing with her own profound loss: first one granddaughter, then another shortly after losing her husband of forty-six years. All within a year. While her marriage was far from perfect, it was a source of stability and strength for most of her life. This tangled web of grief was a heavy load for both of us to carry.

I wasn't capable of feeling concern for my mother's pain because I was fixated on the crushing weight of my own. I went upstairs and flung myself on my bed. My reaction to the angel wasn't my mother's fault, nor her well-meaning friend's. I was inconsolable. All the pain and grief and rage and helplessness of the past few weeks rushed out of me. I don't know how long I cried, but eventually I felt my mother's arms come around me and she cradled me in the bed, unmoving, until the worst of the flood was over. "I'm sorry I cannot take away your pain, sweetheart," she said in a gentle voice. "If I could, you know I would in a heartbeat." Outside I heard thunder boom as a spring storm rolled in, darkening the room's light.

Cindy called a few hours later. My eyes were still puffy from the angel incident and my mother was making tea. Cindy still didn't know I'd terminated my pregnancy. I couldn't bear to tell her yet and dampen her joy.

"Guess what, Cheri?" Cindy, excited, asked when I picked up the phone.

"What?" I said, dreading her answer.

"I just found out the sex of my baby. It's a girl!"

I couldn't pretend anymore. Her words ripped the bandage off to find the wound I thought was healing was a raw mess. I started weeping.

Concerned, Cindy asked, "What's wrong?"

"Rachel's gone, Cindy," I said with the weight of anguish in my voice. "I just lost my baby girl."

"Oh," Cindy said, the excitement draining from her voice. "I'm so sorry, Cheri. What happened? I hadn't heard anything." I was already raining on her parade.

"I know, it's not your fault, we haven't told many people," I said. "We got bad news at our twenty-week sonogram. Rachel was really sick and her chances of survival were near zero. Dr. Andersen recommended that we terminate the pregnancy. It's all so fresh and raw. I just can't talk right now. I hope you understand." I got off the phone as quickly as I could.

Cindy's call exposed the jagged shards dwelling in my heart from Rachel's loss. How could I be the good friend that Cindy deserved and share in the joy of her pregnancy when my child was now gone?

A few days later, I sent Cindy a text.

> Cindy, I hope this note finds you well. I am so happy to hear that you and Richard are expecting a little girl of your own. I know how long and hard you've fought to get here. I hope you can cherish every moment of your pregnancy and that your delivery goes smoothly.
>
> The loss of Rachel is incredibly painful, and I'm afraid that being around my grief would diminish your joy and ultimately damage our relationship. You deserve to be happy and celebrate the life that is growing inside you. I wish things were different and we could have gone through this experience together, but I feel I must step away from our friendship while I try to heal from this tragedy. When the worst of my pain has passed, I look forward to reconnecting with you.
>
> Until then, know that I wish you the very best.
>
> Cheri

That was the end of my friendship with Cindy. She didn't see my note as a gesture of love. She said I abandoned her and was too selfish to be happy for her.

Maybe I was being selfish. I hated myself for being jealous that Cindy was carrying a daughter when I lost mine.

When Rachel died, everything changed. I changed. And I would never be the same person again.

I didn't just lose Rachel on that exam table in Houston. I lost my marriage. I lost Cindy. I lost the dream of being able to experience the motherhood journey alongside her. I lost God. I had even lost the feeling of closeness with my mother. And I seemed to be losing everything else, too.

I soon realized all these losses were related. The part of me that died when Rachel died affected the relationships around me. Some of the damage was permanent. It was like a row of dominos, with one act of grief starting a chain reaction causing one domino of pain and loss to fall, and then another. Later, I'd call this the ripple effect of loss.

I desperately wanted a distraction from my grief. I couldn't hang out with my dance friends because I didn't want to pretend I was okay or inflict the toxicity of my grief on them. I had no energy to make superficial conversation or pretend that I cared about their lives when I didn't even care about myself. So I turned to the one thing that had always given me confidence and joy: dance.

I bought some private lessons with a professional instructor. He rented space at a private studio, which contained a small but clean dance floor with old oak floors and mismatched mirrors lining two walls. Short ballet barres were set up in front of one bank of mirrors and a rainbow of yoga mats were tucked neatly into cubbies in one of the corners.

We were practicing the Viennese Waltz, one of the most

beautiful and purest of ballroom dances. It had a breathless speed the traditional waltz lacked. Like the regular waltz, it's a rotary dance where you and your partner are constantly turning. Just when you feel comfortable spinning in one direction, the momentum reverses to go the other way. At a pace of 180 beats per minute, twice that of the regular waltz, it can feel like a runaway merry-go-round if done poorly. This was exactly the kind of exhausting diversion I needed to take my mind off my pain.

The instructor was walking me through a turn, showing me a reverse fleckerl (pronounced FLAYK-er-uhl) followed by a contra check, where the woman extends one leg to the side while maintaining a graceful posture, when a gush came from between my legs. In horror, I felt thick, warm liquid run down my thighs and calves, over my ankles and onto my rhinestone-adorned dance shoes, forming a puddle of carnage on the wooden floor. I was wearing a skirt to help feel the movement of the dance, so there was only a thin scrap of fabric to hold back the tide. My shocked instructor took a step back, at a loss of what to do as I hemorrhaged blood in the middle of the dance floor.

"Oh shit, I'm so sorry!" I said, alarmed and mortified at the same time. My instructor scurried to a tiny linen closet by the bathroom and came back with a wad of paper towels. I cleaned up as best I could. Thank God no one else was there. My male instructor was gracious, but obviously uncomfortable at witnessing such a personal female moment. I gathered my things and ran out as quickly as I could. Apparently, even dance provided no refuge for me.

This last bleeding incident was too much for me, and I made an appointment with Dr. Heartsong. Like my fertility doctor, my OB-GYN and I had grown close and were on a first name basis. "I'm sorry, Cheri," she said after she examined me, "it looks like there's still some tissue that wasn't removed at your prior procedure that is causing you to bleed more than you should. Normally, small bits of tissue pass in the first few days after a D&C, but some of your tissue appears to be stuck, and it's preventing your uterus from recovering."

My eyes widened. "So, some of Rachel is still inside me?" I asked.

"Well, most likely a part of the placenta, the organ that formed with and fed your baby," Dr. Heartsong hedged. "We'll have to do another procedure, a dilation and evacuation, or D&E, to remove the last of the tissue."

I knew I was still carrying my baby emotionally. I didn't know I was also carrying her literally. She'd been with me this entire time.

The D&E followed the same general process as the D&C, but since there was no living fetus to manage this time, it could be done by my regular OB-GYN. "It's what we do when a woman miscarries and her body doesn't pass all the uterine material," Dr. Heartsong assured me. "Your uterus will be able to heal after this."

I wondered if I would ever heal from this.

This time, they would give me general anesthetic for the evacuation procedure, where the doctors would remove the last vestiges of my daughter. Dr. Heartsong came in just before they were going to put me under. She could see the pain and distress on my face when she entered the room.

"Are you doing okay, Cheri?" she asked.

"Dr. Heartsong, don't wake me up from this," I pleaded, still weeping. "Let me go be with Rachel. Just let me go. Please."

Dr. Heartsong looked at me with a compassionate smile, saying softly but firmly, "I know it's hard. You're going to get through this." With that, the world went out of focus as I gave myself to the darkness.

CHAPTER 12

FINDING WORTH

I LIVED IN DARKNESS FOR A LONG TIME.

Eventually, no one wanted to talk to me about my grief, and I didn't feel much like sharing. They either avoided me like the plague, or they tiptoed on eggshells around me. They treated me like I was fragile. To a certain extent, I could understand, because I felt like I was made of glass. A thing that would shatter with the next hand that touched it.

I never felt so alone. I missed the feeling of Rachel moving in my belly. The future yawned before me vast and empty. Barren. If there were any glimmers of hope I couldn't see them, so I stopped looking.

I became a hermit. I didn't want to see anybody. I didn't want to talk to anybody. For months, my whole life revolved around work. Gaston and I shared the same dwelling, but that's all we shared. My nightly ritual of Cabernet was my sole source of comfort and refuge.

Like I'd done hundreds of times before, I dragged my garbage bins out to the curb one Wednesday evening so they'd be ready for pick-up early on Thursday morning.

"Evening, neighbor," a quiet voice said in a subtle Southern drawl. Dully, I glanced over and saw a man of medium build wearing a crisp pair of Wrangler jeans and a blue button-down oxford shirt, still wrinkle-free even with a full day of wear on them. It was typical tech business casual attire until I noticed his intricately carved leather belt adorned with inlaid turquoise and pointy-toed ostrich cowboy boots, exuding a distinctly New Mexican vibe. Worth gave me a small wave as he positioned his bin next to mine, within easy reach for the garbage truck. I may have become a despondent hermit, but out of all the things that had left me, politeness wasn't one of them.

"Hi, Worth," I twitched my fingers and gave a half-hearted sideways smile in the general direction of my next-door neighbor as we both went back for our recycling bins. I knew Worth from our typical neighborly pleasantries and innocuous small talk exchanged over the years. He'd been a high-tech executive and then worked as a developer in Austin's burgeoning real estate market. I couldn't help noticing Worth had great hair for a man in his early sixties—thick and a lovely shade of white. He had an understated elegance about him, with a look reminiscent of Ralph Lauren. Something about his presence felt peaceful and trustworthy, but I couldn't quite put my finger on it.

When we met back at the curb, all bins now accounted for, Worth paused and looked at me again. I had told the neighbors I was pregnant when I found out and started shouting the news from the rooftops, but that was several months ago. I guess the absence of my protruding belly, combined with zero signs of newborn celebration and my obvious depression had caused him to put two and two together. I rubbed my hands up and down my sides self-consciously. He smiled. A gentle, caring smile that felt like a warm blanket. Then he asked the question no one else dared to ask me.

"How are you doing, Cheri?"

Mysteriously, after a thirty-second exchange over garbage bins, I didn't feel the urge to hide anymore as tears started to flow down my cheeks.

His face filled with compassion. "Do you need a hug?"

"*Yes!*" I sobbed, and let my neighbor hold me up while I broke down.

As the storm eased, he discreetly stepped away. It didn't feel like an abandonment or that he felt embarrassed. It felt like he was giving me enough physical space to make sure I knew he had no ulterior motives. Even a polite distance away, his physical presence still managed to hold the emotional space for me—almost a spiritual space—waiting patiently as I caught my breath. "I can't imagine what you are going through," he eventually said, just before the silence grew awkward, "but I have some experience with loss. If you ever want to talk, you're welcome to come over for a cup of coffee. I've been told I'm a decent listener."

Blotting my eyes with my sleeve, I gave him a small smile. *What do I have to lose?* "Thank you very much, Worth. I might have to take you up on that."

The following week, I asked if Worth was available for a chat. As we sat in the comfortable black leather chairs in his living room, he let me talk without judgment. Sharing my thoughts with him, I felt at ease for the first time in a long time. At the end of our talk, he told me he had trained to become a grief counselor who specializes in neonatal loss several years ago. *How had I missed out on that important tidbit of information?*, I thought to myself. No wonder he was so compassionate and understanding. That coffee chat became a regular weekly visit.

I wouldn't go anywhere else. I wouldn't talk to anybody else. But I'd talk to Worth.

The coincidence was almost enough to make me believe in God again. Almost, but my anger was still a thick fortress I kept around myself.

Worth never tried to give me advice or tell me what I should or should not be feeling. Instead, he listened with empathy. After I'd purged the sharpest edges of my pain, he posed some questions for me to ponder.

"What kind of self-care would bring you comfort right now?"

"What can you do to start finding purpose in your daily life again?"

"What would be a small step or goal you could set for yourself in the coming days?"

It made me think. "Well," I answered, "I have no baby, but I still have the fifteen pounds I gained from the pregnancy. I can start exercising." Running seemed like a safe and solitary activity to meet my goal. So I took up running around Lady Bird Lake, the place I had once dreamed of taking Rachel. It's a wide spot in the Colorado River that splits downtown Austin into a north side and a south side. Wide paved paths meander along the riverbank and green expanses of lawn play host to gnarled oaks and wildflowers. Sometimes I'd catch glimpses of turtles, ducks, and snowy white egrets as I watched a rainbow of paddle boarders and kayakers make their steadfast journey up and down the river.

Gradually, my mind and body started to heal. Slowly, I felt my self-worth begin to re-emerge and I was able to put one foot in front of the other.

Aside from running, the second thing I needed was some time alone to relax and deal with my pain. I had been working myself nearly to death and was burned out. I wanted to decompress and gaze upon something beautiful. I decided I would take a two-week trip to the Caribbean with stops in St. Thomas and St. Croix. Perhaps the purity of the crystal-clear azure water would renew my soul—I hoped the change in latitude would change my attitude.

I did not invite Gaston on this trip, and he didn't ask to go along. I wagered he needed a break from me as much as I needed one from him. As I packed, I threw in the typical things—swimsuit, hat, sunscreen, and a book called *Heaven Is for Real*. I'm not a big read-for-pleasure person, sticking mostly to nonfiction that would answer practical questions about business and relationships. My mother bought the book for me because she'd heard it might bring me comfort. It had been on my bookshelf collecting dust. But beaches and books go together, right? Maybe now I'd be receptive to what it had to say.

Chapter after chapter, I sat in a lounge chair on a Caribbean island beach drinking fruity cocktails and crying behind my sunglasses. Not exactly the picture of bliss promoted on postcards of paradise, but it felt right.

The book recounts a little boy's near-death experience. One of the people the boy saw on his brief journey to heaven is a child he'd never met. Once revived and safely back on earth, the boy revealed a family secret: a sibling his mother had miscarried prior to having him . A little girl. She didn't have a name because her mother never named her. *I'm grateful my baby has a name*, I thought. I believed in the purity and innocence of that little boy's testimony. If his window into heaven was true, I could finally envision Rachel in a better place, free of the pain and physical limitations of her earthly body, and that gave me some comfort.

I also indulged myself in a ninety-minute massage in a cabana overlooking the ocean. The masseuse's expert hands gently pressed on all the tense muscles where I had stored the anguish of losing my baby. I wept unapologetically as I shed layer after layer of heartbreak and loss. It felt good to be vulnerable enough to allow someone to touch me again, even if it was a stranger.

As the two weeks drew to a close, I knew the trip had served its purpose. Rachel would always be with me. I still grieved and would always mourn the loss of my little girl. From time to time, I would find myself revisiting the memory of what she could have been whenever a sound, a smell, or an image came across my path that reminded me of her. But for the first time in weeks that felt like a lifetime, my steps became a bit lighter. Rachel's soul had found rest, and now mine could finally lay her down to sleep.

I was ready to move forward. And there was one thing I knew for sure. I had to become a mother.

"How has this loss changed your perspective on life relationships and priorities?" Worth asked during one of our sessions after I returned from the Caribbean.

"I'm done with Gaston," I said firmly. It was good to hear it out loud. "Last night, he did something that, in my opinion, proves he isn't willing to do what it takes to be a parent."

"Oh?" Worth asked mildly. "Tell me about that."

So I did. I told Worth what had happened the day before.

"I want to try again for a baby, Gaston," I said, as I summoned him for a heart-to-heart after returning from my trip.

Gaston jumped up like I'd kicked him. I guess he was surprised I was speaking to him at all. "Try again?" he said slowly.

"I know I'm not going to be at peace until I become a mother."

"We're not stable enough to try again," he said shortly. "Cheri, we barely talk to each other."

"You're right," I said, and I saw Gaston's eyebrow lift. I couldn't remember the last time we'd agreed on anything, either. He would love this next part. "But I don't really care. I realized on my trip that I won't feel fulfilled in life if I don't realize my dream of becoming a mother. I'm going to do this with you or without you. The fertility paperwork we signed states I get the remaining embryos in a divorce, but I don't want to wait for a divorce to be finalized." I took a breath. "I don't want to force you into something you don't want to do, either. Tell me, what do you need that will allow me to move forward with our embryos?"

Gaston paused for a long moment, deep in thought. Then he looked at me. "I don't want to be involved with any children if we're not together anymore."

I paused, unsure if I'd heard him right. "Are you saying you don't want to be a father to your biological children if we're divorced?" I asked, to clarify. Gaston had let me down a lot over the past few years, but this was a new low.

"Yes, that's what I'm saying," he said, almost nonchalantly. "I still hope we can work things out, but if we can't, then I want to walk away completely."

I was incredulous. I racked my brain to understand his reasoning. *This must be Gaston's way to gain control over the situation*, I thought. Over the years, I'd felt that self-preservation was his top priority. I guess this was no different. Except it *was* different—it was our kids and their future. Our relationship had been limping along like a wounded animal after Rachel's diagnosis. This was the final death blow. How could I ever move forward with someone who could walk away from their child?

I found a template online for a voluntary relinquishment of

parental rights. It spelled out all the rights and responsibilities that Gaston would be released from if we decided to separate, including relinquishing the right to have time with the child and care for them in all respects, including making decisions about their education, discipline, and religion. It also meant he would have no financial obligation to the child.

The words on the template jumped out at me and turned my stomach. "I relinquish my parental rights freely, voluntarily, and permanently." "I realize that I should not sign this affidavit of waiver of interest in child(ren) if there is any thought in my mind that I might someday seek to gain custody of this child(ren)."

The whole time we filled it out, I thought Gaston would change his mind. For once, he didn't. The next day, we went to the bank and got it signed and notarized (the look on the banker's face said he couldn't believe it, either). With our signatures still wet and shiny, the document looked all neat and legal.

We had both drawn our lines in the sand. I *would* become a mother. Gaston had made his position clear, both with actions and now words, down to the dotted line. He didn't want the responsibilities of fatherhood if we weren't together, and I had no desire to be with him anymore. Still, I wasn't ready to go through another divorce with all its trauma and emotional upheaval. Document in hand, I opted for the indifferent status quo while I got about the business of getting pregnant again.

I made an appointment with Dr. Babymaker to start a new cycle and prepare myself for another embryo transfer. There were eight frozen embryos that had resulted from our last IVF cycle. Once my body was ready, it would be go time.

"I'm on my own now," I told myself after I collected my supply of oral medications, creams, and suppositories from the pharmacy, "but I *will* become a mother, come hell or high water."

When I returned to work, I felt a greater sense of strength

and purpose. I knew my journey of grief wasn't over, but I had crawled out of the depths of despair and was back on course to become a mother. I was still a shadow of my former self—feeling disconnected from my friends and from my mom. And now my marriage was falling apart. I would keep that news to myself for the time being.

While my marriage and friendships crumbled, one work relationship rose to fill the void.

I met Hunter while working as the marketing leader on a new acquisition. He was the sales leader, so we were two halves of the whole that was needed for revenue growth. Essentially, the company I consulted for had acquired a smaller company, and it was our job to kick-start sales of the new products to our clients worldwide. My company was massive (top fifty in the Fortune 500) and was regarded as the Wal-Mart of software, meaning their distribution network was vast and powerful. With a new product to sell and a global rolodex of clients to sell it to, the opportunities were endless. Together, it was our job to achieve the business case that was set forth at the time of acquisition—in other words, make tons of money to make the investment worthwhile. And we killed it every day.

Hunter was charming and dynamic. Funny. Intelligent. Sarcastic with a sprinkle of mischief. He had a bald head, and I had a secret thing for bald heads. He was a compassionate leader who cared about his team. A father of two kids, he managed to balance both work and family.

I'd only met Hunter on the phone. It was pre-COVID, but this was the tech world, so we were already used to working remotely. But the phone couldn't hide Hunter's deep, commanding voice with the trace of gentleness. I found his layers intriguing. He was everything Gaston wasn't, and I couldn't help being drawn into orbit with him.

Four months into the project and one month into my new doses of fertility medications, the company had its annual user conference at Walt Disney World in Orlando, Florida. Thousands of people from around the world came for the massive event. It always fell on my birthday in June, so for the three years I worked for the company—for the three years I desperately tried to become a mother—I became a year older in every child's version of paradise. It was excruciating. The timing this year couldn't have been more poignant, as I was scheduled for my embryo transfer the day after I returned from the trip.

I wasn't even supposed to be at the conference. If Rachel had lived, I would have been home with my newborn in a blissful, sleep-deprived haze. Instead, I would be rubbing salt in that well-worn wound. But this was the coming-out party for the new acquisition, and I had to be there with bells on. There was also a small thought that kept poking the back of my mind. *This could be fun.*

Hunter and I met the night before the conference started to compare notes and strategize before day one of the event. We went to an Italian restaurant at the conference hotel. We'd been working via phone and video calls for months, but now we were face-to-face over osso buco and a pricey bottle of Cabernet.

After the shop talk was done, the conversation turned personal. Hunter had been married for fifteen years, but they had grown apart. Of course, he was on the road a lot, which is true of many salespeople, but he also felt betrayed by his spouse in similar ways I felt betrayed by mine.

"But I love being a dad," he said firmly. "My youngest, Stephanie, just had her first piano recital last week. She chose to do 'Stairway to Heaven,' of all songs. She had her best friend accompany her on a flute. I told her I expected a bigger house when she became the next Taylor Swift. And my oldest, Ben, is in a soccer league—we're on the road almost every weekend with his tournament team."

I grinned. "Sounds hectic and wonderful, Hunter." Then I sobered. "I wish I had kids. Gaston and I have been trying for years, and we're now doing fertility treatments. There have been some...disappointments." I hesitated, not wanting to let my guard down too much, or shut down the conversation by bringing in something too heavy. Gaston was a much safer topic. "And Gaston's been a bump on a log through most of it. I'm having to go to all these appointments and take all these hormones that make me crazy, and Gaston forgets to take an STD test, the one thing he needed to do," I complained, the story bringing up a welcome echo of the old frustration to banish my sorrow.

"Wow, did you hit him?" Hunter asked dryly.

"Oh, I wanted to," I laughed. Talking to Hunter felt safe for some reason and I was elated to be having a meaningful conversation with a man again. "But the doctor ordered us to go home and make a baby the old-fashioned way. I've never had angrier sex in my life. It was the worst!"

Hunter raised his right hand to rest under his chin and looked at me for an overlong moment as candlelight flickered in a votive between us. I felt myself grow warm. "Really? That bad?" he said slowly. "Because when I have angry sex, it's usually the best."

I nearly spit out the sip of wine I'd just taken as I felt my womb clench. *Was he flirting with me? My body certainly thinks he's flirting with me!* I didn't want to put too much stock in his words and let the conversation flow to safer topics after that, but my body kept zinging with new awareness, like a limb that was trying to wake up after being in one position for too long.

The next night was a gathering of the whole integration

team. We had recruited the best of the best to work on this lucrative venture. Everyone liked each other and knew they were doing good work under our leadership. The feelings of camaraderie and collective winning permeated the space. I even felt attractive for the first time in months. My body had a few new curves from the lingering baby weight I'd put on with Rachel and the new black dress I bought hugged them like they were meant to be there. I was still getting used to them. After a conversation with a teammate came to a natural conclusion and the other woman drifted away, I made a discreet adjustment to get a seam near my bustline to lie better. Sensing eyes on me, I looked up quickly to see who'd caught me in the act. From across the room, Hunter's gaze bore into mine. My body on a hair trigger from all the hormones, I immediately flushed hot and felt that clench again.

There's something happening here. But we still had a job to do, so I quickly glanced away and went to strike up another conversation with a teammate I hadn't yet spoken to.

The last night of the conference was the big party. My company had bought out EPCOT, so we had free reign of the theme park for hours. It meant unfettered access to all the rides and attractions. Everyone was expected to go. The conference had been a resounding success for our team—attendees were abuzz about our success. Personally, I had handled interactions at the smaller team events fine since I knew the people, but the thought of a huge event in a massive crowd of strangers when my emotions were at the end of their rope was more than I could take.

"Are you going?" Hunter asked after the last conference session got out. "I know the whole team will be there. They've earned a victory lap."

"I don't think so," I said slowly, feeling a little guilty. "I know

I should be showing up for them, but I'm exhausted, and these fertility drugs I'm on have thrown me all out of whack."

"Do you need someone to stay with you?" he asked. The question looked like platonic co-worker concern on the surface, but underneath was an edge that had my body suddenly sitting up to beg.

In the back of my mind, a little voice told me hanging back with Hunter was a bad idea. We were both married, even if those relationships were strained. But when Captain Picard shows up and says, "Engage!" in that smooth, sexy voice, and the jalopy-of-a-starship you'd long ago left for dead roars back to life at warp speed—a life that reinforces that you *are* still attractive as a woman, that all your womanly parts *do* still work, that you *can*, indeed, feel desire and happiness again—well, you can't help but buckle up and boldly go.

That night, we went to the hotel's steakhouse for dinner, their best restaurant. We talked so long we shut the place down.

When we were forced to leave, I suggested moving the conversation to the bar, but we knew all our colleagues would be there by now and our alone time would be over. Instead, Hunter suggested we continue the conversation in his room. I was happy to keep going on this joyride, curious about where it would lead. Once inside the room, we took up seats in the small sitting area. Meanwhile, the pheromones and tension kept building up in the small space until you could cut it with a knife. An ache built up in my poor hopped-up girl parts and, lacking any sense of propriety, they started screaming at me, *Kiss him already!*

You, shush. I told them. *Wait for him to make the first move.*

The sun was just starting to lighten the curtains and I got up to leave. It was 5:45 in the morning and he had to leave for the airport at 6:00 am. Hunter rose to his feet, too, rubbing his hands on his dress pants. *So he's feeling it, too*, I thought.

Well, now or never.

At the door, I turned to face him fully. Only inches separated us in the narrow foyer. "Are you ever going to kiss me, Hunter?" I asked. Or at least, I would have asked, if he hadn't jumped me when I opened my mouth.

It was a kiss that could wake the dead, soft and sensual and strong all at the same time. I rose to it like I'd been underwater for months and he was my last chance for air.

"I'll cancel my flight," Hunter breathed when we separated. But despite my unruly body that screamed *Yes!* I knew I was chock-full of suppositories and creams that would make intimacy awkward. Plus, something didn't feel right about going down that road just before I was about to get my embryos transferred. Motherhood was still my top priority, even then.

With a Herculean effort, I told him no. "I'm not ready for that," I said. "Go catch your plane." I urged him out the door to catch his ride to the airport. He reluctantly complied. When I was confident he was in the elevator, I laid down and gave myself four glorious orgasms in his bed.

Even though we didn't seal the deal, it was enough that he'd breathed new life into me. I could finally see some light again. Going back to my hotel room to pack for my own return flight, I felt a spring in my step that hadn't been there the day before. I'm pretty sure I could have flown from Orlando to Austin on endorphins alone.

It didn't take long for reality to bring me crashing back to earth. Only a few hours later, to be precise, as the miles put more and more distance between me and The Most Magical Place on Earth. I was getting my embryo transfer procedure the next day.

What did my time in Orlando mean for my future? Probably nothing. Hunter and I were both married. Perhaps it was just a moment, a fantasy within a fantasy setting. Nothing really happened except a kiss, anyway. *But what a kiss!* my happy body reminded me with a twinge. It felt like my DNA had been rewritten in those few minutes and I'd passed a point of no return, at least emotionally if not physically.

Meanwhile, I stood on the precipice of becoming a mother.

When I got home from the conference, I avoided Gaston. While exchanging the usual civilities, I hoped he didn't notice anything different between the me before the trip and the me that came back. I just said I was exhausted from the week and went to bed at 7:00 p.m. Hundreds of miles now separated me from Hunter, so I reluctantly tried to exit the world of Orlando and reenter the real world of Austin.

But the glow did not go away.

The next morning, at Dr. Babymaker's office, Nurse Barbara asked, "Are we going to transfer one embryo or two?"

It hadn't occurred to me to transfer two. "Is that an option?" I asked.

"Of course," she responded. "Sometimes they'll transfer more than one to increase the chances of a pregnancy, since not all embryos implant."

"I thought that was more the case when there was a question of egg quality and didn't count for my spring chicken embryos," I said dryly. *Was my humor starting to come back, too?*

"Well, normally that's the standard process." She paused, seeming to gather herself to choose her words carefully, "but I know you've been trying for a while now, and the odds of a viable pregnancy with two is always better than one, no matter the egg quality." Her eyes softened for a moment. This was the nurse who'd called to tell me the good news about Rachel, had been there through my miscarriage scare, and had heard about the tragic outcome of my pregnancy. She couldn't offer direct advice, but I knew she was rooting for me.

I've always wanted two children, I thought with my returning optimism. *Why not try for twins? It would be a one-and-done and I won't have to go through this again.*

"Yes, let's transfer two," I said firmly, rolling the dice.

For a second time, I watched the live camera feed as the embryologist collected two thawed embryos into a catheter from the clean lab, walked them to my exam room, and handed the catheter and its precious cargo to Dr. Babymaker, who would use the catheter to go up the birth canal and deposit the embryos in my uterus. Even though God and I weren't talking much these days, I sent up a silent prayer anyway. *Please, let this procedure work so my family can be complete.*

I think it was the first time I'd talked to God since Rachel died.

In the recovery room, I got a text from Hunter. "What are you wearing?"

I laughed out loud. "A hospital gown," I irreverently texted back.

"Ooooh...sexy..."

"Yeah, my doctor just impregnated me," I teased.

"Bummer, I was going to apply for that job." His text sounded mostly joking, but it made me wonder.

"Too bad, you were too slow," I wrote. I couldn't help yanking his chain after he'd taken so long to make his move in the hotel room.

The gravitational pull between us strengthened, and the messages with Hunter continued over the weekend. I had gotten a taste of life again and I wanted more. Other than the babies that were hopefully taking root, Hunter was the only thing that mattered.

The next work week was a blur. My personal and professional lives collided and now meetings weren't just meetings, they were rendezvous. A chance to connect with Hunter. Even in group meetings, our exchanges were filled with inside jokes and double entendre. In between meetings, we would exchange messages to sustain the connection that was forming between us.

On Friday, I decided to knock off work early and head to Ski Shores to look at the water. Ski Shores was a local legend. It started in 1954 as a hamburger stand for campers in the area and grew in popularity because of its prime location on Lake Austin. It was gentrified now as a full-service restaurant decked out in vintage 1950s décor, complete with a metal roof and weathered wooden beadboard in turquoise, brown, and red hues to carry on the nostalgic vibe. Just a few minutes from my house, it felt like a different planet. A more serene one.

I ordered a virgin margarita and sat down to gaze at the water. I pictured myself there with Hunter. Just as my muscles were starting to relax in the warmth of the early summer sun, I got a call from Gaston.

"Hi, Gaston, what's up?" I said, maybe a tad too happily.

"Who's Hunter?" he said sharply.

I bolted to a stand, caught off guard not only by his vehemence (his actions repeatedly showed his lack of concern for our relationship) but also by his snooping. *He must have seen notifications come up on my computer*, I reasoned with one half of my brain. The other half attempted to do damage control.

"He's the guy I'm working with on the acquisition," I said. "I've mentioned him before."

"Are you having an affair?" asked Gaston bluntly. For a few

seconds, I was speechless. What would I call my relationship with Hunter?

"No…I'm not," I assured him, but the tentative note in my voice said otherwise.

"Ha!" Gaston barked, like he'd caught me with my hand in the cookie jar. "I read your DMs, Cheri."

"So now you're spying on me?" I asked, trying to distract him by going on the offense. "Gaston, why do you even care? Our marriage has been over for months. You've made clear to me you don't want kids, even your own, and that's *all* I want." I was on a roll now, all the pent-up anger and hurt spilling out of me, a toxic sludge that had been waiting for a chance to be released. "I saw everything I needed to know when we found out Rachel was going to die. Our relationship is going nowhere, and I don't want to bring a child into this world who might see our sham of a marriage as a model to follow."

When I paused to catch my breath, he coaxed, "Come home so we can talk about this." He kept his tone calm but stern, as if I was a rebellious teenager that needed a dressing down but he was taking the high road.

"There's nothing to talk about, Gaston, we're done," I asserted, now exhausted by the conversation.

He muttered, "Fine, have it your way. I have to get out of here."

"You do what you need to do," I said. I was through pretending I cared.

I came back home to an empty house. A quick note on the counter said he'd gone to Houston for the weekend to see his family. It was a relief. I was so tired of faking it. I didn't care if he ever came back.

Hunter and I eventually consummated the affair Gaston accused me of having. First, in Houston a couple weeks later, and then on subsequent work trips. I found it funny when we'd be on the same conference call at opposite ends of one hotel room with me wearing nothing but his dress shirt. The sex was good—shake-the-rafters good. Truly, we were a force of nature, made even more intense due to the hormones I was still taking to ensure the pregnancy took. We were perfectly in sync—personally and professionally. It was something Gaston and I had never shared.

Two weeks into my whirlwind affair, I got another call from Barbara. "Congratulations!" she reported happily. "You're pregnant! Come in next week and we'll take a look."

My three-week ultrasound revealed that I was most definitely pregnant...with *TWINS*.

Twins? I thought, a wave of panic rippling through me. I honestly hadn't expected both embryos to implant. *What have I done?* The document Gaston signed made it crystal clear he wouldn't be around. I could envision being a single mother of one baby just fine but having twins was a different story. I didn't even want to think what breastfeeding twins would be like!

Gaston had moved his stuff to an apartment while I jetted around with Hunter to work functions. A week after Barbara gave me the good news, Gaston called. It was the first time I'd heard from him since our last fight.

"Have you gotten the pregnancy results yet?" he asked without preamble when I picked up.

I was in no mood to be polite, either. "Why do you want to know?"

"Because it's my baby," he said, as if the answer was obvious and I was being especially dense.

It was amazing how angry he could make me when he wasn't even in the room. "*Your* baby? You made it clear in the affidavit you signed that you wanted no part of *your* baby if we split up."

"I changed my mind," he sniffed. *Of course he did.* The man who couldn't be there for his wife and daughter when hard decisions had to be made and disavowed any involvement with his future children now wanted to crash the party?

"You're kidding me," I said flatly. "Go to hell." And I hung up on him.

Ironically, Gaston was the only person who wanted any part in this pregnancy. I felt isolated, even more so than in my grief because at least that loneliness was self-imposed. My co-workers and friends treated me like a leper, like someone whose fate was already decided. No one called me to check on how I was doing, or even mentioned the twins. There were no cards of congratulations, no talk of baby showers, and no questions about how I would decorate the babies' room.

No one dared to be happy for me in case it all went wrong again.

CHAPTER 13

INTO THE WOODS WITH BABY A AND BABY B

HERE WE GO AGAIN.

My palms were sweating and I felt light-headed as I exposed my belly on another exam table to do my three-month sonogram. Déjà vu in the worst way. I did some deep breathing to stave off the panic attack I could feel lurking in the corners of my mind. It was a good thing I was lying down.

I had a different technician this time, Nicolette, but I could tell she was aware of my medical history because she was over-the-top in her peppy assurances.

"Two babies," she chirped. "Heads look good. Spines look good. Feet look good. Twenty fingers and toes—" Nicolette grinned, "in total, of course," she finished with a lighthearted giggle. "Looks like you're rocking this pregnancy, Ms. Bergeron! I'll go get Dr. Andersen for the final assessment." She gave me a last quick smile before replacing her instruments and heading out the door.

Dr. Andersen came in with the same calm self-confidence he always displayed and sat down to review Nicolette's results.

"I like what I'm seeing, Cheri," he started. "The anatomies of both Baby A and Baby B seem to be in order and consistent with what we'd expect at twelve weeks. I don't see any signs of a recurrence of the issues we had with Rachel. You've been taking the folic acid, correct?"

"Yes, absolutely," I said quickly. I would do anything in my power to prevent this pregnancy from going wrong. I felt my body start to relax, then jump with excitement at his next words. "Now for the fun part," he said, clapping his hands together, his eyes twinkling, "would you like to know the sex of the babies?"

"Of course!" I said, his confidence infectious.

Dr. Andersen expertly ran the probe around on my belly, looking for telltale body parts. "Baby A is a boy, no doubt about it," he said with a smile before moving the probe to Baby B.

A boy? I hadn't pictured myself having a boy. *OMG, what if I have TWO BOYS?!* I thought, as my mind started to race. As a single mom, they could decide to tie me up in an old-school game of Cowboys and Indians and there would be nothing I could do about it. Before I went into full panic mode, Dr. Andersen interrupted my train of thought. "For Baby B, all signs point to a girl."

One of each! I thought with glee. "That's wonderful!" I said.

But Dr. Andersen didn't respond to my enthusiasm. He continued to scan the babies as he made a curious face. He leaned in to get a closer look at the monitor. All my fears came rushing back with his next words.

"I'm seeing a slight anomaly on Baby A," he said, his tone puzzled. "There's a cloudy spot in the lung area. We'll have to keep an eye on that. It's likely something minor, but we'll be able to get more details as the baby grows." He turned to look at me. "I'd like to see you in thirty days for another sonogram."

Thirty days. That was a little soon. But I was a high-risk pregnancy, now on several fronts because of my age, the twins, and my history with Rachel's condition. "Okay," I said slowly, trying to read his mind. "Is there something I should be concerned about, Dr. Andersen?"

He smiled to calm my anxiety. "I wouldn't worry about it. I know you've had a rough time. Take care of yourself and let's check back at sixteen-weeks' gestation."

I tried to temper my emotions and not read too much into his comments as I straightened my clothes after Dr. Andersen left the room. *Don't jump to conclusions, Cheri*, I told myself firmly. *Everything's going to be okay.*

The next few weeks flew by. Business was good and I continued to travel. I wasn't accountable to anyone, so I could come and go as I pleased. I felt freer than I had in a long time.

I went back to see Dr. Andersen at the sixteen-week mark, four months into my pregnancy.

"I'm still seeing a spot on the lungs of Baby A," Dr. Andersen said, not quite alarmed but not totally relaxed, either.

"Do you know what it is?" I asked, chewing my lip. These medical mysteries were killing me.

He gave a half shrug. "It's hard to say. It may be nothing. Often these cases can be resolved with minor surgery, or it may even resolve itself prior to birth...," he hesitated, and my stomach twisted, "but I'm also seeing excess amniotic fluid around your baby boy, which is something we'll need to manage."

"Why would there be too much amniotic fluid?" Everything was getting curiouser and curiouser, and like Alice, I felt the rabbit hole getting deeper and darker.

"It could be a variety of things," Dr. Andersen explained. "Our biggest concern is what could result, namely preterm labor." He held up a hand to stop me before I panicked. He probably saw all the blood drain from my face. "The amount of amniotic fluid can be managed with medication. I'm going to refer you to Dr. Eleanor Shadowvale. She's an OB-GYN specializing in maternal fetal medicine. She'll be the best resource to help you navigate the rest of your pregnancy."

"But I already have an OB-GYN," I said. I really liked Dr. Heartsong.

Dr. Andersen nodded. "Yes, but based on your risk factors, we need to be proactive here. Dr. Shadowvale has special training to treat medical complications related to high-risk pregnancies. You'll be in good hands."

Despite Dr. Andersen's upbeat assurances, my heart sank. What was wrong with my baby boy? I tried to steady my nerves, but I couldn't help feeling like my world was unraveling once again.

This is my punishment for all my past mistakes, I thought, which seemed to be a message on perpetual repeat in my head.

Dr. Shadowvale shared the same assessment as Dr. Andersen when I went to see her. The lung spot was nonspecific. It could be attributed to a variety of health conditions ranging from minor to severe. And we likely wouldn't know exactly what we were dealing with—or how to treat it—until I gave birth.

The excess amount of amniotic fluid is called polyhydramnios. It would need to be managed to ensure I would carry the twins to term. She prescribed a nonsteroidal anti-inflammatory drug called indomethacin to reduce the amniotic fluid level. But with twins, it was a tightrope to walk. It would improve the levels of fluid on my son by decreasing them, but it would also decrease the normal amount of fluid around my daughter.

And if the amniotic fluid got too low, causing the amniotic sac to break too early, it was game over for both babies.

The medication would buy us time and sustain the pregnancy. The minimum gestation was twenty-four weeks, which is medically considered the "age of viability" because it's viewed as the earliest age a fetus can live outside the womb. This is why, even in progressive states, abortions are usually banned at twenty-four weeks—because after that point a dependent fetus could become an independent baby. At that age, they'd hit one pound each, the tiniest of preemies. They'd require weeks in an incubator and other medical assists to make it to a point where they could breathe and eat on their own. But they'd have a fighting chance.

I measured my life in two-week increments, the time between my check-ups with Dr. Shadowvale. "I'm not happy with the way Baby A's lungs are maturing," she said at my twenty-eight-week appointment. "We need to take some additional steps to accelerate the baby's lung development. We're going to administer an antenatal corticosteroid shot. Be prepared, the size of the shot can be intimidating."

Shit, as if I haven't suffered enough. She wasn't kidding. I nearly passed out when I saw the imposing four-inch needle coming toward me carried by Dr. Shadowvale's nurse. It looked like the penicillin shots out of the dark ages that cruel nurses tortured me with as a kid. *Holy crap! Who do they think they're injecting? King Kong?* I thought with alarm, using every relaxation technique I'd learned during my hormone treatments to keep it together as I felt the nurse insert the massive needle into my hip. "We'll need you to come back in two days for the second dose," she said on her way out.

Was this a doctor's office or a torture chamber? There wasn't anything I wouldn't do for my children, but this was pushing it.

As the race to save my babies' lives loomed larger in my mind, Hunter receded further from it. Turns out, he had a lot more to lose in discarding his marriage than I did with mine. Mainly, he felt a tremendous responsibility to his kids and didn't want to parent from afar. And how could I fault him for wanting to be a good dad?

I knew our relationship was one of circumstance, and prospects for a bright future were a long shot, especially considering our less-than-admirable beginning. My biggest priority wasn't, and never had been, maintaining the courtship, anyway. It was becoming a mother—and I needed to concentrate on keeping my babies inside me long enough to be born. So, having done his part to help me recover myself and my fighting spirit, Hunter faded from my life to remain only a memory, its happiness tinged with remorse.

I would come to regret the affair. Not because I had been unfaithful to Gaston. His actions had betrayed our vows long before my transgression. I regretted it because my actions had fallen short of my own values, and that wasn't the kind of example I wanted to set for my children.

Fortunately, my dive back into motherhood brought another kind of support and companionship back into my life: my mother. Soon, it didn't seem like she'd ever left. She accompanied me to every ultrasound. She was there when the twins passed one pound. Then three. Then four. It looked like we were going to make it!

"I just met your new neighbors," my mother chirped as she came in from walking her dog, Raggie, one day. Johnny and Colleen had just purchased the house to the left of mine. Admittedly, I hadn't taken much notice of them because they decided to complete some renovations before moving in. I was in recluse mode anyway and wasn't inclined to be social.

"They're so nice," my mother proceeded to explain in spite of my lack of interest. "He's a retired fighter pilot in the Texas Air National Guard and had been an air traffic controller at Austin Bergstrom International Airport. Colleen has been a great support to Johnny's military career. It doesn't sound like they have any children. And Raggie took to Johnny right away," she remarked. "He sat down on the curb and Raggie jumped right into his lap!"

I was always amazed how much information my mother could learn about complete strangers in a ten-minute period. "Great, Mom," I said, trying to placate her and move on from the conversation.

My mother paid no attention to my blasé attitude. "I'm going to bake some cookies and take them over tomorrow," she said with a smile.

"Knock yourself out, Mom," I said dryly. Little did I know the impact these neighbors would make on my family later.

The closer I got to my due date, the more I found myself battling with another man from my past. Gaston. His newfound desire to be a father infuriated me. He had not participated in any of the ultrasounds or medical appointments. Nor had he made any purchases or assembled any baby gear to accommodate the arrival of twins. And with twins, the normal mountain of baby paraphernalia an expectant parent needed to amass was doubled. Based on the document he signed, he wouldn't be entitled to see them in the hospital, but I didn't want the arrival of my babies to be filled with bitterness and conflict, so Worth mediated a settlement where Gaston could have visitation with the babies after they were born. We haggled over several details, but I insisted on picking their names. I chose Brandon for Baby A, an Old Irish name meaning "prince." It was a name given to deep thinkers. I reluctantly agreed for his middle name to be Gaston's last name. Baby B would be called Lauren Renee, Lauren for the laurel tree, a symbol of triumph and wisdom, and Renee which means "born again" in French. These babies were my second chance. My redemption. My fait accompli. With those details settled, I could focus on my children rather than fighting with him and adding more stress to my already stress-filled pregnancy.

We signed the mediated agreement six weeks prior to my due date. *Now I can relax,* I thought. Turns out fate had a different plan.

CHAPTER 14

BRANDON'S STORY

AT THREE O'CLOCK THAT SAME FRIDAY AFTERNOON IN JANuary, I had my regularly scheduled appointment with Dr. Shadowvale. As she began my thirty-four-week ultrasound, I saw a look of concern come over her face. Without mincing words, the doctor bluntly said, "Cheri, your baby boy is in distress. His heart rate is dropping. We need to get you across the street to the Mercy Hospital emergency room to have your babies immediately."

It was D-Day, aka Delivery Day. The day we'd known could come at any moment. I reached out my hand as panic and elation doused me in equal measures. The person who caught it and returned an encouraging squeeze was my mother.

Mom acted as both birthing coach and significant other in the delivery room as the doctors prepared me for an emergency C-section. "It'll be okay, Sunshine, women have been having babies since the beginning of time," she said, "so just lie still and let the doctors do their work."

I'm not sure if her words were to distract me from all the commotion as extra equipment started to arrive in preparation for preterm twins, or to distract herself.

My son, Brandon, was born at 5:00 p.m. weighing four pounds and four ounces. When Brandon was born, there was no crying. *Why isn't he crying?* The doctors and nurses rushed around in a frenzy. *Is he breathing?* My prone position and the curtain walling off the surgery zone below my waist prevented me from seeing anything.

"Mom, what's going on?" I whispered desperately. But she shook her head sadly. The doctors wouldn't let her beyond the curtain, so she heard as much as I did.

"I don't know, sweetheart, but you'll be the first person to know when I find out. It looks like they're taking Brandon out of the room."

Putting my concern for Brandon on hold, I concentrated on my daughter. "Here she comes!" the delivering doctor said. It was 5:03.

A collective sigh of relief filled the delivery room when Lauren let out a soft but distinct newborn wail of protest at being evicted from her nice warm bed. She was weighed and came in at a decent four pounds and twelve ounces.

I couldn't hold my daughter since I still needed to be closed up, but they brought her over to me so I could see her for the first time—a beautiful little girl with porcelain skin, perfectly formed pink cupid's bow lips, and when she blinked them open, the most beautiful blue eyes I'd ever seen. I finally had my little girl. After a few minutes that felt like a split second, the nurse whisked her away, but I wasn't sure why.

In the recovery room, as I slowly regained feeling below the waist, my mother wouldn't stop pacing. Back and forth. Back and forth. When she wasn't pacing, she was leaving the room to hunt down the nurses to speak with them in hushed tones. I was still high on painkillers and the lingering effects of the anesthesia, so I wasn't fully aware of what was going on.

"When can I see my babies?" I asked impatiently as she came back into the room for the umpteenth time.

My mother looked pale. "I'm working on it," she said simply. What she didn't say was that Brandon and Lauren were both in precarious conditions. She wanted to be sure I had a chance to see them in case the worst happened.

I don't know how she did it, but my mother badgered the right person into agreeing I could be allowed into the NICU (neonatal intensive care unit) to see my babies. It was against hospital policy and rarely happened, even in the worst cases. *Maybe I need to rethink which parent had given me my tenacity*, I thought idly, as my hospital bed was wheeled down the hall by a couple of nurses. When I got to the NICU, it became clear why it was against standard practice.

I was unprepared for what I found.

The NICU was a large sterile room, holding maybe thirty to forty incubators and cribs. Screens divided the treatment areas as an army of doctors, medical assistants, and nurses walked around endlessly, attending to the preemies. A cacophony of beeping heart and oxygen monitors, all with their own type of beep to stand out in the crowd, barraged the ears. Regular alarms from these machines kept visitors in a perpetual state of anxiety, never knowing if it was serious or just a loose sensor. Other than the beeping, the room was completely silent, which, for a room full of babies, struck me as uncanny. Unsettling.

Brandon's situation was especially dire. An incubator to regulate body temperature, I expected, but the array of tubes and wires and IV ports and tape and the chorus of beeping machines was something out of a sci-fi horror flick. He was unable to breathe on his own. A massive machine called a forced air ventilator was keeping him alive by mechanically pushing air into his lungs. I could barely see my son through all the paraphernalia of modern medicine. It was unclear whether he would survive.

Lauren was a little better. She, too, was placed in an incubator and had a tube in her nose for supplemental oxygen and a feeding tube in her mouth, but those were the only outward signs she needed help to live.

While I was physically only a few feet away from my babies, it felt like miles. I couldn't touch them through the closed incubators. All I wanted was to hold my babies like other new mothers, but I could only look at them and worry. After a few minutes, they wheeled me out of the NICU.

I lay there in my recovery bed, powerless as my children clung to life. It was all so confusing. My babies were not seriously premature. Thirty-four weeks gestational age just squeaked into the "late preterm" bracket and was run-of-the-mill from a NICU perspective. At thirty-seven weeks, they would've been considered full-term. And four-plus pounds was hefty compared to the delicate one-pound preemies that occupied other incubators.

Back in my room, I counted the minutes after post-op until I could head back to the NICU in a wheelchair. When I did, I found a team of medical attendants at Brandon's bedside, their concern palpable. The nurses rushed around hurriedly tending to his needs. I couldn't tell what they were doing, but their pace told me it was urgent.

I took turns standing beside the incubators of my sweet babies, so tiny and helpless. *This has to be my fault. I'm the reason they're suffering.*

These thoughts spun around my brain until Dr. Sophia Valerian, the head of neonatology, or, as I would affectionately come to think of her, the Head Bitch in Charge, introduced herself and gave me the rundown on what was happening with my kids. Her petite five-foot-two-inch frame, short brown hair, and blue scrubs didn't look intimidating, but her demeanor made it clear she called the shots.

"We've done our best to stabilize Brandon," she said directly, "but it's touch and go. We need to run some additional tests. It appears his lungs are significantly underdeveloped. You were thirty-four weeks into your pregnancy, correct?"

"Yes," I confirmed. Maybe now I'd get some answers to this mystery. "The maternal fetal medicine doctor knew there was an issue with his lungs, but we had no idea it was this serious."

"Hmm," she wondered, projecting confidence even when she didn't have the answers. "We're going to do our best to keep Brandon stable. He's on a specialized neonatal ventilator that is essentially breathing for him. It's a delicate task since he's so small. We're keeping him sedated so he doesn't resist the process."

I appreciated she didn't pull any punches, but I couldn't help the tremble in my voice. "Is he in pain?"

For the first time in the whole conversion, the doctor's eyes softened a little. "We will make him as comfortable as possible."

I jumped on her statement. "That means he's suffering." When she didn't respond, I knew. Every breath Brandon took was torture. The act of living was hurting him. And I could do nothing about it.

"Lauren's stats are encouraging," she said, trying to give me some good news, "though her lungs are also underdeveloped for her gestational age. We feel confident that we can help move her along. Expect it to take some time before she's ready to go home." Eagle-eyed, she surveyed me, noting immediately that, between the lingering pain from the surgery and the emotional pain I'd sustained since the births, I was about to fall over. "Why don't you go back to your room and rest. I'm sure you've had an exhausting day. I'll be here all night, and we'll update you on any developments. In the meantime, I suggest you start pumping so you can stimulate your breast milk production."

Knowing she was shooing me out of the NICU, but not knowing what else I could do to help my babies, my mom wheeled me back to my room. The realization I'd be using a pump was one more sucker punch on top of all the other hits. I couldn't breastfeed my children like a normal mother. I couldn't even try. Instead, I had to sit in my lonely hospital room strapped to a cold, unfeeling machine like a cow, my breasts exposed to whomever waltzed into the room, while my babies were nowhere in sight.

My mother helped me get the breast pump situated. I wasn't used to all the flanges and tubing and valves, though it was simple enough when I got the hang of it. I had the hospital-grade double pump, so I was able to do both breasts at once. As I turned on the pump and it began to rhythmically pull at my breasts, my uterus contracted with the stimuli, which felt like someone stabbed me in the gut and crotch simultaneously. But at least pumping gave me something to do.

Mom planned to stay with me through the night, sleeping on the reclining chair stationed in the room's corner. At 1:00 a.m., we were both jolted awake by the room's phone ringing. *This can't be good.*

"Ms. Bergeron," the nurse on the other end said, "please come to the NICU now. It's Brandon."

I didn't wait for the wheelchair to arrive. It was only eight hours after the doctors had split me open from navel to pubic bone, but I started the long walk down the hall to the NICU. With every step my incision throbbed, and I could feel the pain meds wearing off with this new demand, but nothing was going to keep me from my baby. My mom acted as my crutch, holding my upper arm to steady me as we traversed the maze of hospital halls to the NICU. When we entered Brandon's treatment area, it was clear the doctors and nurses were on edge. Brandon's oxygen monitor going ballistic probably had something to do with their tension.

Dr. Valerian approached me, her look grave. "We're having trouble maintaining Brandon's oxygen levels, Ms. Bergeron. The ventilator is at the maximum pressure we feel is safe for his lungs, but his oxygen saturation is dangerously low." I glanced at the monitor, which read 82 percent. Even as I watched, the decimals crept slowly downward. She followed my gaze. "We want to see levels of at least 93 percent."

"What happens if it keeps dropping?" I asked, dreading the answer.

Dr. Valerian didn't sugarcoat it. "Anything below 80 percent is life-threatening."

Tears streamed down my face. My missions of motherhood always seemed to end in tears.

Unaware of my dark thoughts, Dr. Valerian plowed ahead. "He's fighting really hard, but I have to be honest with you, based on what I'm seeing, there's a chance he may not make it. I'll call you again if he's in critical distress." She glanced at me, then offered the only comfort she could when medicine came up short. "If it would be helpful, we have a chapel in the hospital. I can call the chaplain for you."

I could read between her caveats. *She's preparing me for Brandon's death.*

My legs started to buckle underneath me. I didn't know how much more I could take. It all seemed so surreal that another child could be taken from me.

"Yes, please," I said hoarsely, "have the chaplain come."

The pain of walking to the chapel was a sort of penance. I refused to use the wheelchair after that first trip to the NICU. Once there, the hospital chaplain, my mother, and I knelt. Huddled together, we prayed that God would save my baby. It did not escape me that the last time I'd prayed like this was when I almost miscarried Rachel. The renewed trauma had me on the verge of hyperventilating.

How could this be happening to me again? How could You be so cruel, God? How could You do this to me? To them? Why must You punish innocents to punish me?

At three in the morning, the deepest part of the night and what some call the witching hour, my mom took me back to my room. As I waited to get the call that my son was dying, my mother cradled me in her arms on the hospital bed as sobs spilled from the depths of my soul. It felt like hours, but it could only have been minutes when I felt a soothing hum against my cheek.

"*...when skies are gray...*"

My mother was singing.

"*...please don't take...*"

It was the longest night of my life.

"*...away.*"

The sun came up and the call never came. I woke at 7:00 a.m., realizing I hadn't heard the phone. My first thought: *Is he dead and they failed to call me?*

I left my mother sleeping, curled up on the hospital bed, while I summoned the strength to make it to the NICU on my own. I entered the unit to see my son was still alive. He'd made it through the night. I caught Dr. Valerian's eye, and she walked over to me. "It's quite astonishing, Ms. Bergeron," she reported, "we were able to stabilize him. His blood oxygen saturation is at eighty-seven percent. In my fifteen years in the NICU, I've never seen this before. We're not out of the woods by any means, but it's an encouraging sign."

I broke down and hugged her. "Thank you," I sobbed. "Thank you for saving my son. And please, call me Cheri." I knew I was going over the line of the doctor-patient relationship, but I didn't care. By now, I knew Dr. Valerian had three children of her own. This was something only another mother would understand.

"You're welcome," she said, giving me a quick squeeze back before stepping away. "We'll keep doing everything we can for him. I have two nurses attending to him twenty-four hours a day. We'll need to do blood work and additional tests. We should know more in the next twenty-four hours after I consult with a pediatric pulmonologist at Dell Children's Hospital. I also want to do some genetic testing on Brandon. I plan to send off a blood sample to the Mayo Clinic so they can do a full chromosomal analysis. We'll get the test expedited, but it will still take seven to ten days to get those results back."

I only halfway heard the rest of her plan. I trusted Dr. Valerian. She could have said she'd speak with the president and needed to get a sample tested on the moon and I would have nodded along. All I heard was I'd get more time with Brandon, and I was grateful for that.

I spent the morning hours standing at my son's bedside. He was so tiny I could barely see him past the ventilator tubes, but I did notice his body had some unusual characteristics. He had a broad forehead and wide-set eyes. His torso was stocky, appearing out of proportion to his small arms and legs. His little face looked pained, as if he was crying but couldn't make a sound. My heart broke to see him that way.

Delicately, I reached out and laid my hand on the incubator.

It was the closest I could get to touching him. "I'm going to get answers for you, Brandon," I vowed, "just you wait."

On day two after my C-section (had it only been two days?) the hospital told me I was to be discharged. I couldn't imagine leaving without my babies, but my health insurance coverage was running out because I was teetering on the edge of medical necessity. I was able to eke out one more day, but on day three they kicked me out.

In the days following my discharge, my mother and I practically lived at the hospital. Johnny and Colleen agreed to watch Raggie while we focused on the twins. I knew I needed to be my children's advocate and went into full-on Mama Bear mode whenever I sniffed out a new answer or piece of information or bit of attention from the medical team that would make my children more comfortable. Gaston, now that the babies were born, was back in the picture. He'd come to stand his own sort of vigil but offered little comfort to me and didn't communicate with the doctors, who all saw me as the go-to parent. It was up to me to do all the thinking and legwork and decision-making, but at least Gaston was physically present for his children even if he was mostly a statue.

The NICU was like a war zone. Each day felt eerily similar. Anxiety, fear, and grief reached a fever pitch most days, left behind by hundreds of harried medical professionals and dozens of desperate parents that had passed through its doors. I swore the smell of crisis was in the walls, a miasma made of sweat, adrenaline, tears, and illness overlaid with antiseptic.

The NICU was closed to visitors for only four hours a day for shift changes, from five to seven in the evening and five to seven in the morning. At 6:30 a.m., I'd head to the hospital, arriving at 7:00 a.m. Then I would stay in the NICU until 11:00 p.m. when I couldn't bear it anymore, only taking a break for dinner when the evening shift change came. They wouldn't allow parents to sleep in the chairs placed in each unit; otherwise, I would have slept there.

When I returned home each night, I went to bed at midnight and set an alarm for my 2:00 a.m. ritual. First, I'd pump breast milk. Lauren was able to receive a small amount of my milk through a feeding tube, which provided some consolation, and the rest went into the freezer. I didn't want my supply to dry up. Brandon was too underdeveloped to get my milk, so he received a cocktail of medicine and formula. Then I would call the NICU's night nurse to get updates on my children. What was Brandon's blood saturation level? What was his heart rate? What other tests were being performed? Was he peaceful or restless? How was Lauren? There were always fewer updates for her.

I would jot down every detail the nurses gave me in my notebook as if documenting them would cause the situation to improve. In reality, the only thing I could do as a mother was bear witness to Brandon's suffering.

On day ten, Dr. Valerian called me into her office. I brought my mother with me. This couldn't be good if she wanted us to be sitting down for it. The room was generic hospital grade with white walls, a wood laminate desk, and standard issue blue office chair. I could tell she spent very little time there. My eyes immediately went to all the artwork, pottery, and cards sprinkled around the space. Masterpieces made by her kids. It didn't matter that I was on pins and needles; their creations brought a smile to my face.

"I have some significant updates from the pediatric pulmonologist," she said, as we sat nervously on the other side of her desk. "I have a theory of diagnosis." My throat tightened and I steadied myself. My mother grabbed my hand and squeezed tightly to relieve both our tension. "I believe Brandon has a condition called congenital pulmonary lymphangiectasia, pronounced lim-fang-jee-uhk-tay-zhuh, that prevents the lungs from developing properly. It's rare. I've never personally seen a case of it, but I have a strong instinct. Hopefully the test results from the Mayo Clinic will tell us for sure."

My heart beating faster, I took a breath, "Well, at least we know…," but Dr. Valerian held up a hand and I went quiet. *There's more? Isn't this enough?*

She continued, "I also suspect Brandon has Noonan's syndrome, which has some similarities to Down's syndrome and explains Brandon's unusual body proportions you've probably noticed. Again, the genetic test results will tell us for sure."

I tried reading between the lines for what this meant for Brandon's future. If it was like Down's syndrome, Noonan's might be challenging but survivable. Lungs that didn't work right were clearly bad. Both conditions together?

I mounted the courage to ask the dreaded question now foremost in my mind. "What are the odds of Brandon recovering from this lymph thing?" I couldn't even remember how to say the words.

"Lymphangiectasia," she corrected. "We call it PL for short."

"Yeah, that one." *Shit, my baby had* two *obscure conditions?*

Dr. Valerian sighed and sat back in her chair. "Unfortunately, the survival rate for infants is low. Most infants with this condition die at birth or within a few hours thereafter. The introduction of advanced neonatal forced air ventilators has helped prolong life, but there's no known cure."

Another wave of heartbreak and disbelief washed over me, a feeling I was all too familiar with by now. *God must really hate me*, I thought. I'd pursued fertility outside the natural order, and now I was being punished for trying to create life artificially.

When I got home from the meeting with Dr. Valerian, I rushed to my computer to learn everything I could about Brandon's conditions. I found myself on the National Library of Medicine website wading through medical journal articles full of jargon. As I combed through them, the words made my heart jump into my throat.

> Presents at birth with severe respiratory distress.
>
> Very high mortality rate within a few hours of birth.
>
> Reported cases are sporadic and the etiology, aka the cause, is not completely understood.
>
> Occurrences are approximately one in 15,000 births.

This last fact got to me. I'm no mathematician, but I started to wonder what the odds were that I would have a child with spina bifida, which was one in two thousand births, and then the next child with PL. I calculated the odds, and it was .0000000335, or 335 *trillionths*, for one woman to have two children with those conditions by chance. I'd never seen a number that small. Mathematicians start using letters to truncate numbers that tiny when they want to work with them in equations. In contrast, the odds of winning a billion-dollar lottery prize are about one in three hundred million. If we applied my level of luck with babies to playing Mega Millions, I would be one of the richest people on earth. Instead, I felt completely bankrupt.

I printed out a litany of articles from medical journals and asked Gaston to read them. "We need to educate ourselves on Brandon's condition." From what I could tell, he never read a single one.

On day seventeen, the results came back from the Mayo Clinic. Once again, we gathered in Dr. Valerian's office.

"Brandon has a chromosomal deletion on 2p16.3. You may remember from biology class that each person has forty-six chromosomes. Brandon is missing part of chromosome two."

"What does that mean?" I asked, trying to take the results from the abstract back to the living child.

"Nothing good," she said starkly. "This deletion is linked with a variety of conditions, including developmental delays, Noonan's syndrome, and schizophrenia. It confirms my diagnosis that your son has both PL and Noonan's."

My spirits sank. I'd been expecting the worst, and now here it was, laid out before me.

Dr. Valerian continued. "It will be important for the egg donor and Gaston to get the same genetic test that Brandon received to see if either of them shares this chromosomal deletion. It would be important information if they want to have more children."

"But," I protested, sifting through a flood of conflicted feelings, "the donor already had genetic testing done."

"That should have caught an abnormality," the doctor conceded. "I'd still recommend she get retested. This particular test is called a microarray, and it is much more detailed and thorough than the standard genetic test."

Talk of future children was insignificant to me. My top priority was my son. "What can we do for Brandon?" I asked.

Dr. Valerian, having delivered her testimony, handed the verdict off to the parents. "That's for you and Gaston to discuss."

"So," I said, wanting that last card on the table, "I assume this means Brandon wouldn't be able to live without the ventilator."

"Unfortunately not," she confirmed. "At present, Brandon's condition is stable. It may not even be a decision you and

Gaston get to make. This kind of complex health condition can create tricky medical ethics dilemmas. It's possible the hospital board would have to be involved in this decision. We'll cross that bridge when we get to it."

In a daze, we left Dr. Valerian's office. I found it ironic that modern medical science had given humans so much power over life and death—and if you believed God made everything, He also made modern medicine—and yet those advances now made it hard to choose: When do you allow a loved one to live? And when do you allow them to die? Compounding the agony, there was a good chance I would be powerless to stop my son's suffering. That call might be in the hands of hospital bureaucrats who didn't even know him. *Where does mercy come into the equation?* I wondered.

It was all too much to bear.

God, how can you stand by letting my son continue to suffer? Even in my mind, my voice was small and lost.

That night, my mother, who'd been staying with me since the births, suggested we call my brother to share with him what was happening with his niece and nephew. Our nerves were frayed, and we could barely think. I told Phillip about Lauren and my hope she'd soon be home with us. Then I told him about Brandon's diagnosis.

"My son is suffering, and the decision may be out of my hands," I shared through my tight throat. Voicing the words made them more real somehow. "I'm not sure what I should do..."

My brother leapt on my words like a panther that had been waiting for the opportunity for its prey to show weakness. "You can't intervene, Cheri. You can't cheat and play God. Let God's will be done and let God take him in His own time."

I was speechless for a second. "So, you'd leave Brandon on

a ventilator forever? Knowing babies with his condition, who don't have access to high-tech ventilators, *do* die?" My throat closed and the next part came out hoarse. "Knowing he's in agony? You haven't been here to see him. I have been watching my son's torment for hours on end."

But the floodgates seemed to have opened for my brother, and he had a lot he wanted to get off his chest. "Look, I held my tongue with the Rachel situation, but I'm not going to stay silent here. I don't condone all that fertility stuff in the first place. None of my friends have had fertility issues. You were off gallivanting around for your job when responsible women were having kids. What did you think would happen? And I don't believe in abortion. Under any circumstance. Now you're wanting to end the life of a second child. Where is your morality, Cheri?"

I felt like a woman being paraded into the public square to be stoned for her sins. His attack blindsided me, but my temperature rose the more he spoke. It was my job to protect my boy from undue pain and suffering. I wasn't going to let my brother's vilification and black-and-white thinking stop me from doing what I knew I had to do for my child.

I cut him off mid-rant. "I was calling for your support, Phillip. I didn't ask for your narrow-minded religious doctrine. I will do what's best for my son."

But even as I defended myself, I felt another type of loss. I needed Phillip to be in my corner. Not because we saw things the exact same way, but because he loved me. After all this time, all the other snubs, I still yearned for my sibling to comfort and support me in my time of need—to listen, to encourage, to trust that my decisions were the best ones for the situation. Instead, I was rejected in the worst way possible, compounding my pain and trauma instead of alleviating it. I felt that he attacked me instead of protecting me, like a big brother should. Protecting me with the kind of unconditional support and acceptance family should give each other. Didn't I deserve that kind of love?

I abruptly got off the phone. I couldn't take it anymore. My mother, who had been on the group call listening quietly throughout the assault, had heard enough. She promptly called him back. "This is not your sister's fault, Phillip. Cheri did not cause this. The doctors now say Brandon's problems are genetic, which means even science says she did not cause this."

"But she deserves it!" my brother yelled, not to be outdone. "She played God! She was flitting around the world, enjoying her job and her fancy lifestyle when she could have been having children. This is what you get when you're selfish and interfere with God's plan!"

Thoroughly incensed, I could see her body rise up to its full height. "You know it's more complicated than that, Phillip," she snarled. "You're not here. You can't imagine how excruciating it is for Cheri and me to sit here and watch that innocent little boy's daily suffering. Who are you to judge your sister?" Then she pulled out the coup de grâce. "Where is your loyalty to our family? It was a mistake to call you."

Then she ended the call. If she suspected this action would start a multi-year rift with her son, she didn't seem to care. I think, if she'd still had her old rotary phone, that receiver would have been rammed home with all the force her elderly frame could muster. *Now, this is Mama Bear*, I thought with respect.

Two days later, I was met by Dr. Valerian as we entered the NICU. "Cheri," she said solemnly, "Brandon's kidneys are shutting down. His condition is deteriorating rapidly. If you prolong this, I'm not sure we can manage his pain." I rushed over to his incubator. Along with his ever-present silent scream, I could see some of his extremities had started to swell in troubling ways, puffing around all the tape holding in his tubes. It was like every aspect of his body was betraying him.

"We've done everything we can for him," Dr. Valerian said softly, coming up to my side. "It's time to make a decision."

There was no choice. It was time to say goodbye. I called Gaston. Then I called Worth. If he could break away from his other obligations, I wanted him at the hospital with me.

The only time I was allowed to hold my son in his nineteen days of life was when he was dying.

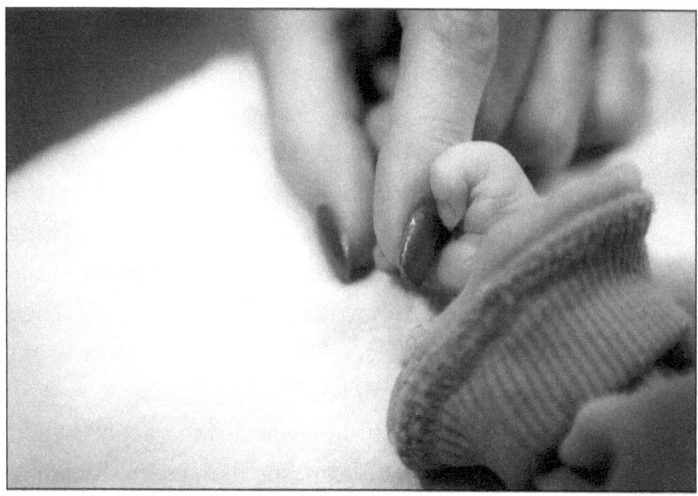

Holding my son's hand in his final hours

Gaston and I took turns holding him as the doctors disconnected Brandon from the ventilator. My mother and Worth were by my side. As life slowly left Brandon, I held him close. "I love you, my sweet boy," I whispered. "It's time to go be with Jesus, where you will be free to run and laugh and play and your pain will be over. Say hi to your sister for me. I will find you both in heaven."

I didn't let him go until he stopped breathing. Gaston left, but I stayed alone with him in a private room after he passed, waiting for the medical examiner to come. I was with him until they took him away.

The whole NICU mourned. Even the beeps seemed to hold a moment of silence. The doctors and nurses were used to performing medical miracles every day, but all their efforts had been unable to save this one precious little boy.

Brandon was gone. Another child was taken from me.

Overcast skies loomed over the cold Saturday in February of Brandon and Rachel's memorial service at Remembrance Gardens. Gaston was there along with dozens of family and friends. Dr. Valerian and many of the nurses came to the service, some on their day off, which I found extraordinary.

I never wanted my children buried in a cemetery, so Brandon was cremated, and his ashes put in an urn shaped like a crescent moon. I had memorial stones made for each child and placed them under an ancient live oak, its huge spreading branches reaching toward heaven. Little stone paths wound through the garden, which was covered in flowers and butterflies in the spring. Nearby, in the same garden, two other stones rested, one blank that is meant for me, and the other one carved with my father's name on the left-hand side. My mother's name filled the right side, listing her date of birth with a blank for her date of death, to be added later. We wanted to be close to the children even if it was only symbolically.

I sat next to my children's stones and said my last goodbyes. I don't remember everything I said. The grief and pain flowed out of me like a river while friends and family watched, devastation written on their faces. I admired their courage to be present for such a heart-wrenching scene. Our neighbor Colleen made all the food and arrangements for the reception that followed at our home so my mother and I could focus our energies on mourning and honoring Rachel and Brandon.

My brother and his family attended the ceremony but stood apart from all the other participants, as if passing judgment on the unholy spectacle. They barely said anything to me, only talking briefly with other people who came to the reception. I felt Phillip also snubbed our mother, presumably for her sin of supporting me. I wondered why they even came. *Probably so I could experience their disapproval firsthand*, I thought angrily. *Uncaring, self-righteous Pharisees.*

The memorial stones were still warm from my hands where they'd been placed under the tree when I got a call. It was the NICU. "Ms. Bergeron, come quickly to the hospital. There's a problem with Lauren."

CHAPTER 15

LAUREN'S BATTLE FOR SURVIVAL

IF I WAS SITTING ACROSS FROM YOU IN A DIMLY LIT restaurant sharing my story, this is the point where we would switch from a really good Cabernet to a really strong tequila. Take a deep breath and stay with me, my friend. I promise there are brighter days ahead.

For women, those beings who are blessed to be the carriers and nurturers of life, we never start our pregnancies thinking something bad is going to happen. We trust we will be among the fortunate ones who sail through their pregnancy, navigate the delivery unscathed, and cruise home from the hospital with a healthy child a day or two later. But sometimes parenthood sends us into turbulent waters. Having a preemie is one of those times.

Parenting a preemie is like sailing out into the middle of the deep blue sea in a flimsy dinghy. Each mile of the journey is a perilous balance between terror that you'll hit a big wave and your worst fears will be realized—your child doesn't survive—and desperate hope that you may have a fighting chance of reaching land—getting to take your healthy child home. Each day is a test of your mettle to endure some of the most difficult moments of your life for the well-being of your baby.

Like a sailor in the midst of a hurricane, your survival depends on your ability to seek out and cling to the bright spots and hold on for dear life when seas get rough.

Twenty-four hours after Lauren's birth, I still hadn't been allowed to hold her. I ached to touch her, but the incubator and all the tubes going into her body formed a barrier between us. As I stood staring into her tiny plastic world, the NICU nurse showed me mercy.

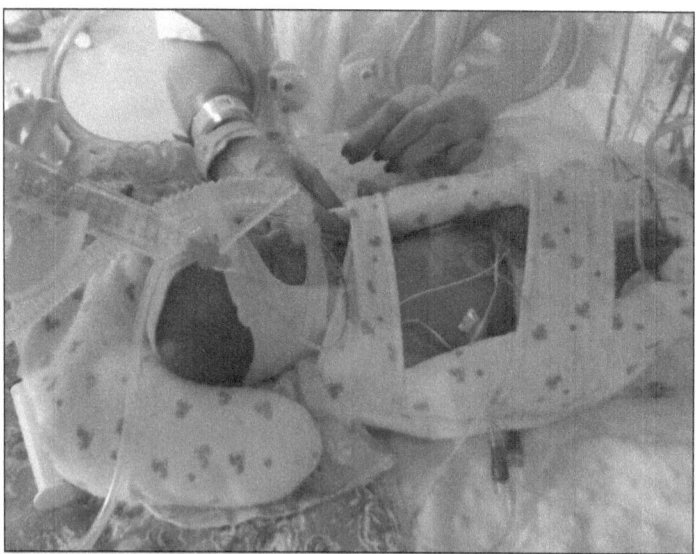

Lauren's first day in the NICU

"Would you like to do kangaroo care, Ms. Bergeron?" she suggested. "We could start tomorrow evening."

"What's that?" I asked, daring to hope something good could come our way.

The nurse moved her arms, mimicking holding an infant up to her breast. "It's like a mama kangaroo snuggling her joey in her pouch. We also call it skin-to-skin because we lay the baby on you chest-to-chest without clothing between you. There are numerous benefits for both you and the baby. Most importantly, it helps the two of you bond. It also provides stress relief and promotes milk production for the mom and helps the newborn regulate temperature and heart rate, improve sleep, sharpen reflexes, and accelerate brain development."

The simple act of physical touch could do that much for both of us? I marveled.

It sounded like heaven. "I'd like that," I got out around the lump in my throat.

The next evening, my mom helped me limp down to the NICU from my room in the maternity ward. The nurse got me settled into a rocking chair near Lauren's unit. I'd worn something that buttoned down the front and a front-clasping bra in preparation and it took no coaxing for me to bare my breasts, any kind of modesty now forgotten with the prospect of holding my child. It took some maneuvering for the nurse to wheel the incubator into position and manipulate all the tubes and wires to lift my tiny girl out of her incubator, still connected to her breathing and feeding tubes, and lay her carefully on my bare chest.

Two days after she was born and a decade after first dreaming of her, I was holding my daughter for the first time. Like the summer sun emerging from behind a cloud, warmth radiated through my body from the point where she rested.

Lauren felt like a feather, so small and light. She had no muscle control, so it was hard to cradle her as she ran almost like water through my hands and arms. Once I got her fluid body balanced, my finger moved unbidden to touch her hot-pink beanie, then her pouty pink lips, then the tiny fingers splayed across my breast. I lightly moved her head into a more comfortable position that freed up the tubes in her nose and mouth, the harsh plastic scrape against my skin a contrast to her delicate, petal-soft cheek. She gurgled, a tiny sound, as the breast milk I'd pumped earlier that evening fed her through the tube, drop by precious drop. I felt some satisfaction that I could provide my milk to sustain her even if it was through a tube. Through the antiseptic and the plastic smells of the NICU, the scent of her reached my nose, an intoxicating perfume like no other.

I sighed in relief as the tension I didn't know I'd been carrying melted away along with everything else in the world. I forgot about the tubes and wires, the beeping machines, the atmosphere of despair and desperation. I didn't notice the nurse covering both of us with a warm cotton blanket, or the doctors, nurses, and parents walking past the opening to our unit. I sat still, all my concentration on the little life now matching me breath for breath, heartbeat for heartbeat. It was just us, we two alone on our island of calm, mother and daughter.

Vaguely, I heard a small gasp of wonder from my right, and I looked up briefly to see my mother looking at us, her eyes shiny with tears. "Pure bliss," she murmured, "the look on your face is pure bliss." Later, she'd tell me witnessing my raw emotion and the connection between us was one of the most impactful moments of her life.

If that had been my last moment on earth, I would die content, having already gotten a taste of heaven.

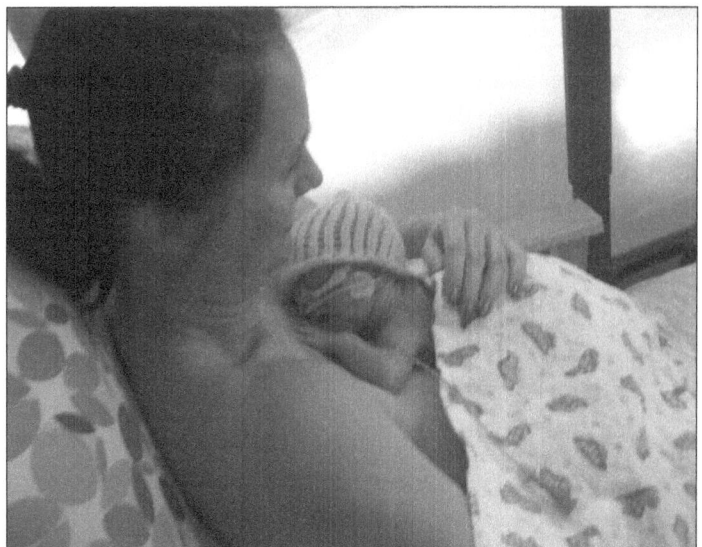

My first skin-to-skin session with Lauren

Each day after I was discharged, I'd make my walk down the long halls from the hospital lobby to the NICU at 7:00 a.m. to be there when it opened. My route passed the nursery where the healthy babies were kept if they weren't in the recovery rooms with their mothers. Inevitably, the nursery held a sea of blue or pink balloons and jubilant families. How I envied those normal families' lives.

In contrast, under the NICU's martial law, everyone had to speak in a whisper, cell phone use was prohibited, and the number of visitors allowed by the child's bedside was strictly limited to two people. "I want a freaking parade when I take my children home," I told my mother as we walked by yet another celebration with what seemed like a hundred extended family members, complete with balloons, flowers, and a cake piled high with pink frosting.

As Brandon struggled, Lauren fought her own battle. The doctors weren't sure why Lauren was having so much trouble. Unlike Brandon, she had no obvious signs of a serious condition. At thirty-four weeks gestational age, she wasn't alarmingly premature. I knew Lauren's birth weight, four pounds and twelve ounces, was also child's play for these doctors compared to the one-pound babies they treated on a regular basis. Yet, it seemed all the important biological systems—her lungs, her digestive tract, her heart—were significantly underdeveloped. Some of the doctors theorized her twin may have arrested her development. In trying to save Brandon, Lauren had paid a big price in her own growth and health.

While not as bad off as her brother had been, Lauren still needed a breathing tube, and she was prescribed a diuretic called Lasix to assist with respiratory distress syndrome, or RDS, because her lungs contained excess fluid that caused breathing problems.

She needed an incubator to regulate her body temperature.

Lauren's issues continued to mount. She had neonatal jaundice, a liver condition that causes yellowing of the newborn's skin and eyes from a buildup of bilirubin, a yellow substance produced when red blood cells are broken down in the lungs and blood. Jaundice is commonly caused by immature liver function, so that organ, too, wasn't working well. She was put on a light treatment called phototherapy, which is a special lamp that emits light in the blue-green spectrum that changes the shape and structure of the bilirubin molecules so they can be excreted from the body. Tiny covers shielded her eyes from exposure to the rays. In the old days before high-tech lamps, nurses would put babies out in the sunshine for this treatment.

Lauren wasn't able to breastfeed. Breastfeeding for an infant takes the energy equivalent of an adult jogging one to two miles.

It was a strenuous activity, especially for a preemie, so she had a feeding tube.

In and of themselves, each of these issues was relatively minor and fairly common among premature babies. All together, they presented a gauntlet of challenges for Lauren to overcome, but the doctors were still optimistic about her prognosis.

Despite the long list of Lauren's concerning health conditions, I longed for a safe haven—a port in the storm—given all the trauma I lived through with Rachel and Brandon. To offset the anguish of watching Brandon's constant suffering, I clung to the hope of Lauren and cherished each of her milestones.

I savored the moments of her first bath in the hospital.

I was relieved when she was able to be taken off the bilirubin light and the covers were removed so I could now see her little eyes. They were blue, like my dream girl.

I lived for our daily skin-on-skin time where I could feel her heartbeat against me and listen to the delicate little noises she made.

I celebrated when she gained fifteen grams.

I relished the opportunity to participate in her daily care, like journaling every detail of her existence: when she slept, every wet diaper, her blood pressure readings and oxygen saturation levels. I assisted the nurses by warming up my frozen breast milk so it could provide nourishment to Lauren through her feeding tube. I pumped to produce more breast milk with the precision and discipline of a military regimen, freezing what she couldn't use in the hope we would need it later.

"I think we can reduce the level of Lauren's supplemental oxygen," Dr. Valerian said to me one morning. "Her blood saturation levels look good, so we're going to slowly step it down and see how she responds."

She's making progress, I reassured myself. I would have to be content with calm seas for the moment.

I rode the high of every morsel of good news. But inevitably, the next day would bring a new wave of disappointment, making it clear we weren't home free. Not by a longshot.

"Lauren's oxygen saturation levels are dipping again," said Dr. Valerian with a tone of frustration. "She was responding so well, but we're having to increase the oxygen again. It's a setback, but we're not giving up. I'm going to order an EKG to figure out what's going on."

An EKG revealed why she was having trouble absorbing oxygen. Lauren had a small hole between the chambers of her heart, an atrial flap that didn't fully close, which prevented her blood from oxidizing properly.

"It's called an atrial septal defect, or ASD, and about ten percent of the population has it," Dr. Valerian informed me. "Lauren's is a little larger than normal at seven millimeters across. Depending on the severity, it could require surgery."

Just add that to the list, I sighed.

Part of that list included Lauren's ongoing trouble with breastfeeding. When she was strong enough, a lactation specialist worked with me and Lauren to teach her how to breastfeed, since premature babies don't instinctively know how to do it. The speech therapist also working with us explained why breastfeeding was so important. "It helps develop language and intelligence," she informed me. But it was a total struggle and I often felt like I failed my daughter when I couldn't get her to latch. Eventually, I resigned myself to the reality I would never be able to breastfeed my little girl.

Ten days into Lauren's life, she developed digestive problems. She was getting my breast milk via the feeding tube, but she stopped pooping it out. When you have a newborn, among other things, you become obsessed with baby poop because it's an essential checklist item for normal body functions. A baby's gut has to work properly. Because Lauren's didn't, every few days she'd get an enema to clear her system. It was an endless cycle: eat, enema, poop.

On day fourteen, the doctors decided to move Lauren to an elemental formula, theorizing she might be allergic to my breast milk. *Great*, I thought, *even my breast milk doesn't work.* Again, I felt inadequate as a mother as all those soft-focus images of mothers wearing cute pastel nursing clothing holding their peaceful child to their breast flamed out like all the other new-mother scenarios I'd imagined.

The struggle was exhausting, but I willed myself to fight against the tide. If Lauren had to fight her way through it, then so did I. No way I was going to leave her side. I just wished God would throw us a life raft.

On day sixteen, I walked into the NICU as I had done every morning. But this time, Lauren's incubator was empty.

"Where is my daughter?" I panicked.

"Don't worry, Ms. Bergeron," the nurse soothed. "Lauren has been moved over here. She graduated to NICU Level I because she's able to regulate her body temperature now. This is a good thing. Level I is the final stage before a baby is cleared to go home."

"Oh, thank God," I said with relief. Then panic was replaced with excitement. *Could I really be close to taking my little girl home?* "Are you saying Lauren might be well enough to go home soon?"

"You'll have to talk with Dr. Valerian about that," the nurse said with a hint of caution. I'm sure she didn't want to speak out of turn or get my hopes up too high.

I had no idea there were levels within a NICU—somewhat like Dante's rings of hell, I reasoned. Brandon was in Level IV, which was the worst. The most life-threatening. As an infant improves, they advance to less-critical stages until they are healthy enough to be released from the hospital.

"Let me show you to Lauren's crib." She motioned to a group of cribs a short distance away. My steps quickened as I caught sight of my daughter. She was now in an open-air crib and dressed in one of the newborn rompers I had purchased for her. It was pink with red hearts on it. I'd bought it for Lauren for Valentine's Day.

"Is today Valentine's Day?" I couldn't keep track of the time of day or the day of the week, let alone holidays.

"Yes, it is," the nurse said, a small smile playing about her stoic face.

I couldn't take my eyes off my daughter. Even though her romper was size zero-to-three months, it was humongous on her, to the point I thought she could disappear in it. I didn't care. It was the best Valentine's Day present I had ever received. *This was true love.*

As I approached her crib, I said, "Hi, sweet girl," and gave her a smile. Lauren turned her face in my direction and looked at me with those beautiful blue eyes. I swear she smiled back at me. For the first time, she looked like a normal baby—tiny, but normal.

"Did she just smile at me?" I asked as tears started to stream down my face.

"It's rare at this age, but certainly possible," the nurse said. "I think she's happy to see you!"

"I'll get you home as soon as possible, my love. I promise."

I rushed into the NICU still dressed in black. I came straight from Brandon's funeral to the NICU. I'd just seen Dr. Valerian an hour earlier for the service at Remembrance Gardens, but now I was meeting with her to discuss what was wrong with Lauren.

"Lauren's digestive issues are worsening," Dr. Valerian informed me, somehow looking like she'd been in the NICU all day.

I'm not sure I can take another crisis.

I'd gotten the urgent call at Brandon's funeral because Lauren was bloating up. It was now day twenty-five and Dr. Valerian was getting increasingly concerned that Lauren wasn't growing out of her gut problems. Now with the knowledge of Brandon's genetic condition, she wondered if Lauren's problems were also genetically based. Lauren hadn't undergone the genetic testing we'd done for her brother. The test was expensive and there wasn't a medical necessity to get the test, so Dr. Valerian hadn't ordered it. Truthfully, I didn't want to know. I didn't want to look at my baby while always wondering when the other shoe would drop. I wanted to dwell in hopeful ignorance as long as I could.

Looking into my eyes the day of my son's funeral, when I'd just been told Lauren wasn't getting better, Dr. Valerian's empathy was written on her face. "Cheri, I know you've had a brutal day. I'm sorry to give you more bad news."

"Just hit me with it," I said. At least I would be getting the unvarnished truth from someone I trusted.

Pursing her lips, she did, "I'm concerned Lauren might have a digestive system disorder called Hirschsprung's disease."

God, please, not another disease I can't pronounce!

"Go on," I prompted, though I wasn't sure I could take much more.

Perhaps sensing I was reaching my limit, she plowed ahead. "Hirschsprung's disease, pronounced hirsh-sprungz, is a congenital defect that affects the lower part of the large intestine. Babies born with this disease don't have ganglion cells in certain portions of their intestine, which are the nerve cells in the rectum and colon that regulate bowel movements." My eyes must have glazed over, because she switched to layman's language. "It means the baby can't poop easily. It can also cause abdominal pain and swelling, or 'abdominal distension' in doctor speak."

"What causes it?" I sighed, guessing at the answer before she said it.

"The disorder starts in utero and can be genetic, affecting one in five thousand infants."

Now the one child I have left might have a rare genetic condition, too?

"How is it treated?" I asked, trying my best to maintain my composure. It felt like I was in a hellish version of the movie *Happy Death Day*, doomed to repeat the worst nightmares of my life.

"If she has it, the affected part of the colon would have to be surgically removed. Left unaddressed, the colon could become infected and threaten Lauren's life."

"But Lauren has been having bowel movements for the last three weeks," I protested. "How could she do that if she's missing those cells in her intestine?"

"If only a small part of her large intestine is affected, it's possible a child can still defecate," Dr. Valerian explained. "Given Brandon and Rachel's issues and Lauren's symptoms, we really can't be complacent about this. We need to rule it in or rule it out."

In the NICU, a parent has very little control or self-determination over their child's care. From the moment you check yourself into the hospital until you and your child are discharged, the doctors are in charge, and they make most of the decisions about the course of your child's treatment. They decide when your child gets care, and they dictate what tests, medications, and treatments will be administered. In many ways, you are at their mercy, along with the nurses following their orders. If I had to relinquish my power to someone, I was grateful it was to a doctor as talented and conscientious as Dr. Valerian.

But something inside me questioned this theoretical diagnosis. I certainly trusted Dr. Valerian. Her instincts had been right about Brandon, so I felt I needed to give her the benefit of the doubt on this issue, too. *Whose instinct should I believe, hers or mine?*

I just buried both of my other babies. I can't bury this one. "Okay, what do we need to do next?"

"We'll have to do a rectal biopsy to see if the ganglion cells are present. Unfortunately, we don't have the equipment or the experts here to do it. There's a pediatric gastroenterologist from the children's hospital who has privileges to diagnose and treat patients at Mercy Main near downtown Austin. Lauren will have to be transferred there to get the test. I'm afraid we won't be able to feed Lauren until she gets it."

The pediatric gastroenterologist only practiced at Mercy Main on Tuesdays and Thursdays. It was Saturday.

"I can't feed my baby for three days?" I said, my voice incredulous. "That's insane." How was Lauren, at her tiny size, supposed to fast for three days?

"We'll do everything we can to make her as comfortable as possible," Dr. Valerian reassured me. Sadly, I'd heard that line before. I knew it was up to me.

My mom and I took turns standing vigil with Lauren, holding her virtually nonstop for those eternal seventy-two hours, except for the four hours per day the NICU was closed. We gave her pacifiers to appease her hunger pains, which she sucked on nonstop. We'd dip them in water so she'd get the sensation of eating, but she had to go back on IV fluids to keep her hydrated. She could survive without food for a few days, but not water.

I don't know how she made it to Monday—I don't know how *my mother* and *I* made it—but we did.

On Monday, day twenty-nine of her life and ten days after her brother died, Lauren and I took an ambulance to Mercy Main. It was like the day she was born all over again as the new medical team reversed all of Lauren's hard-won milestones.

The nurses stripped Lauren out of the cute baby clothes and put her back in an incubator. They put her back on an oxygen tube, which she hadn't needed for a while. She was hooked up to an IV for fluids. It was frustrating and disheartening to see my baby, who'd been gaining some independence, wired and tubed as if we were back to the days when things looked bleakest.

All this, for one damn test?

The pièce de résistance of the whole scene was Dr. Wong, who strode into the room as if he was King Doctor of NICU-land. "We're going to change Lauren's treatment plan," he proclaimed, without having consulted me on anything. And then he proceeded to give me the rundown of which medications he was stopping and which he was adding to her chart.

I held up my hand to stop him. "Look, we're just here to get one test. Once it is done, we're going back to Dr. Valerian. I don't want you to change anything about her medications or her treatment. Let's keep her stable so we can do the test and figure out whether or not she has Hirschsprung's. Then we'll discuss what to do from there."

Dr. Wong glared at me like I was a lowly peasant and walked off.

Instinctively, something deep inside was still telling me Lauren didn't have this condition. I was willing to go along with Dr. Valerian's plan since she thought it was possible and I trusted her. I was not going to extend the same grace to a doctor that hadn't earned that trust. My gut was giving me a big fat *no* on this one, and I was prepared to dethrone anybody who pushed me too far.

Mercy Main was going to keep Lauren overnight while we waited for the test, so my mom and I checked in at the Ronald McDonald House on campus so we could be near her while she was at a strange hospital with strange people. At 2:00 a.m., I went to check on Lauren like I always did and found out Dr. Wong had changed Lauren's medications without my consent. At 5:00 a.m., she was supposed to get a dose of Lasix for her breathing issues, but the medication had been removed from her treatment plan.

"I want to speak with Dr. Wong," I told the head nurse in the NICU.

She looked down her nose at me. "He's sleeping right now. He gave strict orders not to be disturbed."

"Get him up," I demanded in my best Mama Bear voice.

"We can't do that," she said firmly.

Enough of this. I pressed my shoulders back and mustered up my best bad bitch face. "Then he's fired. Let me talk to the next doctor in charge."

The nurse looked at me in shock. "Yes, ma'am," she said.

I marched back to the Ronald McDonald House and woke up my mother. "Mom, Lauren needs us. We need to make sure she gets her medications." Then we marched back to the NICU and sat there until I saw the paperwork confirming she'd gotten her meds.

After that, the hospital staff treated me like Public Enemy No. 1. The NICU doctors weren't used to their authority being questioned and ruled like emperors in their environment. I was the nobody who'd dared to point out one of their own had no clothes on. The staff pretty much ignored us the rest of the night and into the morning hours.

Lauren got her test the next day at 11:00 a.m. "She's negative for Hirschprung's," the gastroenterologist said, "and she didn't need to fast before the test." Then he looked at me over the top of his glasses. He could tell I had been put through the wringer. I got the sense he was annoyed, but not at me. "Feed this child," he said in a stern voice as he departed. *Ha!* My instincts had been right on the money.

I let out the breath I'd been holding for four days. This was the first big break we'd gotten in this merry-go-round of suffering. When I found out my insurance wouldn't pay for an ambulance ride back to Mercy North, the choice was clear. "Screw this," I told my mom. "We're *getting out of here*. I'll pay for it out of my own pocket."

It was the most expensive taxi ride of my life. Lauren didn't require any of the life-saving equipment that resided in the ambulance, but rules were rules. Like I said, the doctors were in charge and my family was along for the ride.

Dr. Valerian and her attentive nurses were a sight for sore eyes. "Welcome back," she said with a small smile. "I heard you caused quite a ruckus. Did you really fire Dr. Wong?"

"Dr. Wong is a pompous asshole," I said as I gave her a big hug. "I had to get back to a place where competent women were in charge."

Dr. Valerian chuckled. "I wish I had been there to watch. I'm so glad to hear the test was negative. I apologize for putting you and Lauren through all that, but we needed to know."

"I get it," I said ruefully.

"Well, let's figure out what we need to do to get you out of here."

That was music to my ears.

Other than having a predictable digestive cycle that didn't require enemas every three days, there was a list of milestones Lauren had to reach before she could be released from Mercy North. Essentially, she had to be free of life-threatening complications that required daily medical interventions.

She had to be able to regulate her body temperature. Check.

She needed a normal heart rate. Check.

She had to be off supplemental oxygen. Check.

"The only thing left is getting her to drink from a bottle on her own," Dr. Valerian noted. "I'll work up a plan with the speech therapist. If Lauren shows signs of good progress, we should be able to discharge her soon."

Over the next few days, Lauren seemed to hit her stride. She began taking to the bottle more readily and she started gaining weight. Dr. Valerian let me know we'd be able to leave the hospital in a couple days.

The day before we were to check out, we held a party for all the nurses in the NICU. We bought each of them hand-blown glass hearts. I penned handwritten notes to each of the nurses telling them specific things they had done that improved our stay. We brought in a catered Italian lunch complete with lasagna, salad, garlic bread, and decadent cheesecake for dessert. We wanted to thank them for everything they'd done to support us through the highs and the lows. They'd become part of our family, and we would be eternally indebted to them. I got the feeling it meant as much to them as it did to us. These women were incredibly passionate and dedicated to the lives of those NICU babies.

On the eve of her release, I got to spend the last night in the hospital with my baby for the first time. Having my daughter sleep beside me in her tiny onesie, swaddled in her plastic bassinet, tubeless and wireless in the silence of a regular maternity room was…terrifying.

I had no confidence in my ability as a mother. All those beeps had worked their way into my psyche until they'd become reassuring instead of annoying. They told me Lauren's heart rate, her temperature, and her blood oxidation level. I had become dependent on them to tell me how my daughter was doing. *How am I going to do this on my own?*

That night, I didn't sleep at all. In between feedings my fitful brain would jerk me awake to reflexively check on her. Touch her. Hold my finger up to her petite nose to see if she still breathed.

Finally, the sun came up. In total, Lauren, my mother, and I dwelled in the NICU for forty days. It was as if I was Moses leading my people across the Red Sea. Instead of navigating all those unruly waves, I felt like, against all odds, I'd somehow parted them. Forty days after her birth, right around her original full-term due date, we brought Lauren home.

Dr. Valerian made a point to be there for Lauren's discharge. "We made it," she said gleefully. Then she laid a hand on my shoulder and waited until I met her gaze. "Lauren's lucky to have you as a mom, Cheri. You're both going to do just fine." She smiled as she pulled away. "Call me if you need anything." As another offer of trust, I now had the doctor's cell number.

As we left the hospital, I took a picture. I still have it by my desk.

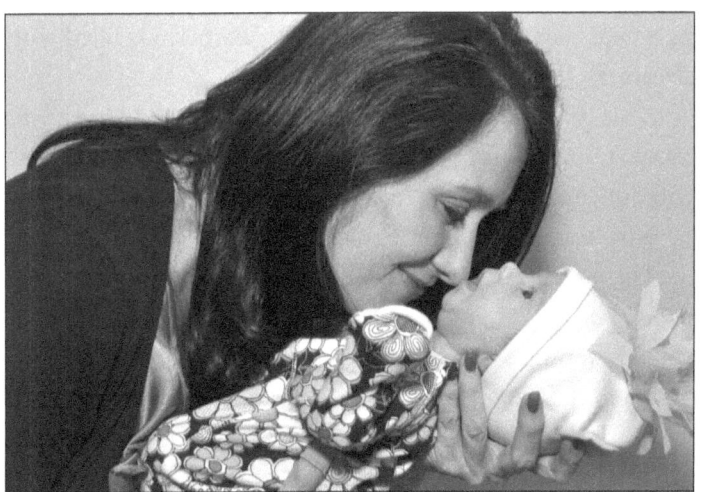

The glorious day I took Lauren home from the hospital

My mother drove us home as I sat with Lauren in the back seat. She was still very small to fit into her car carrier. When our car pulled into the cul-de-sac, I noticed several people positioned by the driveway. Worth's was the first face I recognized standing in the middle of the street. Then I saw Colleen, Johnny, and several other neighbors gathered behind him.

"What are they doing?" I asked.

My mother turned around and smiled. "It's your parade, Sunshine. Welcome home."

I watched as Worth and his Band of Brothers marched down the street to our driveway playing "Pomp and Circumstance" on his mobile phone to commemorate Lauren's all-important graduation into the real world. There was a yellow ribbon tied around the live oak out front symbolizing our neighbors' vigil for Lauren to come home. I looked on in awe as friends and neighbors clapped from their positions across the front lawn and followed us into the house.

As we came through the door, Lauren and I were greeted by a huge display of decorations. Every corner was filled with streamers, balloons, and flowers.

"This is incredible," I said through tears of joy. "Thank you, Mom. I don't think I could have gotten through this ordeal without you."

Now *this* was a proper homecoming.

The people flowed inside and took seats around the living room, and a big pile of gifts wrapped in baby-themed paper spilled over the coffee table. It was a surprise baby shower, my first, and the only baby shower I would receive. My mother's friends from her PEO Chapter, a charitable organization that raises education money for women, had arranged it for us.

I gleefully opened gift after thoughtful gift.

A personalized blanket.

A bottle warmer.

A stroller.

A handmade baby bonnet.

A diaper bag.

A picture frame.

I learned that Colleen had done all the decorating and made the arrangements for the celebration. I was overwhelmed by the love and generosity of the people around me, many of whom didn't even know me.

As the crowd started to dissipate, Colleen approached me. "Would it be okay if I held Lauren?"

I hesitated. Lauren had just gotten cleared to be home, after all. She seemed so fragile and fluid with her lack of muscle tone and I was scared she would break or slip down the proverbial drain if held the wrong way. I knew Colleen and Johnny decided not to have children, but the look on her face revealed her secret longing for motherhood. My heart melted.

"Sure," I said, carefully transferring a sleepy Lauren over to Colleen's welcoming arms. The warmth and joy that lit Colleen's face was miraculous. She looked twenty years younger. I knew it was the best gift I could have given her.

"We made it, sweetheart," I whispered to Lauren that night. I was grateful to drop my sails, thankful for the now calm waters around us, filled with love.

But of course, that isn't the end of the story, because unlike a fairy tale, real stories don't end.

I wish I could tell you it was smooth sailing from then on. After the trauma of the birth, losing Brandon, and Lauren's white-knuckled journey in the NICU, I was on pins and needles with Lauren for the next two years.

Similar to many preemies, Lauren's development was delayed. She missed milestone after milestone. It was five months before she learned to roll over. Six until she could sleep through the night. Fifteen months before she crawled. Between my PTSD and the doctor's concern about whether Lauren had an undiagnosed genetic condition, we about drove the poor child crazy.

The intensity of Lauren's reflux was terrifying. My hypervigilance led me to hire night nurses so my mother and I could get some rest a few nights a week. I could let my guard down knowing someone was watching her. The first night nanny was a Brazilian woman who was trained as an actual nurse. We propped Lauren up in a bouncy seat in her crib to keep her elevated because of her reflux. The nurse would feed her a bottle and Lauren's eyeballs would bulge out of her head as she gagged and gargled like she was drowning. She quit the next day.

I was so worried about Lauren maintaining her body temperature, I put a space heater in her bedroom, jacked it up to 80 degrees, and gave her heat rash.

When I got rid of the heater, I decided to swaddle her. At one point, my daughter couldn't sleep and got so frustrated she busted out of it like a deranged patient at an insane asylum, only she wasn't the one who was mad.

One night, I thought her lips looked blue, so I ventured out in the middle of the night trying to find a twenty-four-hour pharmacy to buy a pediatric blood oximeter to check her oxygen saturation, only to find out her fingers were too small to register any readings.

I knew my worry and hypervigilance pushed the boundaries of absurdity, but my fear wasn't allowed to dissipate, as Lauren continued to have developmental delays and ongoing health issues. My whole being was kept on high alert, like a car alarm that wouldn't turn off.

Turns out Lauren wasn't allergic to my breast milk after all. Her digestive issues were so severe because she had been so little, but they lessened as she got bigger and bigger.

The doctors were head cases, too. I mean that literally. Concerned that Lauren's head was growing too fast for her body, they suspected she had macrocephaly (an abnormally large head). I actually had to get her head examined with an ultrasound at Dell Children's Hospital. The test came back negative. She was fine.

They also worried Lauren might have cerebral palsy because she had too much tone and tightness in her legs and hips, causing her legs to scissor. Her muscle tone issues meant physical and occupational therapists were added to her repertoire of specialists. They wanted her to get into a fetal position and do tummy time, but she had no strength in her body to get into the most basic of baby positions.

I called Dr. Valerian in tears. "No, Cheri, Lauren doesn't have cerebral palsy. It's just going to take her some time to catch up developmentally. Try to relax and enjoy your daughter."

How could I do that when I couldn't see beyond the swelling waves ahead and wondered if one was a tsunami?

Thankfully, Lauren was resilient enough to survive not only her health issues, but also my neurosis and that of the well-meaning professionals around us.

Doctors say it takes three days of development out of the womb to make up for every day missed in the womb. Most children can and do grow out of the problems caused by prematurity. Many of Lauren's issues would, eventually, lessen or resolve. But it was a long, arduous road, especially in the first year, when so many milestones were delayed.

Despite all of it, there were many moments of joy.

When Lauren was five months old, I finally felt she was well enough to have a baby portrait taken. You know, the ones parents typically do when their child is days or weeks old. We still didn't go many places, so I booked the photo shoot with a professional photographer to occur at my house. It was early summer, when everything in Texas still looked green and lush right before they start to get scorched by the intense June heat. We would do the shoot in my backyard. I'd gone on Etsy and bought a bunch of Winnie-the-Pooh-themed knit diaper and cap sets. In one photo she was placed in a big yellow ceramic flower pot labeled "Hunny." Then she was Eeyore, complete with detachable tail. I was dressed in pink to match her Piglet outfit, and I couldn't resist curling my bare feet in the soft spring grass. The photo shoot was something that felt normal in my whole abnormal journey to motherhood.

With each outfit change, a new person came into the frame next to Lauren. Me. My mom. Worth. Colleen and Johnny—our whole village. With tremendous adversity comes tremendous joy, and we celebrated how far we'd all come.

Pooh was right. That tiny girl had filled all of our hearts.

I'm getting big! Mommy and me at five months.

Lauren's posse. The family that God built.

For Lauren's first birthday, I threw a huge party. Twelve months in, she was much more stable. She took her first steps that day—right on schedule.

That night, an inescapable thought started to take root.

I'm not done.

I'd always dreamed of two little girls. Perhaps I should try again?

Only this time, there would be no one in the daddy box.

Thank God.

CHAPTER 16

GENETIC RUSSIAN ROULETTE

THREE MONTHS AFTER HE DIED, I FINALLY GOT AN ANSWER to Brandon's genetic mystery.

I was at home. It was 6:00 p.m. on a typical Wednesday night and I had just finished work. I got up to answer a knock at the door. It was Gaston.

"Hi," he said.

"Hi," I replied. This short exchange pretty much summed up our relationship at this point. "Come on in. Lauren is still asleep."

Now that Lauren was home from the hospital, Gaston came over for regular visits. Based on the terms spelled out in the agreement Worth helped to mediate, he got to see her three times a week for three hours at each visit.

Like most newborns, Lauren took five to six naps per day and was only awake for a couple hours at a time. This meant that she often wasn't awake during his visits. That left just the two of us. Can you say, *awkward*?

The routine was predictable. Gaston would walk into the living room and take a seat. He would sit down on the couch and look at his phone. I did my best to ignore him and go about my business. Only this time, Gaston wanted to talk.

"I have something to tell you," Gaston said, a little too casually. "You may want to sit down."

"Oh?" I wasn't accustomed to Gaston initiating conversation. I was occupied washing and sanitizing some of Lauren's baby bottles, but they could wait. I walked the short distance from the kitchen to the living room and took a seat on the sofa opposite him.

"I got the results back from Mayo Clinic," he started.

"You did?" I asked. My mind went from wondering if I had to buy new bottle nipple brushes to fully focusing on my estranged husband and his news. I wasn't exactly sure when we would get those results back. Since there was no longer a health emergency, I knew Gaston's test results would take longer than Brandon's to come back.

"Yeah, the test was positive," he said glibly. "I have the same chromosome thing that Brandon had."

I sat in stunned silence. Apparently, he couldn't bring himself to use the word *defect*. The results must have come as quite a shock since he prided himself on being the picture of physical perfection. *How the hell could this have happened?* My mind started to race and roll back the clock on the events of the last two years. All I had were questions.

Why hadn't the doctors done genetic testing on Gaston at the start of the fertility process the way they had been done on me and the donor?

Were Rachel and Brandon's issues related?

Why hadn't the genetic counselor recommended genetic testing for Gaston after we found out about Rachel's condition?

Those answers would have to wait.

"When did you find this out, Gaston?" I asked slowly. I could feel beads of sweat start to gather on my forehead and chest as my nerves took over.

"A couple days ago," he said shortly.

"A couple days ago?" I responded in disbelief. "Did you not think that information was important enough to tell me as soon as you got the test results?"

"I didn't figure it would make a difference," Gaston said, oblivious to the fact that my blood was starting to boil. "Lauren is fine."

"Lauren is far from fine, Gaston. She's had so many issues already, and we have no idea how this genetic issue could manifest itself down the road."

As usual, Gaston was clueless.

Man, I really knew how to pick 'em. I chose Gaston because he possessed the one ingredient that I needed to become a mother, namely sperm, and even that was a bust. Rationally, I knew this wasn't Gaston's fault—he had no idea he was carrying a genetic doomsday weapon—but on top of all the other willful acts of betrayal, this was the icing on the cake.

Boy, this was one fucked-up fairy tale.

After getting the news, my first call was to Dr. Valerian.

"I know it's a shock, Cheri," Dr. Valerian said emphatically when she answered her cell phone. "I wanted to tell you as soon as I saw the results, but I couldn't breach Gaston's confidentiality."

My son and I suffered immeasurably, but Gaston's the one with the rights. I couldn't blame Dr. Valerian. I knew her hands were tied. Violating Gaston's confidentiality could get her fired.

"I get it," I relented as my blood pressure slowly lowered. "Do you think that Rachel and Brandon's conditions are related?"

"I'm confident they are," she said.

Now I had answers for both my dead children. This was no accident or coincidence. Even worse, it could have been prevented.

"That's very unfortunate and highly unusual," Dr. Babymaker said of the Mayo Clinic's test results. I sat across from him on the same couch where my fertility journey started.

"Why does the clinic test the female for genetic defects and not the male?" I pressed, trying to be respectful, but I'm sure he could tell I was very upset.

"Gaston had no known family history with those conditions. It's statistically rare for there to be a problem with the man's sperm." *But I had no known history of defects when you tested me*, I thought cynically, *and neither did the donor*.

I wasn't satisfied with that answer, so I interrogated further.

"Why wouldn't the genetic counselor agree it would be a good idea to get Gaston tested after we learned about Rachel's condition?" I asked, hoping for a better answer than the last one. "I had asked her about that specifically when we met to get her guidance about Rachel."

"I can't say for certain," said Dr. Babymaker. "You'd need to ask them, but I suspect it's because there are many factors that can cause spina bifida and genetics is only one of them. Perhaps the counselor thought that your age combined with nutritional factors were the likely cause."

This is a load of crap, I thought.

"How much would it have cost to get Gaston tested?" I asked.

"Between one-thousand and twenty-five-hundred dollars."

Brandon's medical bills for the nineteen days he lived totaled $750,000.

I wanted to scream, but at whom? Two children tragically died for less than $3,000. I'd spent $50,000 on donors and fertility treatments alone. I'd gone to the best fertility doctor in Central Texas—arguably still the best. They'd required a test for sexually transmitted diseases of two married people, but not one that would have saved my children and my family from a lifetime's worth of loss, pain, and suffering.

For a hot minute, I pondered the idea of a lawsuit, wanting someone to be held responsible for all the trauma and pain we'd been through. But deep in my heart, I didn't believe Dr. Babymaker and his team were to blame or even the misguided genetics counselor. They were following the standard practices and thinking of the time. Truth be told, the system was flawed, the conventional wisdom patriarchal and dead wrong.

"Okay, one last question, Dr. Babymaker," I said, mustering all my courage to ask the question I was most afraid to have answered. "What are the odds that another child would end up with a terrible disease if I used more of our frozen embryos?"

Dr. Babymaker dropped his head for a moment and let out a sigh. The break from his usual collected confidence was telling. "I'm afraid the odds are very high," he said, his tone resigned. "Both the sperm and the egg carry half the genetic information from the mother and father. The odds of a child inheriting Gaston's genetic defect and the conditions that go with it are fifty percent."

It's genetic Russian roulette, I thought to myself.

I had six embryos waiting to be brought to life, but they were all doomed.

If I wanted to have more children, I would have to start over.

As angry as I was by the circumstances, there was one bit of God's mercy in all of it. Brandon lived long enough for me to get answers. So, in a way, Brandon saved his potential sisters and brothers from suffering the same fate as him.

He also saved me. There was nothing wrong with me. God didn't hate me. I wasn't being punished for my past choices. I was even open to the possibility that God didn't work that way. What if He loved me as His child as much as I loved Lauren?

My next move would put that theory to the test. Would God be with me as I started over? I couldn't help but wonder if my luck and blessings would change with a clean slate.

CHAPTER 17

BRAYDEN AND THE GIFT OF NORMAL

SOME WOMEN HAVE THEIR MOTHER PRESENT AT THE birth of their child.

Mine was present at conception.

The story goes like this.

Gaston and I were legally separated and were living separate lives a year into Lauren's life. He still actively managed a business we started together, and I didn't want the stress of disentangling that ownership while managing Lauren and her ongoing health issues as a single mom. Other than the business, all other property issues were formalized in a separation document called an Asset and Liability Partitioning Agreement. Between that and our signed Parenting Plan covering all the child-related issues, we were in a stable place. To me, the big issues were resolved. I was happy to live life on my own terms and have Gaston out of my home, my purse, and my bed. A formal divorce seemed like a technicality—a can that could be kicked down the road.

Our financial and romantic lives were separate, but Gaston was now tied to me in a much more permanent way as Lauren's biological father. Armed with Gaston's DNA test results, I felt better prepared going into another pregnancy. I still had the dream of two little girls. But I felt it appropriate to give Gaston a heads-up, since he was still a part-time member of my household.

"I'm thinking of having another child," I said to Gaston as he grabbed a glass of water in the kitchen. It still felt strange having him around the house, but I wanted to keep things as civil and comfortable for Lauren as possible. I didn't want him to be my husband anymore, but I wanted Lauren to have a better relationship with her father than I'd had with mine.

A look of horror came over his face as he looked back at me, water missing the glass and running all over his hand. "You aren't thinking of using our embryos, are you?"

I rolled my eyes. "No, of course not! I would never take a fifty-fifty chance of more tragedy given everything that happened to Rachel and Brandon." Gaston would later file a formal revocation of consent with the fertility clinic to make sure those embryos would never be used. At least we agreed on that. Even if Gaston's sperm wasn't a genetic gamble, I would never tie myself to him again as a co-parent. Sharing Lauren was challenging enough.

"Okay, good." Gaston's look of relief was obvious, and I couldn't blame him. He had always been concerned about the level of financial obligation that came along with kids. The last thing he wanted was to pay child support for another one. But then I smiled like the cat that ate the proverbial canary.

"No, this time I'm getting a sperm donor as well as an egg donor." Gaston went silent as he stared long and hard at his glass on the counter.

"Good for you," he said. "I hope it works out."

My smile got wider. *Good for me, indeed.* The road ahead wouldn't be easy, but it would be much easier without him hanging like an albatross around my neck.

I knew I'd have to start from scratch with securing new donors and creating new embryos. The first thing I did was go back to the former egg donor to see if she was still available. She was now married and looking to have children of her own. She wasn't interested in donating again. In fact, she was concerned about her own fertility.

So, this time, I decided to find a donor that looked like me. For Lauren, we'd picked a donor that had Gaston's features, a match for his blue eyes and light brown hair. My features were darker, more continental, and I kind of liked the idea of a little girl with my straight sable hair and sass.

Starting over meant another big financial investment. I didn't feel I could afford the private donor agency I'd used before, which would add $10,000 to $15,000 to the price tag. I remembered Dr. Babymaker mentioning his practice offered a selection of egg donors. There wasn't as wide a selection of female donors, but all the candidates had gone through the same medical, genetic, and family history vetting as the private agency.

One particular donor caught my eye. No names were used to maintain anonymity, but each donor had an assigned number. Hers happened to be my lucky number. I nicknamed her "Lucky Lady #5."

Lucky Lady #5 had donated before and completed one successful cycle for another would-be mother. She was a college student with a 3.9 GPA who was studying business. She was an athlete. "I have a larger-than-life personality and limbs so long I wasn't always in control of them." Upbeat and funny, a lover of theater and debate classes, she wrote, "My friends expect to see me on *SNL* one day. I live to make people laugh"—which was also something I liked to do. As a bonus, she was a stunning brunette.

As I read her profile, I felt a kinship. It felt right. So I picked Lucky Lady #5 for my egg donor. *That was pretty easy and straightforward*, I thought to myself.

The sperm donor selection would be much more entertaining.

Scrolling through sperm donor profiles is a lot like online dating, except you know you don't have to put up with all the awkward dinner conversations. I could try on all these men as baby daddies without having to come up with excuses to leave early. And I could quietly learn some of the most intimate parts of their lives, like their full genetic rundown, without ever having to leave my home. I hadn't had a sexual partner since Hunter and I called it quits, and taking care of a needy infant doesn't lend itself to casual dating, so my sperm bank exploration provided ample fodder to fuel my fantasy life. I knew I wanted the donor to be tall, dark, and handsome. Someone with good hair and an undeniable charm that was more than surface deep. He would be smart…funny…ambitious.

The sperm bank had a facial recognition search feature that matched photos of faces to the list of sperm donors. Type in your husband, a family member, or a famous person and the technology would sift through the donors to pop up the ones that matched the features of those individuals.

"Hey, now," I purred when I found this bit of technical wizardry, "for a good time, call…"

…Bradley Cooper.

No hit.

…Blake Shelton.

No hit.

...Patrick Dempsey.

No hit.

...Hugh Jackman.

No hit.

"Zac Efron," my nanny, Sam, suggested, looking over my shoulder. Her full name was Samantha but she insisted we call her Sam to make it easy for Lauren to say.

After the Brazilian nanny bailed after her first shift, there was a series of others. All of them fell asleep on the job. I wondered if it was even humanly possible to do a night shift with Lauren when the agency sent me Sam. She was the one person who could stay up all night in a warm, dark room filled with the sound of lullabies. Turns out she was also wonderful with Lauren. I hired her full time. She traveled with me and Lauren when I needed to go on work trips and quickly became a fixture in Lauren's life.

I started typing her suggestion and hesitated. "Nah, too young. I want to put something in the cradle, not rob it."

"George Clooney," my mom piped up from my other side. Were Sam and my mother signing up to go on this quest? It looked like everyone in the house wanted in on the action. Thank goodness Lauren couldn't talk yet, or we'd be looking for someone bearing a striking resemblance to Mickey Mouse.

"George Clooney," I typed methodically, grinning at my mother's excited squeeze on my shoulder as the search engine churned.

No hit.

"What about that one?" my mom said, pointing to one of the profiles that came up as we went back to the main page.

"Oh, no," Sam giggled, "he looks like a dentist."

My mother tipped her head and narrowed her eyes at the

much younger woman. "And what's wrong with dentists?" she huffed. I squinted at her choice.

"You know, he looks a bit like Dr. Babymaker..." I stopped myself at my mother's glare. Was *she* now blushing?

"Well, what do you think of this guy?" Sam said, gesturing toward a moody-looking figure with tousled hair and a black leather jacket. I studiously turned to my twenty-something-year-old nanny's choice, trying really hard not to look at my mother.

Mom waved her hand dismissively. "He looks like he could be in a motorcycle gang. Let's steer clear of the bad boys, please."

I barked out a surprised laugh. "The description says he's outgoing. Maybe he's the *leader* of the motorcycle gang," I quipped, getting into the game.

As we dove deeper into the files of the sperm bank, still playing the game, I was stunned at the abundance and quality of sperm available to buy. Or maybe, I shouldn't have been? It was almost as easy as getting lucky on bulk trash collection day by finding a vintage Chippendale chair discarded along the side of the road.

Where had the sperm bank been all my life?

Unfortunately, my wish list of men was running dry, and it was taking me longer and longer to put names into the search bar. Then my mind switched from celebrities and entertainers to other famous men.

"Hmm," I typed, "John F. Kennedy Jr." I always had a thing for John John with his tall, athletic physique and signature dark wavy hair. The computer thought for a moment, then...

Bingo!

"Oooh, I like him," my mom said approvingly, leaning over my shoulder to squint at the screen.

"Me, too," Sam piped up. "Grade A for sure," she giggled again.

I skimmed the little bit of information I had for Donor 726. The donor interview questions were so thoughtful for the women. Each egg donor wrote short essays about their life aspirations, their families, and their reasons for wanting to donate. Very personal stuff. With the men, it was bare bones. It seemed most men couldn't be bothered to even write their hair color. Or, long ago, it was determined by someone in charge of the sperm bank intakes that men didn't need to explain themselves. I got the impression the bank staff were lucky to get the guy to talk for five minutes before he went into a booth to jerk off in two.

Instead, it was up to the female staff member to fill in the blanks of what was known about the donors based on their interviews with them. "Donor 726 is exceptionally cute with boy-next-door good looks and a great smile. His tall, lean build is often dressed in sporty clothing." What wannabe romance novel writer on the sperm bank staff was charged with doing this description?

"His best characteristic is his outgoing and friendly demeanor." Well, that was a gimme. It's not like you'd sell a guy by saying he was a rude jerk with anger issues. Was this before or after he'd made his deposit?

"He has gorgeous hazel eyes and wavy black hair that pairs well with his tan complexion." A bit reminiscent of wine tasting notes, but I'll play along. Our Romeo was sounding pretty good so far.

"Donor 726 is strong, confident, and assertive." Okay, I like a strong man.

"He goes after what he wants in life and takes advantage of new opportunities that come his way." That one sounded like me.

"He maintains an active lifestyle through sports like football and swimming, but also enjoys quieter pursuits such as reading and playing chess." Smart as well as athletic?

Yes, I thought, after forgiving the profile writer for her cheesy copywriting. Mentally, I rubbed my hands together in glee. *He'll do nicely.*

I couldn't help feeling a bit like a mad scientist splicing two strangers together to make my ideal child. This wasn't exactly every girl's dream of how to make a baby, but there was something exhilarating about it. Though I couldn't help feeling a small twinge. *Am I playing God again, or is God guiding me on this journey of creation?*

To make sure, I asked for God's help by sending up a prayer. *Direct my steps, Lord. Help me know if this man is the right choice to be the father of my child.*

I decided I would sleep on it. To my surprise, I slept better than I had in months. It was hard to explain, but I had peace about it. This was the guy. I ordered four vials of sperm, which was way more than I needed. A bit of paperwork and a couple thousand dollars later and it was done. Easy peasy lemon squeezy, as the kids say.

My humorous fantasizing at the sperm bank couldn't quite overshadow the reality that had led me there. Brandon's medical bills totaled three-quarters of a million dollars. I got premium sperm for $2,000. Which path to motherhood was easier? Which carried less heartache? I knew making an embryo with other people's genetic material wasn't everyone's fairy-tale way to build a family, but if it was going to help me have a healthy baby, I was willing to throw the fairy-tale fantasy to the curb.

Things went smoothly on the egg donor side as well. Fourteen eggs were retrieved, and twelve viable embryos were achieved when they were introduced to my vials of super sperm. I would only transfer one this time.

My mom was in the room when the embryo was transferred. We sat together, her hand in mine, as we watched the embryo go into the catheter and get handed to Dr. Babymaker to place inside me. I hoped the third time would be a charm.

During the waiting game of the next couple weeks, many doubts filled my head. Was I crazy to go through this again? What if genetics weren't the only issue? What if it *was* the environment? I was forty-five now. Was my body just too old to have a successful pregnancy?

We were about to get that answer.

"You're pregnant!" Nurse Barbara told me for the third time. Once again, she pulled rank to be the one to deliver the happy news. My joy was tempered with fear at what the future would hold, but I was hopeful we'd solved the issues that needed to be solved.

With Lauren's health on the upswing, my friends, family, and co-workers weren't quite as reticent to celebrate with me, though it was the kind of celebration similar to a bride who was on her fourth marriage. This would be my fourth child. I didn't want to make a big fuss about this pregnancy. I got a couple cards from friends, and co-workers who I'd known for a while would ask me how I was feeling, but no showers, no luncheons, no fanfare. It was more like, man, I sure hope things work out for her this time, this mother deserves a break.

Yet, this pregnancy meant everything to me. I was wanting, no, *needing* God to give me the gift of normal with this child.

Week ten and the blood test to check for chromosomal abnormalities came. Down's syndrome was the most common, caused by an extra chromosome number twenty-one. It affected one in seven hundred babies.

I went in to get my blood drawn. By this time, I had gotten over my fear of needles. I mean, what choice did I have? Lauren and nanny Sam accompanied me to the lab. As I walked into a treatment room, I was greeted by a perky young phlebotomist. She was about twenty-two and sporting a noticeable baby bump. Before she put the needle in, she took a stab at making some conversation.

"Is that your family out in the waiting room?" she asked.

"Yes, my daughter is out there," I said, referring to Lauren.

"Oh, yes, I saw her. She's lovely. And your granddaughter is adorable, too."

I did a double take. I was sitting there pregnant and she thought I was a *grandmother*?

If she wasn't sticking a needle into my arm, I would have sucker punched her. I laughed it off, but it stung a little. *Was I too old to become a mother?*

Enough with the self-doubt, Cheri, I reassured myself. *Screw the societal norms. You will be a great mother.*

My anxiety jumped when the clinic called with the results. Every milestone triggered my PTSD. "The test was negative for abnormalities. Everything looks good," the nurse said cheerfully, happy to give me good news. "Do you want to know the sex of the baby?"

I let out the big breath I'd been holding and felt light-headed as my pulse dropped back to normal. "Yes, please," I said into the phone. I couldn't wait to have my other little girl.

"Congratulations. It's a boy!"

Huh? My heart stopped, but not in a good way. There must be a mistake. "That's great!" I forced out as the nurse hung up. The panic that had receded with the negative test results came roaring back. This couldn't be. I was convinced I was going to have a second girl. That's what my dreams had told me.

I felt my heart start to race. I wasn't prepared to have a boy. I was on the verge of a panic attack, and to add to that, I felt consumed with guilt for reacting that way about the sex of my baby. Aren't mothers supposed to be happy to have a healthy child, no matter the gender? My mother and Sam were all set to celebrate the good news with me, so my reaction threw them for a curve, too.

I took my concerns to Worth.

"Girls are safe," I told him as he brought me a cup of hot chocolate. I blew on the steam as if by breath alone I could cool it enough to drink. That illusion of control now seemed silly to me, but I went through the ritual anyway.

"What do you mean by 'girls are safe'?" Worth asked. He sat across from me on his front porch, his untouched black coffee resting on a well-worn rattan coaster on the side table next to him. He liked to let it cool off in its own good time.

I stared down at my cup. It was hot. Using the handle, I rested it on the crook between my thighs and belly, letting its warmth seep into me, to my baby, through my clothes. "I'm having a son. What if he lies to me? What if he hurts me the way the other men in my life have? What if he rejects me?" I thought for a moment as Worth waited, serene as a statue. "What if he pees all over me?"

What if he dies?

Worth looked at me, his expression infinitely kind. "What if he doesn't?"

I leaned forward and straightened up. *What if he doesn't?* The thought had honestly never occurred to me.

"Have you considered the possibility this little boy could be a fresh start for you, Cheri?" said Worth as he gently touched my hand.

I'd tried to control so many things in my life and discovered, painfully, I could not. But in those moments of chaos, I found there were sparks of hope. Of growth. I didn't have to keep licking my old wounds. If I wanted to be a good parent to this little boy, I had to let the past go. I couldn't let it paint this relationship with the same brush as my previous ones. Not the relationships I had with my father and brother. Not the relationships I had with my husbands and lovers. Not the relationships I had with my children who didn't make it. An open mind and open heart, that's what I needed. It was up to me to break the pattern.

I have to give this little boy a chance. Maybe he would even help me heal.

After my conversation with Worth, my outlook shifted. Perhaps this was my chance to build a healthy relationship with a man. A chance to show one how to treat a woman. I would demand I stay open to the possibilities this innocent man-child would bring into my life.

But I did buy a dozen pee-pee teepees to protect myself from infant golden showers. Just in case.

At twenty weeks, Dr. Heartsong ordered the quad screen to test for neural tube defects like spina bifida. *Okay, Cheri, here it comes.* I braced myself for the blow I'd felt too many times before.

Dr. Heartsong called me personally. "Cheri," she started as my breathing quickened. *Why was she taking so long?* "Everything looks fine." I blinked as tears gathered in my eyes. Relief spread through me, so much I had to sit down. I expected adversity and when it didn't come, I didn't know how to handle it.

My mom and I went in for my twenty-four-week sonogram with Dr. Andersen. I clutched her hand as he ran the probe around my bare belly. "Everything looks great, Cheri"—by this point all my doctors called me by my first name—"your son looks healthy."

I fought myself with every piece of good news. I wanted

to relax and enjoy my pregnancy, but I also wanted to protect myself if everything went south again. I was afraid to hope. *Was it really going to be this easy?*

When we got home, jubilant after this last big developmental hurdle was crossed, I noticed Sam looked uncomfortable.

"What's up?" I asked her.

Sam let out a breath, looking pained, "Cheri, I've decided it's time for me to change careers. I'm thirty, and I think it's time that I got a real job. I'm thinking about going into sales," she said.

Not great timing, I thought.

"Oh?" I said, surprised. "When are you thinking about making that change?"

"I start my new job in two weeks," Sam said sheepishly.

"That's wonderful, Sam, we wish you all the best," I said through my shock. She'd leave three months before my due date. *Was this the shoe I expected to drop?* I scrambled to put together a plan to hire a new nanny and get her up to speed, fast. I hired a nanny agency to expedite the process.

And then Faith walked through my door.

Literally, the young woman's name was Faith. She was an eighteen-year-old with a slender five-foot-six-inch frame and straight strawberry-blond hair who had been homeschooled her whole life. She was the fourth of seven children, the ultimate middle child with three siblings on either side of her. The experience of taking care of her younger siblings and a depth of knowledge in child development had made her wise beyond her years. I liked her instantly and hired her almost as fast. My instinct proved to be good this time. We found we had very similar personalities, though hers was a softer, more grounded version.

Faith went with me for my routine thirty-four-week appointment. This was when everything went to pieces the last time, and I clutched Faith's hand to stave off the anxiety that threatened to overwhelm me in the waiting room. Sensing my fear, Faith brought my attention back to the present. "So what are you going to do about the nursery situation, now that you'll have two babies?" she asked calmly, her voice breaking through the storm circulating in my mind. I latched onto her question like the lifeline it was.

"Lauren will keep her old room, and I'll redecorate one of the guest rooms," I said, my voice hesitant and small. "I'm not sure what I want it to look like."

Then my teenage nanny patted my hand gently. "We'll get through this, Cheri, try some deep breaths."

My prior pregnancies had wired me for the worst possible scenarios. I had no faith and my anxiety lurked to pull me down when I doubted. So God thought He'd help me out by sending me faith personified.

"He looks wonderful, Cheri," Dr. Heartsong said during the ultrasound. "He's a little shy. See, his face is buried in his umbilical cord. My, he's going to be a big one."

I couldn't see his face. My son teased me, never letting the probe get a good picture of him, almost like he didn't want to reveal himself. With Lauren, her beautiful little profile and perfect button nose had shown up on every sonogram. But this baby was a mystery man. Who was he going to be? How would he stack up to every other man in my life who had mistreated or abandoned me? Why wouldn't he let me see his face?

Dr. Heartsong and I agreed that I would deliver by C-section at thirty-eight-weeks. I know some women view natural childbirth as a badge of honor for womanhood but…*screw Mother Nature on this one*. I'd suffered enough pain and trauma for a lifetime with my previous pregnancies, thank you very much.

This was one thing I could control, and I was happy to take that unpredictable variable off the table. "Please schedule with the surgeon and check in with the hospital for that week," said Dr. Heartsong.

My surgery ended up falling on exactly thirty-eight weeks gestation. I'd be the first procedure of the day.

It was really going to happen.

I'd gone through an entire pregnancy at forty-five without any health issues. Not one. And more importantly, neither had my baby.

I hadn't been able to plan my children's births the first time. My scheduled surgery presented a new but welcome problem.

Second babies are interesting because you have more bodies to shuffle. My mom, who was now living with me permanently, would take care of Lauren that first night while I was in the hospital recovering. So who would be with me?

"I'll be with you," Faith said.

Interestingly, I didn't have any hesitation with having my young nanny be my significant other to share the first night with my son.

The night before the procedure I couldn't sleep. My anxiety was back, running in circles around my brain. *Will there be a last-minute crisis? Is it possible that everything will go as planned? Had we caught every problem there was to catch?* I had every indicator things were fine, but my PTSD gripped me as we headed toward the point of no return, when my son would become his own separate person.

That night, Faith sat with me in my room just holding my hand. She didn't say anything. What was there to say? She didn't make any promises that everything would be alright. Because how could you? I concentrated on the warm pressure of her palm and fingers and prayed.

God, please protect me and my son. Please help me deliver a healthy baby boy.

The next morning, I arrived at the hospital at 7:00 a.m. for check-in and pre-op preparations. Even though I wasn't having labor contractions, I focused on controlled breathing to relieve my anxiety. I smiled awkwardly when Dr. Heartsong came into the room.

"Here we are," Dr. Heartsong said to me cheerfully, perhaps too cheerfully for seven o'clock in the morning.

"Yes, here we are," I echoed, rubbing my hand over my belly with trepidation.

Dr. Heartsong could see the panic on my face. We'd been here many times before.

She paused for a moment and put her hand on my stomach. "It's going to be okay, Cheri. Your son is healthy, and we're going to bring him out into the world today. Try to relax."

"Thank you, Dr. Heartsong," I said as a tear ran down my cheek. "I'll try."

"You'll do just fine," she said. "I'll see you in there."

The process for a cesarean section (C-section for short) is a relatively straightforward one. Like the last time, I was completely awake throughout the process. First, the anesthesiologist administers the epidural by inserting a needle and a catheter into the lower part of the back. The catheter remains in place to deliver pain medication as needed throughout the procedure. The majority of the medication stays in the spinal canal so it is safe for the baby.

After the epidural was set and doing its job, Dr. Heartsong came into the operating room along with two assistants. It takes a while as the team painstakingly makes incisions through each layer of skin and muscle. Then she opened the uterus and the amniotic sac. I couldn't quite make out their words to each other amidst the beeping and the sound of the oxygen mask on my face. I felt some pressure on my body as the team navigated their way through my insides.

There was a moment of silence that seemed to last forever.

The next sound was music to my ears. At 10:11 a.m., my son let out a strong, resounding cry. It was the cry of a healthy, vibrant, eight-pound-one-ounce baby boy. I gave birth to Brayden Michael with my mother by my side. Brayden means "brave one" and Michael was for the archangel, the leader of God's angels and highest in virtue.

"Would you like to meet your son?" a nurse said to me. Dr. Heartsong was busy closing me up.

"Yes, very much," I said, a smile blooming on my face. I was finally going to lay eyes on the face of this mysterious man who had been dwelling inside my body for nine months. The nurse brought him beside me.

This was the big moment. The moment I had waited for. I looked at him for the first time and thought...*he looks like an old man.*

Okay, I know every mother is supposed to say their baby looks like an angel when they come out of the womb. Truth be told, Brayden wasn't especially cute when he came into the world. He looked like a cross between a grumpy old man and an alien, complete with his freakishly long and unwieldy fingers, toes, arms, and legs that I'm sure his egg donor would have recognized.

But he was *my* grumpy old man. What a blessing it was to be fixated on those unimportant cosmetic details in a lighthearted way. It was the first joyful birth I had known.

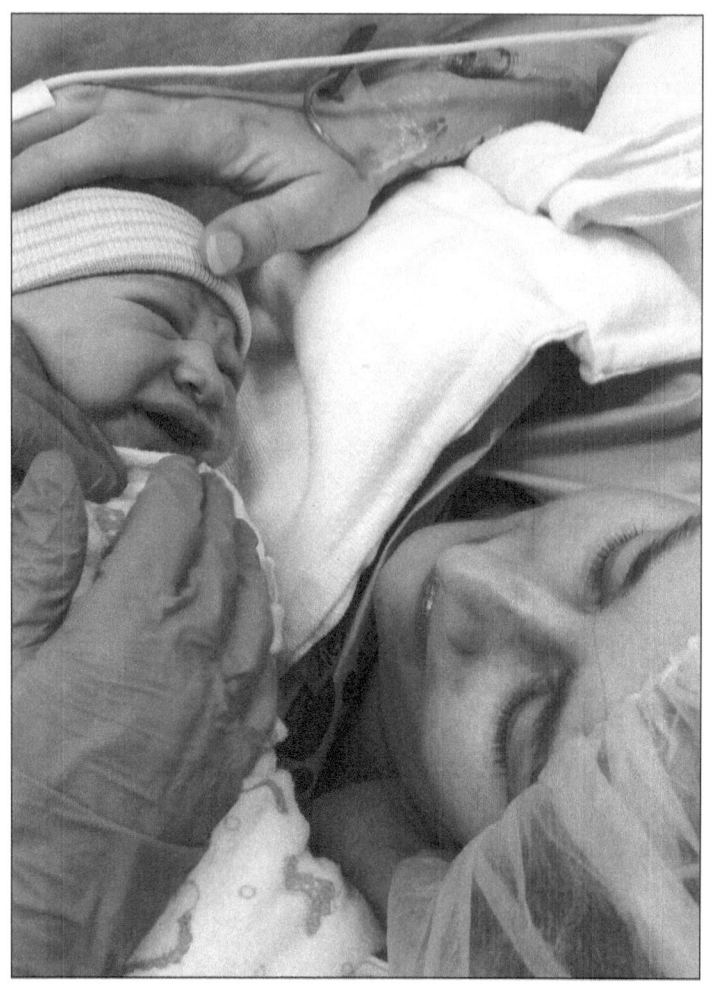

Meeting Brayden for the first time

Johnny and Colleen came to visit us a few hours after the birth and were among the first people to hold him. After a C-section, most women are in the hospital for two to three days. We bolted from the hospital twenty-two hours after the birth. I wanted to get out of there as fast as I could. It was just two weeks shy of my forty-sixth birthday.

Right after Brayden was born, my mother had a trip planned to Houston to attend the graduation of her grandchild, one of Phillip's daughters. Faith stayed with me for that first night in the hospital and for the next three days at home as I recovered. She was with us when we got a clean bill of health and were checked out of the hospital. She rode in the car and kept an eye on my newborn as he sat propped up in the car seat for the first time.

And she was with me when I put Brayden in his new nursery.

I'd chosen to decorate the room with Peter Rabbit. I wanted to revisit that small brown bunny with white belly and ears, which looked so much like the stuffie Ruth brought to Aurora that first night in our home. I felt it was appropriate that the well-dressed, mischievous bunny was raised by a single mother. The quote on the wall above the crib read, "Even the smallest one can change the world."

My small one certainly changed my world, and my perception of what motherhood could be like. Even after Brayden's textbook gestation and birth, I still struggled to take each positive step at face value.

A big defining moment was when I went to breastfeed him for the first time. I was filled with feelings of doubt and inadequacy. Would he latch successfully? Would I produce enough milk to satisfy him? I bared my naked breast like I was baring my very soul, wondering if he would accept my offering or reject me as had happened to me with men so many times before.

To my amazement, Brayden latched on like a champ! I was finally able to nourish my baby naturally. We were in perfect sync. Soon after, I happily gave the Cadillac breast pump away. I nursed him for over a year, to the point he could switch to regular cow's milk.

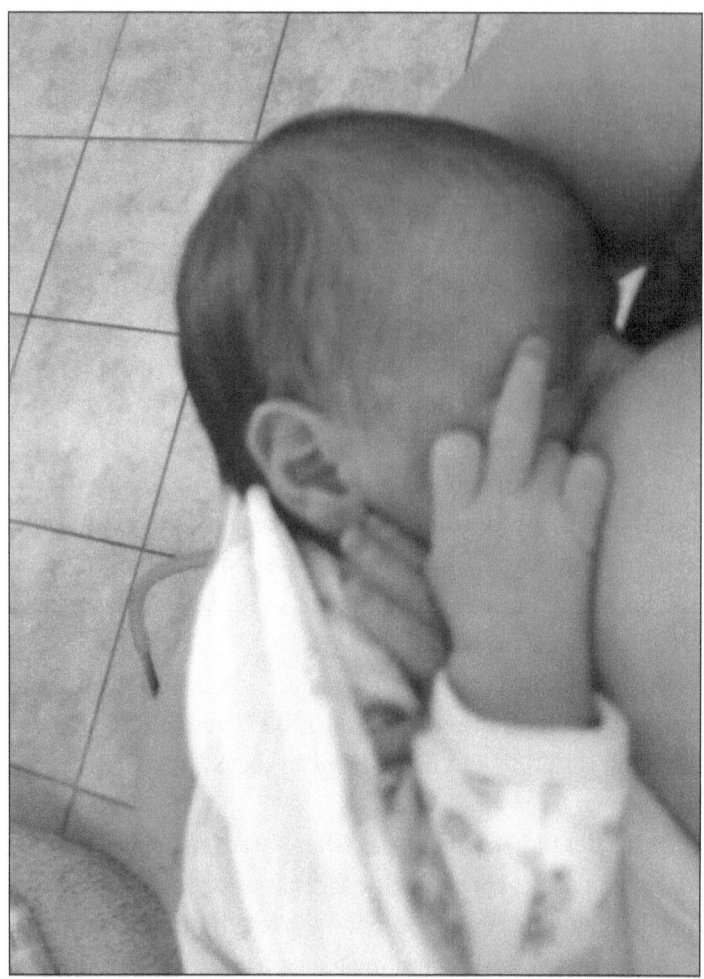

Leave me alone! I'm eating.

The months seemed to fly by with Brayden. Every milestone in his first year came on schedule. It was the gift of normal I'd prayed for, which allowed the hypervigilance I'd carried around with me since Rachel to slowly melt away.

Thank you for healing me, little boy.

Shortly after Brayden was born, Gaston filed paperwork

with the Texas courts declaring Brayden wasn't his son and that he had no rights or responsibilities where he was concerned. Gaston's filing spelled it out in no uncertain terms:

> The purpose of adjudication is to establish that Defendant is not the legal father of Brayden ▆▆ born on ▆▆. Defendant requests a finding for the court that he is not the legal father of Brayden and is not legally responsible for the support of the child, Brayden.

The declaration was a relief. Finally, I had a child that was completely mine. But my elation also came with the realization that I would be raising this child on my own.

Faith became, in many ways, a trusted advisor and surrogate co-parent. She was there for me every step of the way. She helped with the day-to-day raising of my children and modeled a gentle way of disciplining. As a partner, this eighteen-year-old young lady ran circles around Gaston.

I found myself watching her as she negotiated the regular testing and squabbles of young siblings. She would hear the children out and acknowledge their feelings, then set limits that emphasized safety and love.

One day, she tried to get Lauren to pick up her toys, but Lauren was intent on doing something else. So tender and gentle, she said to the toddler, "I understand that you want to go play with your dolls right now, but it's not safe to leave your blocks out where someone might fall over them." After giving her explanation, Faith sweetened the pot with a game. "Let's see which one of us can pick up the blocks the fastest!" Then she had a "race" with Lauren, going slow enough that the toddler could get to most of the blocks a moment before her nanny could. "All done! Give me a high five for such a good clean up!" Giggling, Lauren slapped at Faith's raised hands and then went to her dollhouse.

Faith showed me a way to parent that was different from the paternal autocracy I'd been raised with. Honestly, it felt strange to be learning how to kindly manage my children from a woman young enough to be my daughter.

Throughout the first four years of Lauren's life, I continued to take both children with me on business trips. I was determined not to allow my work to deprive me of precious time with my kids. Faith would travel with us to look after the kids, and my mother would tag along to support Faith. It was the closest I would ever get to having an entourage.

When Brayden was almost two years old, I was called away on a business trip where it wasn't practical to take the children. This was the first time I contemplated my own death since Rachel, only this time I decidedly did *not* want to go into that good night. My mind ran in the familiar circles. What if the plane crashed? What if the taxi got into a car accident? What if I didn't come back? Who would take care of Brayden then? Lauren would go with Gaston, but Brayden had no one. My mom was getting on in years, and I wouldn't ask my brother to adopt him after what he'd done to me. He'd see Brayden as an abomination. Who could I trust?

Tentatively, I sat down with Faith one evening after the kids were in bed. This would be a big ask. "I know you love Brayden as much as I do," I started. She nodded. "And you know I have this business trip coming up and am getting all the paperwork in order in case the worst happens."

"Yes, Cheri, I know," she said, then waited patiently.

"I would not ask this of you if I had family I thought would be capable of caring for and loving Brayden as I do. Would you be willing to be Brayden's godmother and guardian, and look after him if something happens to me?" Then I waited on pins and needles. I hadn't realized how important her answer was to me.

A smile slowly spread over Faith's face, so warm it felt like the sun briefly broke through the night pressing on the windows. She didn't hesitate. "Of course, Cheri! I'd love to be Brayden's godmother. You know you can count on me to be there for him should he need anything. I will love him like my own."

Those were the words I needed to hear. A weight lifted from me. Brayden would be safe and loved, come what may.

My family was now complete. My daughter, who saved me from despair and gave me the desire of my heart. My son, who healed me by giving me the gift of normal and setting my heart free of guilt. My mother, who held me up. Colleen, Johnny, and Worth, who served as my village of love and support. And my Faith, who showed me the way forward. It felt like we could go on like this forever, to live happily ever after in the fairy tale we'd created for ourselves.

But like most fairy tales, something sinister was lurking in the shadows to mess it all up.

CHAPTER 18

THE DADDY BOX

I IMAGINED THE SURVIVORS OF THE CHERNOBYL NUCLEAR disaster would understand the feeling that gripped me one hot June evening as I stared at the formally worded email in my inbox. It was a jumbled feeling, somewhere between disbelief, outrage, and pure unadulterated fear, the culmination of catastrophe when your life goes up in a mushroom cloud.

But of course, like with every Chernobyl Moment, my predominant feeling was shock. *How could Gaston do this to me? To us?*

It started innocently enough. Lauren didn't want to go with Gaston when he came to pick her up. She was now four and her health had stabilized. Both Gaston and I were doing our best to encourage Lauren to be comfortable spending time with both parents, but she refused to go with Gaston when it was time for her visits. She would work herself into a worrisome hysteria of crying and hyperventilation. We didn't want to add to her trauma.

As we'd done with so many of her development issues, we sought guidance from an expert—a child play therapist who said Lauren had separation anxiety. The way to remedy the stress of leaving her mother was to give Lauren choices about what she wanted to do. If she wanted to go with Gaston, she could. If she wanted to stay at the house and play with Gaston, also fine. The therapist advised making the activity with Gaston more appealing than staying at home. We'd offer her Chuck E. Cheese or a great bouncy house, kid wonderlands of amusement and culinary delights.

But Lauren didn't take the bait. Nine times out of ten, she'd choose to stay home. As further enticement, we started to do group outings as one big supportive village. Gaston watched Lauren, Faith looked after Brayden, and I split my time between both kids.

Gaston was a regular fixture in my house several times a month. He'd come to family dinners. He'd open presents with us on Christmas. He'd go to the zoo. I believed this peaceful coexistence was the best way to make sure our divorce didn't have a negative impact on Lauren. The counselors we worked with agreed.

With Gaston constantly underfoot, Brayden saw him as a kind of uncle or family friend. Gaston was a fun playmate when Brayden played with him and his sister. Occasionally, Gaston would bring chicken nuggets and French fries for Brayden when he picked up food for Lauren. But unlike other members of the extended family—my mother, Colleen, and Faith—Brayden never went anywhere alone with Gaston.

"Why doesn't Brayden go with Daddy?" Lauren asked me one day when I was encouraging her to go to Target to pick out a new toy with Gaston. At four she was starting to get a better grasp of family relationships.

"Because he's not Brayden's daddy," I said to her calmly. "He is your daddy, but your brother has a different daddy. You get to spend alone time with your daddy." I tried to keep it simple.

"Who is Brayden's daddy?" Lauren asked innocently.

Good question, I thought to myself. I better come up with a good answer. And fast.

However, the child therapist suggested I had time. Age four would be a good age to explain this family relationship to Brayden as well. We didn't exactly keep anything secret—Brayden was never encouraged to call Gaston "Daddy"—but the abstractions of kinship seemed too much for a two-year-old to handle, so we'd wait another couple of years before making things clear.

Over time, I started to share with Brayden that his story was different from his sister's. I read to him *The Pea That Was Me: A Single Mom's Sperm Donation Story*, by Kimberly Kruger-Bell. I told of how he was created with superhero sperm (what little boy doesn't revere superheroes?). Slowly, I revealed his special story of creation. But I still waited for the four-year mark before explaining in plain terms that Gaston wasn't his father.

We slogged through those next two years in our half-step forward, half-step back family dance. We stopped seeing the child therapist after she determined that Lauren had moved past her separation anxiety. "She can separate. Continue giving her choices, and she'll eventually grow out of it," was the last piece of guidance we received. We also engaged a parenting coach to guide us and mediate our parenting disagreements. She asked Gaston for his plan to get Lauren to go with him, a plan which never manifested.

Despite the therapists' reassurances, Lauren continued to resist going alone with Gaston. He handled the frustrating problem with his daughter the way he normally handled problems, by being passive-aggressive about it. This would occasionally bring our simmering divorce to a boil.

"What do you expect me to do here, Gaston?" I would say, when he blamed me for Lauren's resistance. "It's not like I can force her to go any more than you can."

Trying to get Gaston to keep his word felt about as fruitful as trying to nail hot Jell-O to a wall. He gave up his rights to all his embryos, which included Lauren and Brandon. Then he wanted visitation rights. Then he wanted equal custody. I hired one incompetent attorney after another to help untangle the divorce and custody mess, but our negotiations always broke down. To me, attorneys were a waste of money. I figured two reasonable people with integrity should be able to work out the custody situation. Frankly, I thought we'd already worked it out. Just because Gaston had a change of heart didn't mean all these things were up for renegotiation. *At least I didn't have these issues with Brayden*, I thought, relieved.

In the midst of the legal in-fighting, I tried to keep our extended family time pleasant. A month after Gaston's forty-ninth birthday, I had a Father's Day celebration at my house and invited his father, who was visiting from out of town. There were decorations, mimosas, and brunch. I bought gifts and even made a cake. It was a peaceful, happy day. Finally, it felt like we had a truce.

Turns out, it was more like a Trojan Horse.

Four years after filing papers declaring to the world that he wasn't Brayden's father, Gaston reversed his position—again.

There it was in black and white on my computer screen as I opened the email from Gaston's attorney. My eyes blurred with tears as I read it.

...establish that Defendant is the legal father of Brayden ▓▓▓ born on ▓▓▓. Defendant requests a finding from the court that he is the legal father of Brayden and is legally responsible for the support of the child.

...requests that the Court order a custody evaluation to include psychological testing and evaluation of the parties.

...appoint an amicus attorney to represent the best interest of the children.

...the parties and the children to undergo an assessment with ▓▓▓, Alienation Assessments and Treatment.

In one fell swoop, Gaston asserted that I was an unfit mother of Lauren *and* that he intended to become Brayden's father against my will.

It was just a week after I'd entertained him at my home for Father's Day so he could spend time with Lauren.

Brayden had turned four about a month earlier. It was a critical date in child custody battles, as now an amicus attorney, or "friend of the court," would be legally appointed on Brayden's behalf as an advisor to the judge. Because the amicus was there to advocate for the best interests of the child, rather than either of the parents', the amicus's opinion was assumed to be impartial and carried substantial weight with the judge.

A hearing on Gaston's claims about Brayden would be held in one week.

It felt like a premeditated ambush accompanied with a virtual stab in the back, delivered in my own home. I had no attorney at the time (which I'm pretty sure Gaston knew) because I thought the heat of our custody battle had cooled.

I was wrong. It appeared that Gaston wanted to catch me off guard so he could take my son. I was living through yet another episode of *The Twilight Zone*.

As concerned as I was about the accusation against me with Lauren and what this could mean for our future, I knew that protecting Brayden had to be my top priority. After all, I didn't have a choice with allowing Gaston to help raise Lauren. He played a role in her creation and shared her genetics. But I did have a choice with Brayden, and I'd fight tooth and nail to be allowed to raise my son the way I wanted.

I frantically searched for a new attorney. I knew I'd need a good one this time. I scoured the internet for reviews and found Jimmy Evans. His reviews included words like "diligent," "accurate," "knowledgeable," "thorough," "cool confidence," and "gets results."

Okay, I need to speak with this guy.

He took my call even though he was on vacation in Florida. "Why not get a DNA test?" he asked.

"That's what we need to petition for. It'll be an open-and-shut case after that," I agreed. Though it frustrated me to no end because Gaston *knew* his sperm hadn't been used to make Brayden.

"Let's meet in my office when I get back on Sunday," Jimmy said. The hearing was just four days away.

I'll never forget the day I met Jimmy. The office was closed on Sunday. I got there before him and sat on a bench outside waiting for him to arrive. In the distance, I heard the faint strains of AC/DC's "Are You Ready." As the music got louder, I saw Jimmy drive up in his 2018 red Jeep Rubicon with the top down, music blaring, and his trusty border collie, Annie, in tow. He looked like he had just come from a run sporting a blue activewear performance pullover, gray running shorts, and blue tennis shoes. He was a couple inches shorter than me, and I figured he was about my age.

Jimmy's fair complexion and sandy-brown hair mixed with hints of gray coupled with his boy-next-door looks caught me off guard. As he escorted me into his office, I noticed a wall full of pictures of him with his wife, kids, and extended family. *Was this my white knight? My pit bull divorce attorney?* I'm not sure what I expected, exactly. Perhaps I had envisioned an intimidating larger-than-life giant with big muscles and dark, slicked-back hair to slay Gaston and his troll-like behavior.

I quickly realized Jimmy's unthreatening exterior was one of his secret weapons. The guy was shrewd and knew his shit! I'm guessing his opponents never saw him coming. I started getting him up to speed, but there was a lot of baggage to unpack. "I can't figure out his angle, Cheri," he said. "We'll just ask for a DNA test. Don't worry too much about the hearing. Since you just hired me, I'll ask for a continuance from the court so I can prepare. I'm sure the judge will grant one in this situation."

Four days later, we sat in the courtroom as Gaston's female attorney gave an Oscar-worthy performance waxing poetic about how Brayden needed his father. "Brayden hasn't seen his daddy in two weeks. That little boy misses him," she simpered. "Ms. Bergeron has been keeping them apart ever since this lawsuit was filed. Brayden's devastated." She made these statements without any knowledge of how Brayden had handled the time without Gaston. Truth be known, Brayden hadn't skipped a beat in his absence. He was the same happy boy he always was. It was all I could do to sit on my hands and keep from screaming profanities in the middle of the courtroom. Gaston sat there with a pitiful look on his face, presumably to garner sympathy. From my seat on the other side of the courtroom, it appeared he had rehearsed and perfected the victim role. Everything that came out of his mouth felt like a lie. And I could say nothing about it or jeopardize everything.

Jimmy asked for a continuance, but the judge shook his head. "No, Ms. Bergeron, I see here your divorce has been pending for six years," he said, gesturing toward documents on his desk, "we're going to have this hearing today."

We were not prepared. Our backs were against the wall, and they knew it.

Jimmy took me out in the hallway during a short recess. "Cheri, we need time to mount a strategy on this. I don't know what the hell's going on here. I recommend that we agree to visitation because Gaston is still your legal husband. If we go forward with the hearing, there's a good chance this won't go our way. We'll reset this hearing in a few weeks."

I was speechless. It felt like a bad dream. *No, more like my worst nightmare.* "But Brayden has never been away from me," I managed to protest.

"I know," said Jimmy. "This is a raw deal. It's only temporary. We will get to the bottom of this, but it's going to take some time."

I had no choice but to concede and grant Gaston unsupervised visits with my son. The son no one should have been able to take away.

After the hearing, my normally calm and polite mother, who'd been sitting in the courtroom watching the whole fiasco unfold, went nuclear. An avenging superhero, she flew at her target, her gauzy, royal-blue Chico's cover-up fluttering like a cape, and cornered Gaston in the hallway outside the courtroom.

"You should be ashamed of yourself, Gaston Beauvain!" she yelled, using his full name. "We welcomed you into our family and now you're trying to take Cheri's son from her? You know this is wrong. How can you live with yourself?"

Gaston, who'd shrunk under her admonishment, went into a speech that sounded prepared. "Cheri's been preventing me from being a dad to Brayden. She alienated Lauren from me, turning my own daughter against me. Why else would Lauren not want to spend time with me?" he whined.

"Cheri has given her time to help you with Lauren, Gaston. You're just too selfish to take responsibility for the situation that you helped create. I guess it's easier to blame everyone else for your failures, isn't it?"

Gaston gaped like a fish at her saltiness. He knew it was uncharacteristic of her, and Gaston prided himself on maintaining his nice-guy image.

I saw his tight-lipped lawyer start clicking her heels and move rapidly in our direction, like a witch on her Ferragamo broomstick, so I laid a hand on my mother's arm. "Mom, we should go," I murmured. "I want to go home and spend time with my children." As much as I jumped for glee internally at my mother taking a stand with Gaston, the reality was, we were still in the courthouse of my ongoing custody battle and there were cameras everywhere. I would not unleash my anger on Gaston here.

My seventy-seven-year-old mother was surprisingly strong and tugged herself free. She pulled herself up to her full height of five feet, four inches and crooked a finger at my ex. Gaston looked frightened. "I swear to God, Gaston, you will take my grandson away from his mother over my cold, dead body. I will spend every dime I have, if necessary, to make sure you never get to see so much as a hair on Brayden's head."

Then she turned on her sensible black Mary Janes and we walked out of the courthouse together.

"Thanks for standing up for me, Mom," I said as I gave her a hug. It was a small glimmer of light on a very dark day.

How would I explain this to Brayden?

I cried when I told Brayden he'd have to leave me. "I'm sorry I brought this man into our home," I told him, trying to put it in words a four-year-old would understand. "I thought he was safe. Mommy's working to fix this. But for now, you'll have to go with Lauren on visits with Gaston without me."

"But I don't want to go," he said, sounding lost.

"I know, sweetheart. It will be okay. I need you to be brave." I felt my cheeks grow wet despite my best efforts to hide my distress.

"Don't cry, Mommy. I'm a big boy," he said solemnly, his big eyes standing out in contrast to his red Spider-Man T-shirt like he was a modern-day Little Red Riding Hood.

I never should have let the wolf in the door.

Gaston had made his intentions toward Brayden perfectly clear in those court documents filed after he was born. How could the courts give him a do-over on that? I believed Gaston had betrayed me before, but this was by far the worst because I was confident he knew his story was a lie.

From the day the lawsuit was filed, Gaston was no longer welcome in my home. We were required to do the handoff at a neutral spot—a park close to my house. Every time I had to hand over my son, I felt like I was handing him over to a kidnapper. The more I had to give him up, the more I wanted to hold him close. Lauren was struggling, too. Sometimes she wouldn't even get out of the car, so I had to pull her out. Watching my children suffer this way was even more difficult than my own suffering, if that was possible.

In the midst of all this hardship, my children and I clung to each other for survival. We'd sleep together in the Big Bed, as they called the California king in my bedroom, every night until the trial was over, holding on to each other for dear life.

I met with Jimmy in his office two weeks later, desperate for some answers. He was pissed off that Gaston's attorney got the upper hand in the initial hearing. Jimmy wasn't accustomed to losing, and he wasn't going to take this lying down.

"How can Gaston get away with this?" I asked Jimmy in absolute bafflement. "He's not my son's biological father, and he knows it. We've been living separate lives for the last six years, for Christ's sake."

"Our team has spent hours researching this, Cheri. He's going for the 'presumed father' statute," Jimmy explained.

"'Presumed father'? What's that?" I asked, even more frustrated and confused.

Jimmy took a breath, then dove into one of the most anti-mother laws I'd ever heard of. "If a child is born during a marriage, the husband is the presumed father. This presumption can be refuted with a DNA test. However, due to Texas law, there are certain circumstances where the court can deny a paternity test, if it feels that terminating the parent-child relationship would not be in the best interest of the child. The standard for determining whether it is in the child's best interest depends on how much the man has acted in a fatherly role." Jimmy looked at me seriously. "In essence, the court can deny us a DNA test and declare Gaston is Brayden's legal father if Gaston proves he has acted like Brayden's father. Admittedly, it's an obscure part of the Texas Family Code that isn't used very often, but those are the grounds he's standing on."

Stunned, I sat across from Jimmy in his office. "I can't believe this is happening," I said in disbelief. "What can we do?"

"The burden of proof for the presumed father statute requires 'clear and convincing evidence,' which is not as strong as the 'beyond a reasonable doubt' standard you see in murder trials, but it's still a high bar to meet," Jimmy explained.

Relieved, I sank back in my chair. "Well, that should be a slam dunk for us because Gaston hasn't been in a fatherly role for the past four years."

Jimmy held up a hand to temper my relief. "Don't be so sure. Not all judges follow the law. If you get a judge with strong personal convictions, he may decide to go with the 'what would be the harm?' argument, since Lauren is already under joint custody and granted paternity, anyway."

My simmering anger leapt and I felt my face flush. "What the fuck would be the harm?! What *wouldn't* be harmful in forcing my son to have Gaston as his father when it's a lie?"

To me, it was like Lauren was the hamburger and the court was saying to Gaston, "Would you like fries with that?" But Brayden wasn't a side of fries. He was an innocent little boy who'd only seen Gaston as a neutral accessory to his life at most.

"Brayden is his own person. He is not an appendage to his sister," I declared. "I won't allow my son to be used as a poker chip in Gaston's power play." But deep down, I knew it might not be up to me.

"Look, a lot will hinge on what the amicus thinks," Jimmy explained. "I've known LeFou for many years. The duty of an amicus attorney is to be impartial toward the parents and objectively represent the child's best interests. Let's pray he can see through all this nonsense."

There's no way I would be late to my first meeting with the amicus attorney. He officed out of a small rundown house in Georgetown. Unlike the polish of my attorney's office, this one looked like it was occupied by a used car salesman, complete with cheap artwork and particleboard furniture. I sat in the makeshift reception area waiting for LeFou to come out for our meeting.

LeFou plodded out of his office, his heavyset five-foot-ten frame making the hardwood floors underneath him creak. He was quite a sight with his black cockatoo haircut and goatee, ill-fitting khakis, hand-me-down green plaid sportscoat, and brown cowboy boots. He exuded an awkward vibe like a backwoods country boy who was trying to look intellectual and sophisticated but missed the mark by a mile.

I got a bad feeling about him immediately. *Keep it together, Cheri,* I told myself. *This guy has a lot of power over the future of your family.*

"Tell me about Brayden's relationship with his father," was his opening salvo. *Oh boy, we were off to the races.*

"Gaston isn't Brayden's father and never has been. I had Brayden completely on my own," I stated bluntly, my irritation palpable.

"That remains to be seen," he said without flinching.

"Okay, well, Gaston and I weren't together when I had Brayden, and he has only been around my son while he was at my house spending time with Lauren. That hardly makes him a father."

"Fathers come in all different shapes and sizes," said LeFou. "Maybe he wasn't given a chance to be a dad."

Was this guy on drugs? I wondered. Then the amicus proceeded to tell me his story, although I don't remember asking. He was a stepfather himself, having adopted his wife's child from a previous marriage. He was raised by a man who wasn't his biological father. The amicus appeared to be a firm believer that every child deserved to have someone in the daddy box.

My bad feeling grew to the size of a cantaloupe in the pit of my stomach.

I'm screwed.

CHAPTER 19

THE MEASURE OF A FATHER

I SOON REALIZED THAT MY UNCONVENTIONAL PATH TO create Brayden came at a price.

Because I'd used an anonymous sperm donor and there was no physical man to check off the daddy box, Brayden was vulnerable to be claimed by a man who had no blood ties and hardly any social ones. Because Gaston had occupied the same space as Brayden. Because we were legally still married with a pending but incomplete divorce. Because he claimed he'd acted as a father. If I'd had an affair and the father could be proven, Gaston wouldn't have a legal leg to stand on.

Part of the traditional motherhood fairy tale says you need a man's love before you can have a child's love. A family can't be proper without a spouse. It can't be proper if these spouses aren't male and female. If a mommy's checked off, someone needs to occupy the daddy box. But in a modern world of advanced medical science and proven fertility practices, a man becomes a choice, not a necessity. Sure, it's hard to raise a child alone, but not impossible. And if your partner doesn't contribute or improve the life of the child, then what's the point of having him around?

But the antiquated fairy tale and its values are hard coded into our family court system. I was going to have to fight with everything in me to protect and defend a family that bucked against accepted norms.

Brayden's amicus attorney wasn't supposed to be swayed by this fairy tale. He was supposed to be objective and neutral.

What a crock of shit.

I suspected LeFou started coaching Gaston's attorney and began orchestrating things in Gaston's favor. Out of nowhere, it seemed, Gaston started sending me child support payments for Brayden, four years after the fact, which I, of course, refused. He created a bedroom at his house for Brayden—Lauren had one for the last six years even though she'd never slept in it. The man who in my view was notoriously stingy with his money turned into Daddy Warbucks, buying Brayden a mountain of toys, and then videotaping him enjoying them so he could use it as evidence against me in court.

It appeared to me that the attorneys were conspiring to delay hearings to give Gaston more time to build his fatherhood evidence after the fact. The hearing that Jimmy promised would happen in a few weeks took five months to resolve.

In addition to the amicus attorney, Brayden was required to go to a child therapist who would also weigh in as an advisor to the court about whether or not I'd remain Brayden's sole parent. All of these outsiders were now in a position to tell me what was best for my own son. On top of that, I paid the tab for their pricey hourly rates.

After that fateful moment in my night-darkened kitchen, when Jimmy called to say the amicus would suggest denying a

DNA test so Gaston could be named Brayden's father, against Jimmy's advice, I called the amicus again to talk to him alone. I needed to know why he was doing this.

I also needed to record the call without my lawyer being culpable.

"Do you believe that Gaston is Brayden's biological father?" I asked him point-blank.

"No, I don't think he is," the amicus said.

"And do you think Gaston's been in a fatherly role with Brayden these last four years?"

"No, but I don't think Gaston's been given the opportunity." That claim would catch me in a double bind, leaving me in a no-win situation and setting Gaston up to be named Brayden's legal parent.

But Gaston wasn't a parent to Brayden. Neither in genetics, nor in practice. Yet, if he could convince the judge to deny the first condition and accept the second, or even the promise of the second, he could be made Brayden's father by the State of Texas.

It seemed that the amicus wanted Gaston to be named the father no matter what the evidence said, simply because he believed that every child should have one.

While I waited for my case to be heard, I had to turn over my son to Gaston on Thanksgiving Day. It was the first holiday we had spent away from each other.

All I wanted for Christmas was a DNA test.

In December, the fateful day came when my case would finally be heard before a judge. Travis County operates on a rotating docket system, so we didn't know which judge would hear the case. Each hearing was like playing a game of judicial *Wheel of*

Fortune, hoping you would spin the wheel and get assigned an impartial and even-tempered judge.

Even in that hearing, the amicus sought to delay the proceedings. Fortunately, this time, Judge Solomon had read enough of the previous court transcripts to know that something wasn't right. "We're going to have this hearing," he said, looking straight at the amicus and Gaston's counsel.

The hearing was like a mini trial. It would be a full week of testimony from experts and witnesses on both sides. Gaston's team had to prove to a "clear and convincing" level that he had been a father to Brayden. It was our job to show he wasn't. At the end of the week, the judge would decide if he'd grant a DNA test to prove beyond a shadow of doubt Gaston wasn't Brayden's genetic father.

Gaston's team would go first.

The amicus sat at Gaston's counsel table as if he were Gaston's second lawyer. How ridiculous that I had to pay half of his steep hourly rate to finance Gaston's effort to take my son.

While part of a custody battle is about the role the father plays in the child's life, another, maybe larger part of the judge's decision was based on my own conduct. The conduct of the mother.

For as much as Gaston was on trial, so was I.

There was the question of my intentions. Did I present Gaston as Brayden's father in public? Did I treat him as my son's father? Even the fact that I'd given one of Brayden's school pictures to Gaston came back to haunt me. Why did I do that? I'm sorry, but I gave his picture to a lot of friends. My neighbor and Brayden's godfather, Johnny, also had a picture. Did that mean he had a paternal claim, too? I texted a few pictures to co-workers. Did they also have a claim to my child?

Gaston came with us on a work trip. I figured he could have

more time with Lauren, and I appreciated his willingness to be flexible on his allotted visitation days when I had to travel for business. That got reframed as a family vacation.

Then my family was put on trial. How weird was it that I'd created a family out of my elderly mother, some neighbors I'd only met a few years before, and a young nanny who I'd made a godparent? That I was playing nice with my estranged husband? Was the court expected to believe this band of misfits constituted a family?

And though I had carried, birthed, and raised them, I was not genetically related to my children. This seemed to give Gaston a stronger claim to Lauren and an equal claim to Brayden. Blood, for Gaston and the men who would rule over my family's future, was thicker than love. Without a genetic entitlement, the legitimacy of any caring and committed relationship could be questioned. Even Faith's love and dedication to my family came under fire, since her paycheck, it was argued, could be considered bribery.

And the hits kept on coming.

Gaston went so far as to say he wasn't sure what embryo was used to create Brayden. "Maybe it was one of mine," he suggested, even though the clinic had his revocation of consent on file.

"So did you go back to the clinic and check which embryo had been used?" Jimmy asked. "Did you sue the clinic, or try to get clarification?" Of course, he hadn't, but now the judge had doubts, especially about a process most people outside of the fertility world barely understood.

"But I still don't know if I'm the father…," he hedged, continuing to sow that seed of doubt.

Instead of bringing forth objective, credible witnesses that would provide empirical evidence supporting Gaston's case, he paraded his family members forward one by one to plead his case. I learned that Gaston had a girlfriend for the last seven years I didn't know about. She'd never met me or my children, so I wondered what in the hell she could testify to other than the bullshit Gaston had fed her. Gaston's sister also took the stand to plead his case. Her account of past events with Brayden were, I felt, richly exaggerated—truly the stuff of fairy tales.

The icing on the cake was a legal expert they paraded into the courtroom, who claimed I didn't have the right to pursue a pregnancy without Gaston's consent. Apparently, my legal husband owned my uterus along with the fruits of it.

After two days of being debased and marginalized, it was my turn to go into battle with Sir Jimmy wielding his sword beside me.

Despite Gaston the Ogre's attempts at revisionist history, it wasn't difficult to show that he hadn't been in a fatherly role with Brayden. Other than still being legally married to me and spending some time around Brayden that occasionally involved buying him fast food, Gaston scored a big goose egg on the big and small things that a father does for his child. He wasn't involved with Brayden's conception, prenatal development, birth, or parenting. He didn't supply any of Brayden's basic needs or financial support. He hadn't even taken him anywhere without me until after his suit was filed.

Jimmy meticulously slashed Gaston with each and every piece of evidence that showed he had not behaved as a father to Brayden. He saved the death blow for last.

"Since two of your other children died of genetic diseases that were attributed to your sperm, if you thought Brayden was your child, wouldn't you rush to get him a DNA test to ensure he doesn't have a condition that would need medical attention in the future?" Jimmy struck.

Gaston's charade of innocent bewilderment gave way to sourness in a way I felt revealed his true self. "I've been advised not to answer that." In my mind, it was a coward's way of saying he would refuse to take the DNA test that would show whether Brayden was at risk of carrying life-threatening genetics.

The courtroom sat in stunned silence. Gaston's refusal to put his presumed child's welfare above his own spoke to Gaston's true measure as a father—and by these and the other objective measurements, he came up woefully short.

Brayden's therapist, Dr. Eldertree, took care of the part of the presumed father statute that asked if it would be harmful to remove the fatherly relationship from the child's life. "It would not," he testified emphatically. "In fact, it is my professional opinion that to *continue* the relationship would cause more harm."

"Obviously, Dr. Eldertree is not objective here," Gaston's attorney countered, "since Mr. Evans has worked with him on a prior case."

Predictably, the amicus also dismissed the therapist's claims, as he'd also ignored all the other testimonies brought to the court by my supporters. Faith. Brayden's school principal. Even Dr. Heartsong gave a statement after she'd witnessed one of our carefully chaperoned outings, which was unheard of for a doctor to do in a custody battle.

Of the eight or so custody cases in Texas's history that used the presumed father statute to prove the man's role as a father, Gaston's involvement was the lowest of them all. Gaston was the biggest loser of any presumed father who'd taken his case to court.

I was the last one to take the stand. "No child should be forced to live a lie," I stated, as I looked Gaston and the amicus in the face. "Gaston isn't Brayden's father and never has been.

His flimsy claim to Brayden on the grounds that we're still legally married is tantamount to kidnapping. Brayden and I deserve to live in the truth, and Brayden deserves to write his own story. It would be a travesty for the court to force fit someone into the daddy box where they don't belong. Gaston has never been Brayden's father. Not in deed. Not in DNA."

Then we rested our case. I prayed to God that it was enough.

The court adjourned and Judge Solomon went into his chambers to consider the case before making his ruling. My heart started to race when he returned to the bench fifteen minutes later. Based on the speed of his decision, this was a slam dunk—I just didn't know who had the ball.

"This is it," Jimmy said, his best poker face on. I couldn't tell if he was confident, nervous, or bracing for a negative outcome.

I reached over to clench his hand under the table, knowing my family's future hung in the balance of the next few minutes.

The judge steepled his long fingers under his chin for a moment, then made his pronouncement.

"It is of this court's opinion that the Plaintiff and the Defendant have lived separate lives for seven years," he said, looking slowly from me to Gaston before his ponderous gaze sought out the amicus sitting at Gaston's table. "And considering the evidence, I'm surprised at the amicus attorney's strong position on this case. But I must follow the law. The Defendant has shown little proof of meeting the law's criteria for a fatherly role to Brayden. Therefore, I must deny the Defendant's parentage of Brayden and order a DNA test be done for the child. Court dismissed." He tapped his gavel down and left.

I got the feeling Judge Solomon knew what he was going to say a long time ago.

Court protocol dictates you're not supposed to show displays of emotion when a verdict is being read. *Screw that!* I thought. I immediately let out a small cry of relief and gave Jimmy a huge hug.

"We did it!" I whisper-yelled. "Thank you for fighting for me and my son."

"It's what we do," said Jimmy, basking in the big win as a smile came over his face. It would be a significant feather in his cap.

Judge Solomon granted my Christmas wish. With that, a wave of relief washed over me. *Was the ordeal really over?*

On Christmas Eve, the results from the DNA test came in. There was a zero percent probability Gaston was Brayden's father. It only took me two hundred days and $250,000 to prove it.

Even with the test results, Gaston refused to relinquish visitation until the court officially ruled against him. "You can't defy the visitation court order!" he howled when he came to pick Lauren and Brayden up for Christmas Day. If Gaston had his way, he'd delay the final court hearing to legally recognize he wasn't in the daddy box until the cows came home. January 17, 2020, the date of the final hearing, couldn't come fast enough.

"Sue me," I said. His attorney could make all the noise she wanted, but everyone would know his point was moot. I didn't even flinch when Gaston refused to give Brayden all the toys he had given him over the course of the trial, which now sat in Brayden's newly created bedroom at Gaston's house. I didn't care what he did now. His reign of terror was over.

So Lauren spent Christmas Day with Gaston. Brayden spent Christmas Day with me.

As Michael Bublé carols played on the stereo and I sipped hot chocolate with my mother, we watched Brayden joyfully open brightly colored boxes on Christmas morning. At that moment on earth, and in my heart, I felt at peace.

PART 3

THE MEANING BEHIND YOUR MISSION

If you're fortunate enough to achieve the mission of motherhood, it's important to realize the battle scars that remain once the main mission is over. It may be necessary to deal with the pain, loss, and trauma that you incurred along the way. Only by confronting those issues head-on can you make peace with the past and become the mother you were meant to be.

CHAPTER 20

HEALING THE PAST

WHAT THE HELL JUST HAPPENED?

January 18, 2020, was surreal. It was the day after the final hearing of the trial. Gaston had been denied parentage and visitation rights. Brayden, in the eyes of the law, had been liberated to live his truth after the DNA test showed no blood relation to Gaston.

The whole thing was bizarre. Unlike my previous challenges with loss and grief, which crept up on me and never really left, the trial debacle turned my world upside-down in the time it took to read one email, and righted itself again with one stroke of a judge's pen. I imagined the feeling was similar for someone wrongfully accused of a crime to be acquitted, or a soldier coming home from a war. Suddenly, my family's crisis was over, the monsters were all gone, and I could wake up from this bad dream.

We were free, but at a cost.

I collapsed, physically and emotionally. I didn't know what

to do now that the oppressive weight of the past six months was lifted from my shoulders. Every day of those six months, I fought for the life I wanted for myself and my children. Every night, I lay awake strategizing about the fight that would come the next day. What questions should we ask in deposition? What ammo could I give Jimmy in my defense? What could the other side blast us with next? My whole being focused on ending the threat to my family.

For two hundred days, it felt like I had been sprinting a never-ending marathon and operating in survival mode morning to night. That was too long. My body and mind were in shambles. Sensing safety, both took a holiday and left me an empty shell of a person. I still had insomnia, but now I woke up because my brain no longer knew how to stay asleep. It didn't know what it needed to think about, only that it needed to think.

Brayden was now safe, but there was another thing my shell-shocked brain found to mull over. Part of Gaston's lawsuit alleged I committed parent alienation with Lauren, asserting this was the reason she didn't like to go with him on visits. If his accusation was proven true, I risked losing primary custody of my daughter. Whatever it would take, this issue had to be quashed.

Gaston's attorney recommended a foremost expert in the field of parent alienation, Priscilla Wiseheart, to evaluate and provide expert testimony against me. Instead, I decided to be proactive and seek guidance from her directly. At first, going to see her was a strategic move so she couldn't be used for any assessment against me, circumventing this new potential enemy by making her my ally. But I also wanted her professional input and advice on whether I was doing anything that was hindering Lauren's relationship with her father.

Priscilla's words caught me off guard when I told her Lauren refused to go with Gaston.

"If you can't get your child to go with the other parent, you are either an incompetent parent or you are an alienator," she told me flatly. "Which one are you?"

You could have pushed me over with a feather. *Holy shit!* I thought. *This woman is a hammer!* It was a 180-degree difference from Lauren's former therapist, who was all about giving Lauren choices and allowing the child to run the show. I'd followed that guidance only to find out it made the problem worse.

"If those are my only choices, I guess I'm an incompetent parent?" I squeaked out tentatively.

Priscilla's crackling amber eyes softened as I explained that Gaston and I had been following the advice of a play therapist who told us to give Lauren choices. "Offering a child too much choice is too big a burden for them. You were misinformed by Lauren's former therapist."

Priscilla had a lot to teach me about how to create healthy relationships with my children, and I leaned into her expertise. The weapon Gaston sought to form against me became my biggest mentor and most valuable resource in how to parent. I started seeing Priscilla regularly. So did Lauren. Even my mom visited her a few times. I knew I needed to learn healthy ways to support Lauren since some of my natural instincts weren't always the most helpful. Gaston's parent alienation claim went nowhere in court. My actions showed I had been helpful, not harmful, in Lauren's relationship with her father.

While one disaster was averted, I had no way of knowing that a new disaster was building steam on the horizon.

I began to realize I needed to dig out of the two tons of trauma that buried me. "I don't think I'm a functioning human being," I confessed during one of our sessions. "I can't stop jumping at every little sniffle or scrape with my kids, thinking the sky is falling." And at that point, it truly felt like it was.

Just two months after Brayden's final hearing, COVID-19 shut the whole world down. Like with the trial, the change was instantaneous. We were supposed to take a trip to Dallas to visit the Great Wolf Lodge water park. It was spring break. I'd heard whispers of COVID-19 and faint rumblings of doomsday predictions, but I was too busy dealing with the aftermath of the trial to pay much attention. Then, without warning, COVID-19 would no longer be ignored. Forty-eight hours later, just about every business shut down, including Great Wolf Lodge. It was heartbreaking because the kids and I were in dire need of some lighthearted fun. *No fun for you*, was the resounding answer in my head, like the Soup Nazi scene in a famous *Seinfeld* episode. Thankfully, my job was mostly remote already, but now everyone else's was, too, and air travel immediately stopped. Texas even threatened to close its borders to people flying in from high-infection states like New York. Schools and daycares closed their doors to in-person classes. I now had to homeschool my four-year-old son and six-year-old daughter on top of working, which any single parent who did it now knows is impossible to do well—two full-time jobs is too much. Thankfully, my mother stepped in to help with Brayden.

My personal trauma had turned into a global trauma, and I was one bitter bitch about it all. *Really, God? You had to throw in worldwide pestilence for funsies?* I'd already lost much of my power and control during the trial. My life plans had been hijacked for months. I was a full trauma sandwich, the trial of my life piled high with helpings of betrayal, powerlessness, character assassination, and a few slices of child loss. A global pandemic seemed like the appropriate side pickle to it all. Sure, now everyone suffered from powerlessness and fear. Now everyone had something to mourn. But no one else had gone through my gut-wrenching eight-year motherhood mission before the final shoe dropped. I was already at the bottom of the barrel and didn't know how I'd sink any lower. *Fuck all you guys*, I thought, *I can't do this anymore.*

I started having panic attacks that I'd lose my entire family. My mother was seventy-seven. There were no vaccines and Gaston's actions suggested to me he didn't want to isolate even as Lauren continued to go back and forth between our houses. "I'm not going to stop going into the grocery store!" he said belligerently when I asked him to consider curbside pickup instead. I'd already lost two babies to disease and nearly another to general bureaucratic assholery. I knew loss was always right around the corner. But I had no control over Gaston's decisions. *This imbecile will bring death and destruction to my whole family*, was the only scenario my mind wanted to dwell on.

"What do I need to do to heal?" I asked of Priscilla. I'd had another panic attack the night before that left me incapacitated on the bathroom floor for an hour after my kids were in bed. I was afraid all the pain I'd internalized would break me as a mother, rendering me incapable of caring for my kids. What was the good of having gone through hell to get my children if I was now going to be a shell of a person who couldn't be the mother I wanted to be? "I need to unload some of this baggage so I can be the mother my children deserve."

"Have you tried EMDR?" Priscilla asked during one of our online therapy sessions. "It stands for Eye Movement Desensitization and Reprocessing. It helps retrain your body and mind to manage your trauma responses better."

"No, I've never heard of it." I'd done individual therapy in early adulthood, marriage counseling with each troubled marriage, and worked with child therapists, but this flavor of therapy was new to me.

Priscilla sat back from her computer screen and contemplated me for a moment. "It's a form of cognitive behavioral therapy used to treat health conditions specific to traumatic events. Most people know it from PTSD circles, as it's a common treatment there."

Desperate for any solution, I grabbed onto this one. It was obvious I had PTSD. "Give me a referral and I'll check it out."

I spent the next four months doing EMDR with a therapist named Whitney Dawnchaser. COVID-19 had created a lot of separation between people. My sessions with Priscilla had turned into video calls. But Whitney possessed an infinite amount of sympathy for my situation, and she took me on as one of a small handful of clients she saw in person. Whitney would bomb the office with Lysol and bleach wipes between clients, going to great lengths to protect everyone from the plague. We sat eight feet apart across from each other in white leather easy chairs surrounded by peaceful pictures of Georgia O'Keefe, and lathered up with sanitizer before and after each session. We even contemplated taking sessions outside. Whatever it would take, because EMDR wasn't a technique easily done remotely.

Typically, EMDR involves the combination of conscious eye movements and a sound, similar to a metronome, that clicks along and provides a safe anchor point to the here and now as the therapist prompts you to talk through your past trauma stories. If the memories become too overwhelming, the sound and motion give you something real to focus on as you let your brain stabilize enough to try again. You can think of the sensory part as a form of self-soothing, like a baby sucks a thumb or an adult drinks a cup of tea.

The goal of retelling your stories is to integrate the survivalist part of you that reacts to them with the cognitive part of you that makes sense of them. You consciously and systematically allow the two parts of the brain to meet in a safe place. Under normal circumstances, those two parts of your brain do not talk to each other. The part of the brain that controls survival, the more reptilian part, stays stuck in the trauma it's gotten used to fearing, no matter what happens after the traumatic event in terms of your rational understanding. You can still be triggered by things that threaten you in similar ways to the first traumatic event, or that remind you of it, and your higher-functioning human brain turns off while your lizard brain takes over. If there's no real threat and nowhere to run, most people will experience panic attacks or turn to drugs or alcohol to dull the intensity of the pain. For me, COVID-19's vague, life-threatening potential was enough to let loose from my mental Pandora's box all my prior losses and the fear surrounding them to overwhelm my waking life.

With Whitney's help, I slowly and methodically relived each of my losses. Aurora. Rachel. Brandon. Gaston's perceived betrayals. Even my childhood wounds. I identified the most vivid visual images related to each trauma. Then Whitney guided me to new insights from each of those experiences. "What understanding have you gained from that situation?" she'd ask. "What good came out of it?" These insights she called "preferred positive beliefs," or the idea that some good comes out of every circumstance, a greater meaning or moral. Then she'd take me back through the stories again.

"Okay, take me back to your worst moment during that time. What were you feeling?

"Now, what meaning can you take from that moment?"

"What did you learn about yourself?"

Each time the feelings started to subside, Whitney would have me bring up the painful memory again. We would do this several times over the course of a session. And every time I went through my stories, the intensity of the feelings lessened until, finally, the emotions were manageable. Not completely gone. Never that. But down to something that allowed me to function instead of curling up in a little ball on the ground, guzzling a bottle of wine and praying for it all to stop.

EMDR taught me that my past could not be changed but my perception and understanding of the events that happened to me could be healed and put to rest.

As my therapy progressed, new insights emerged about the most painful events of my past. I became grateful for the seven months I had with Aurora. I knew I'd made a lasting impression on her life by giving her unconditional love during a formative time in her development. I realized my foster parent experience inspired friends like Eric to pursue foster parenting. When he and his wife couldn't get pregnant on their own and the one IVF attempt they could afford failed, I told him, "Fostering didn't work out for me, but it might for you." They got certified and were called about two sisters, two and four, close to being legally free. A month later, another call, an emergency placement of a two-week-old baby. Within two months, Eric and his wife had a full house with three young girls! The baby even looked like them. They ended up adopting all three kids. My heart warmed to think my experience was the spark that led him to create his own happy family.

I came to some measure of peace with Rachel and Brandon. Even though I still felt it incredibly unfair we hadn't been advised for Gaston to get genetic testing, I was thankful that Brandon lived long enough for us to get answers that would end the cycle of suffering. I'd fought for them and been the best mother I knew how to be in each situation. I knew they were no longer in pain, and I would see them again in heaven.

I realized the affair with Hunter had purpose. While I wish I'd behaved differently, I appreciated that I was finally free of Gaston so I could live a more fulfilling life and would not make my children live in the same household as an unhealthy marriage. I would not be the one to model a dysfunctional relationship as an example to follow.

I affirmed my self-worth as a mother. Despite what my brother told me on the eve of Brandon's death—suggesting that I didn't deserve to be a mother; that I'd wasted my chance when I chose career and travel in my twenties and thirties; that my way of creating a family made me an abomination—I came to terms that my brother and I had fundamentally different expressions of the same values. We both believed in family, but my version made space for unconditional love and acceptance and his interpretation held to a very specific set of rules that needed to be followed to have the right kind of family. My brother was still stuck in his own fairy tale, but I was no longer burdened by mine. We'd have to agree to disagree. And if we couldn't do that, it was best to steer clear of each other for everyone else's sake. I would no longer allow anyone to tell me I didn't deserve my children or diminish the beautiful family I had created.

I came to peace regarding my father. It was not easy. In my dad's world, strong women are uncomfortable things, and it was my strength that led to our conflicts, just as it did with my brother. Looking back, I see it all so clearly. The trauma from my childhood affected my relationships in adulthood, hamstringing them in similar ways. I struggled with the realization I really disliked my father's behaviors and the way he treated me, but I was also a lot like him.

My father used to say to me, "You're strong, like garlic." It was meant to be a criticism, as some find the taste and smell of fresh garlic unpleasant. But garlic has its good points, too. It possesses medicinal properties. It's an essential part of the healthy Mediterranean diet, and Asian food wouldn't be the same without it. It keeps away bloodsuckers like mosquitos and vampires.

When I think about how to talk about my relationship with my dad and my understanding of the traits I inherited from him—the business acumen, the determination, the bluntness, the take-no-prisoners mentality that can tip over into offensiveness—like garlic, they are both ugly and beautiful.

My business acumen granted me the financial wherewithal to become a mother. I used his perseverance and stubbornness to get through my motherhood mission. The traits my father hated most about me were his own, but it was those traits that I most needed when the chips were down.

I also inherited some softer qualities from my father. I got his sensitive and giving heart—it's one of the traits I like best about myself. I got his sense of humor, even the parts that are sarcastic and not always politically correct. I possessed his sense of loyalty and commitment to protect his family. With these reflections, I was finally able to create some balance in my perception of my father. My dad was a product of his times. Like all of us, he had his imperfections and his strengths. He was human.

My dad's confusing childhood epithet now settled around me like a mantle. If I had a choice between being garlic or being milk toast, I'd pick garlic every day and twice on Sunday. Women who are agreeable like milk toast rarely make the kind of impact I wanted to make in this world.

I know the pain over my past will never be completely gone, even if that's what I wanted, but my work with Whitney reduced the amount I carried a good 90 percent. Enough that I wanted to move on to a bigger mission: sharing my experience of motherhood with other women and helping them through their own missions.

To that end, I decided to get trained as a life coach with the Life Purpose Institute. Since COVID-19 still raged, the classes were all online. I enrolled in the intensive option, which would certify me in six weeks. There were only seven other students, plus the facilitating coach.

One exercise was a guided coaching session, a real-life role play of what we would be doing for our clients. We'd act as the client and the coach would walk us through question types we could ask, showing the class how it was done. I volunteered to be the guinea pig and chose a safe topic. I was feeling better emotionally after my EMDR therapy sessions, but those wounds were barely scabbed over. So I chose romantic relationships. After the Gaston debacle, added to my other failures, I'd pretty much given up on the idea of having a man in my life. Strike three, I was out. I figured I wouldn't have much to talk about. *My children provided all the love I needed anyway*, I theorized.

The coach started out slowly. "How do you feel about your romantic prospects right now?"

I shrugged. We were all on video, so I hoped everyone could see my body language. "Mostly, I don't feel. I don't think romantic relationships are in the cards for me anymore," I said, vowing to be honest here for the purpose of the exercise.

"Oh?" the coach said, "and why isn't a relationship in the cards for you?"

I was ready for this one. "I have three failed marriages. I'm over fifty. My headstrong personality is too off-putting to most men. I'm a single mom with two young kids. COVID-19 is still here, and I'm worried about bringing it home to my elderly mother and kids. Who's going to date in this scenario, let alone take me with all my baggage?"

"It sounds like you've done a lot of thinking on this," the coach prompted.

I was just getting warmed up. "I have. It's too big a risk. The whole idea of finding love in a pandemic feels ridiculous."

"But, do you have friends that you believe are happy together?" he asked, expertly sidestepping the period I wanted to put on the matter.

"Well, yes," I hedged, thinking of Ruth and her husband, Cindy and Richard, and many of my college friends who were still coupled.

"So these friends are fulfilled in their relationships?" he pressed.

I didn't quite know where he was going with this. "Yeah, I think they're fulfilled."

He pounced, "So they get to be happy, but not you?"

Suddenly, I was thankful to have a screen between me and my fellow classmates. I felt completely naked and exposed. The coach had hit a nerve I didn't know was still raw, and I started to cry. *This was supposed to be the safe topic!* But the coach had seen the excuses for what they were—a flimsy stick house of avoidance tactics built to keep me safe from more wolves—and blew them all down.

"How do you think so many of your friends got lucky enough to find their special someone?" he asked, keeping the pressure on.

"I guess love found a way."

"Oh, that's an interesting thought," he remarked. The instructor waited for me to recover my composure before pushing me again. "What if you believed that love would find a way?"

Discreetly wiping tears from my eyes with a tissue, I was determined to see this to the end. "I'm not sure I can get there. There's too much water under that bridge."

But a tiny voice inside me whispered, *Was there a possibility of a fulfilling relationship for me, still?*

He paused for a moment, then presented his challenge, "Would you be willing to write 'love will find a way' on your mirror at home, and open yourself up to that possibility?"

Still sniffling slightly but feeling better, I gave a small smile. "Yes. Yes, I will." It was still a terrible time, and the odds were not in my favor, but I'd follow my coach's suggestion and see where it got me.

Once I gained my composure enough to focus on the other participants on the call, I realized the majority of them were crying, too. Apparently our raw, authentic dialogue touched all of them in a significant way. I realized this is what good coaching was all about. I determined to put my money where my mouth was and follow through on this experiment in hope.

I joined an online dating site. I'd done so much "online dating" before, first with the foster children newsletters and then with the egg and sperm donor lists, but now I'd do it for real.

I began my mission of finding love by zeroing in on what I really wanted. I literally created a vision board. I cut out pictures from magazines and made atypical families and glued on phrases such as "blended makes us better," "focus on family," "well-suited for each other." I included the personal mission this ideal man would support. I wanted to help women become mothers and navigate the often challenging world of fertility. I wanted to be an advocate and create a support system for them. I wanted to keep growing as a mother myself as my kids developed and presented me with new parenting challenges. This love match wouldn't be just about looks or physical attraction (though I did put photos of Blake Shelton and George Clooney on my board); it was about compatibility and mutual values. This time, I wanted someone who would be part of my team. Who would give just as much as I did.

I made sure to advertise myself as a mother. I didn't want the typical fiftyish empty-nester looking for fun and frivolity heading into retirement. All my dating profile photos had my kids in them. I wanted to bill myself as a package deal.

Three months later, I met Art. I confess, he did not look like George Clooney (who does?) but he was bald, so *cha-ching!* We matched up in a lot of other ways, too. We were both in our early fifties. Art still had two school-aged kids, a boy and a girl, one adopted and the other unplanned, and wanted someone else with children. "More presents under the tree," was one of his profile lines. He had sole and primary custody over his children for the last ten years, which, after my latest custody battle, I knew was quite a feat for a single dad and matched my own situation. He'd be someone who understood complicated family dynamics. The parallels to my life were just too many to ignore.

One thing I knew for sure was that I did not want to get married. "I lost my ability to get a marriage license due to malpractice," I jokingly told friends. But the reality was I would not open myself up to legal entanglements and vulnerabilities again. I wanted my family and my finances kept exactly how they were, thank you. Since I wasn't looking to get married, I figured it wasn't important to include my sad marriage record on my dating profile, or to bring it up in the first few conversations. Who wants to try to spin the good in that on a first impression? And would a future companion really care that much about my past when he didn't have to put a ring on it?

I invited Art out to my country club. It was home turf for me, so I felt safe, and we could eat outside, which was an essential part of COVID-19-era dates.

Art, like me, didn't beat around the bush. After the entrees came out, he unpacked his baggage in front of me. "I want to get this potential deal killer out of the way on our first date," he started, looking nervous but determined. "I've been married three times," he blurted, then rushed to try to explain himself.

I held up a hand just as he got rolling on his soul-baring speech. "You've had three marriages that didn't work out?" I asked. He nodded, looking miserable despite the sunny, unseasonably warm, February day. "Me, too, high five, try some lamb, it's delicious," I said, brandishing a chop in my hand. As his mouth gaped open, I shoved the saucy meat in and smiled sweetly.

His look transformed to wonderment and I could see the wheels turning as he chewed. "Do you get the feeling we were meant to meet?" he asked. A small smile played about his lips. "That lamb *is* good."

The alarm on my phone went off, interrupting us. It was a reminder that I needed to start a Zoom call for my mother and her sorority friends. I had suggested it as a way for them to maintain connection during the pandemic. None of them were tech savvy, so I stepped in to facilitate. "Hi, Art!" they all chirped, ogling my lunch companion through their screens. To this day, they take some measure of credit for bringing us together, since they were there for our first date.

I wasn't sure about divine intervention here, but over the course of our conversation we did find out we'd both visited the same resort with our kids five months earlier. We'd even been in the pool at the same time but hadn't met, like we were in our own real-life version of the movie *Serendipity*, just missing each other every time we were in the same place. I guess love *did* find a way, or tried several ways, until it finally found me. Or, I found it by putting myself out there.

Art was the first man who saw and valued me for who I was. He wasn't put off by my bluntness, my business success, or my unconventional manner as a woman. He saw my heart and my intentions. Only after I became a mother did I find my person, upending the normal fairy tale of love and family once again with a truly blended family where no one shared the same bloodlines.

Healing, love, family—all of it can find a way. If you believe you deserve it. If you seek it. If you refuse to give up. If you are open to whatever form it takes.

If you allow for grace, and a few tender mercies.

CHAPTER 21

TENDER MERCIES

I HATED GOD FOR MANY YEARS. MY LIST OF GRIEVANCES against Him was long.

How could you bring a child into my home and then rip her away?

Why would you save my daughter early in the pregnancy only to learn she suffered from a debilitating, catastrophic disease?

Why didn't you intervene on the genetic issue with my son? Even if You didn't cause it, You allowed it. Your indifference caused Brandon tremendous suffering.

Undeniably, my relationship with God throughout my motherhood mission was complicated, to say the least. My desire to become a mother was deep. From my study of the Bible, I believed God wanted to grant me the desires of my heart. I believed He would be with me as I pursued this goal. But as the journey unfolded and my disappointments and trials grew, I started to wonder if God was really there for me at all. I started to believe the condemnations coming from people like my brother. That I didn't deserve to become a mother. That my life choices had disqualified me from nurturing life. That God was against me, not for me, and I was being punished for my sins.

That really pissed me off. I put God in the same bucket as every other man who had betrayed me, abandoned me, or stood in my way—if You aren't with me, then get out of my way. I'll do this without You.

"If God loves me, why have I and my children gone through so much suffering?" I asked in one of my Zoom calls with Priscilla. In addition to being a specialist in parental alienation, I soon learned Priscilla had a strong foundation of faith. I figured she'd have some kind of spiritual terra firma when most of her job involved custody recommendations between parents and their children. Her position caused her to be reviled by many. After the legal battle was resolved, our discussions broadened in scope to more holistic parenting issues, including the topic of faith.

"That's the question for the ages, and one that has plagued the faithful ever since God made a bet with the Devil in the Book of Job," Priscilla said.

But unlike the tortured but ever-patient Job, bitterness filled me during my regular sessions with Priscilla. All I could think was, why me? Why was a pandemic happening now? Right on the heels of the nuclear bomb Gaston dropped? Didn't I deserve to heal, after being put through the wringer for so many years?

Priscilla contemplated me for a moment, then posed a question. "Do you know about God's tender mercies?"

Slightly taken aback, I was jolted out of my doldrums for a moment. "No," I said, "I haven't heard that term before."

"It means noticing all the little things that show up in your life during times of trouble. Tender mercies show us that God is always there. Looking for them may help you see the love in all the pain."

Priscilla's idea of tender mercies intrigued me. The phrase comes from Psalm 103:4 in the Old Testament: "Who redeemeth thy life from destruction; who crowneth thee with loving kindness and tender mercies." Doing some research, I found the Hebrew word for "tender mercies" can be translated as *womb*, which struck me as appropriate for a mother. But more modern translations interpret tender mercies as personal and individualized blessings of strength, protection, assurance, guidance, support, compassion, consolation—all the loving kindnesses and spiritual gifts that we receive from and through God when we are at our lowest point.

I must have looked at Priscilla similar to the way a dog looks at its owner with both interest and confusion because they don't quite understand what is being said. Sensing the pregnant pause, Priscilla continued with her explanation. "Tender mercies are the people and events, large and small, that provide us with comfort and peace in times of crisis and turmoil. If you add them all up, you find that God gives us more than we deserve. Our challenge is to recognize those gifts, which is hard to do when humans like to dwell more on what they have lost."

I still wasn't sold. But I respected Priscilla, so I would entertain this idea and see if it took root. *Don't count on it*, I thought to myself.

As the weeks of COVID-19 unfolded, I started to think more deeply about my past traumas. *Were there tender mercies that I had missed?* For instance, my experience with Aurora was—is—incredibly painful. At first, it seemed like God had planned for me to be her mother; however, that story turned out not to be. But losing Aurora wasn't the end of that story. My journey gave hope and determination to others to pursue their adoption missions, which did work out. Those successes showed me that part of my life did have a purpose, and the pain hadn't been in vain.

Aurora also showed me the tender mercies of Serena, who acted as a kind of angel next door to help me through that ordeal and to let me know I wasn't alone. Serena dropped everything to be with me in my hour of need. She was my loving rock that I leaned on to get through that difficult day when I had to give Aurora back to CPS and her distant family. "You gave that abandoned and neglected child the care and security she desperately needed at a critical time in her life," she told me afterward, "and that gift is not wasted. That love is not wasted. That's now somewhere within her, even if she's no longer with you."

When I became pregnant with Rachel, once again I thought it was God's plan to give me my own child, healthy and whole. I was relieved to hear her heartbeat when I feared I had miscarried, but then felt blindsided by her terrible diagnosis and the reality that I had to say goodbye. Furious at getting the rug pulled out from beneath me yet again, in a way even more horrible than Aurora, I stopped speaking to God completely.

I may not have been speaking with God, but He still sent others to comfort me. Devastated by my child's death and abandoned by my own husband, God sent Dr. Andersen and Dr. Heartsong to guide and support me through that medical crisis. He brought Dr. Valerian to be my ally and advocate in the NICU through my twins' fight for life, and to grieve with me at Brandon's funeral. The nurses who cared for my children in the NICU were godsends, as well.

And when I was deep in my grief and pain, unable and unwilling to interact with anyone outside my house, God put Worth in my path as I took out the trash, no less. I was working from home and had no need to leave my house even if I'd wanted to, so God gave me the counsel I needed to start stitching my life back together emotionally and help me recover from the tragic loss of my first child. Worth's sage wisdom and tenderness was a lifesaver, not only with Rachel, but also when Brandon and Lauren struggled for survival. Worth continued to be by my side when my son drew his last breath. He led a parade of angels who came to rejoice with my family on the day Lauren came home. This chorus included my mother's PEO sisters, who surprised me with the only baby shower I was ever given. And then Worth helped iron visitation out with Gaston when I just couldn't think about it.

My neighbors Colleen and Johnny spent ten years looking for a house before they bought the one next door, around the same time I started my pregnancy with the twins. While I was immersed in my pain and oblivious to my surroundings, they couldn't avoid seeing a very pregnant woman living alone next to them. I thought back on Johnny's career as an air traffic controller with the FAA. I wondered how many of my flights Johnny had guided to a safe landing when I was going on and returning from business trips over the years. Johnny and Colleen had lost most of the people in their immediate family to death or estrangement. They never had children. In many ways, they were alone and lonely. From the moment Raggie jumped into Johnny's lap on that curb outside our home, they became woven into the fabric of our lives.

When my mother and I needed to spend weeks in the hospital with Brandon and Lauren, Colleen and Johnny stepped in to watch Raggie for us and keep an eye on the house. They were with us in sorrow to host the children's funeral and with us in celebration when we brought Lauren home from the hospital.

Colleen, who adores my kids, has found fulfillment with

two children who treat her more like a grandmother than a godmother, something that would never have happened if I hadn't needed their support during my darkest hours—with the twins, with Lauren's early health struggles, with Brayden's trial. Since then, the couple has spent every holiday with us, and Johnny became the only godfather, and grandfather, my children really knew.

How is it that two people ripe for being grandparents but with no prospects of blood grandchildren of their own picked a house right next to mine after looking for ten years? Could it be God planned for us to heal each other?

God even brought Hunter when I needed someone to breathe new life back into me and help me get out of the depths of despair after Rachel. Some might wonder if God can really be present in an extramarital affair. It's a blasphemous thought. But I believe God is with us in all situations, even the darkest ones. In war and peace. In birth and death. In joy and sadness. He is with us in our deepest traumas and in our greatest triumphs. In our smallest and biggest choices. He's with us the entire time.

He was with me when Brandon died.

Looking back, Brandon's life allowed his sister to grow and develop enough to be born. In a way, he delivered his sister to me. And God brought me mercy by allowing Brandon to live long enough to provide answers as to why he was dying. God freed me from guilt and condemnation through those answers, helping to restore my faith that there is a larger purpose to life and the suffering that goes with it.

That faith was only a tiny mustard seed when I started over with Brayden. I was full of fear and afraid to hope. God had given me fragments of peace here and there, some relief from my anger and guilt, but I was still terrified I was somehow the problem with bringing children into the world. Brayden proved otherwise. I was grateful God gave me the gift of normal for the first time and that mercy taught me to hope that God wasn't against me.

God brought faith knocking on my front door, quite literally. Faith became my comfort, strength, and surrogate co-parent for many years. Her testimony was one of the most compelling in the whole trial. She'd been with us every step and had seen firsthand the interactions between Gaston and Brayden, and how I talked about and constructed visitations and Gaston's relationships with my children. When Gaston claimed to be caring for Brayden on outings, Faith could say honestly, "I was paid to be there watching Brayden. Cheri and Gaston were there for Lauren." Faith was instrumental in my defense, and a key witness to refute Gaston's revisionist version of events. She became my child's godparent, and ultimately, I became the same for her children. We've done slumber parties and family vacations together even though Faith has a different job and lives in another state. Faith's position as nanny brought us together, but that was just the beginning. Our bond and family connection has flourished over the last decade.

God brought me Jimmy Evans and Brayden's therapist, Dr. Eldertree, who supported me in the battle to protect my son and family. During the trial, I would drive Brayden an hour each way to see Dr. Eldertree for his weekly play therapy appointment. I wanted a male play therapist to talk to Brayden, and there weren't many around. There was a church we would pass on the way. One day, its marquee read, "God is greater than any problem that you may have." We stopped at McDonald's to get lunch after one of the therapy sessions, on a day when I didn't know if I could go on, and the person in front of us paid for our food.

We accidently ran into Dr. Heartsong and her family while

at a restaurant for one of Lauren's many family outings with both Gaston and Brayden. "Are you guys back together?" she asked me.

"God, no!" I said, laughing. She remembered this exchange and was willing to testify that I was not presenting Gaston as Brayden's father at one of the hearings, something Jimmy said doctors never do.

The principal from Brayden's school also testified that Brayden told her he didn't want to go with Gaston. We bonded over being foster parents. She had observed Gaston's interactions with Lauren, so she testified a second time when it came time to finalize the visitation schedule for Lauren.

As crazy as it may sound, I even became grateful for the timing of when Brayden's trial unfolded. Had the amicus succeeded in delaying the hearing a few more months, COVID-19 would have prolonged Brayden's visits with Gaston even longer. Much longer. Virtual hearings instead of in-person ones could have changed the judge's perspective. I shudder to think how different the outcome might have been if Judge Solomon hadn't pushed it forward that Monday in early December 2019. What permanent damage could have been done to Brayden's mental state if the visits had continued.

Then, when I fought the parent alienation allegation, the very person meant to be my enemy and prove I was the parent at fault became my biggest parenting mentor and spiritual sherpa. Priscilla helped put the alienation accusation to bed and taught me how to be the most helpful, loving, and disciplined parent I could be for Lauren and Brayden.

There were countless others who poured their love and support onto me through the months of the trial. Friends, co-workers, even the videographer that taped Gaston and my depositions, all showed us love, and many came to the victory party afterward. In their own large and small ways, everyone lifted me up and helped me survive the unimaginable. Many offered daily prayers on my behalf. A handful of the faithful came to my hearings to bear witness to what was happening to my family and show solidarity. Hundreds of people I didn't even know signed a Change.org petition and contributed money on GoFundMe to support me in my fight.

And while members of my own family condemned me, my mother, my guardian angel, never left my side through all my trials. She was always there to provide love, support, and acceptance through the blue skies and gray, as I limped and struggled against the storm. I leaned on her and sometimes she carried me. As a single mother, I couldn't have created this beautiful family without her.

Finally, when the roughest part of the storm had passed, when I thought romantic love was well behind me after three failed marriages and a slew of unsuccessful relationships, God brought me Art in the middle of a global pandemic, along with two more children to love. Not replacements for the girl and boy I had lost, but certainly symbols of the full family I'd originally set out to create.

The power of these tender mercies is found in seeing the big picture, not in the details of any single one. God weaves people and events together like a tapestry. He works through the compassion of friends and strangers alike to make life a little easier, a little kinder, in our hour of need. And like a tapestry, the threads don't go one way. They move over and under, double back and go across, giving and receiving to share love and hope to make one big, beautiful picture.

I have a photo of my full family I used as evidence in Brayden's court case. I submitted it to the judge when my family was held up as being something unnatural—the words "odd" and "contrived" were often thrown around by Gaston's lawyer. The photo depicts me, Lauren, Brayden, Faith, Colleen, Johnny, and my mother. The wonderful thing about a village is that you can choose who you want to be in it.

My brother once tried to tell me that my life choices made me unworthy to be a mother. He suggested playing God was the worst sin I could commit. And he said these things because of a fairy tale centuries old that told him what a family should and shouldn't be. There will always be negative voices of criticism, judgment, and condemnation. The conversation around women's fertility and motherhood seems to bring passions from all directions out of the woodwork. They will tell you that you are undeserving, that you are a failure, that it's all your fault. That you will never become a mother.

Don't listen to them. They are not the voice of God. They do not represent the depth of love He has for you. Faith may be lost at times, but it never disappears. Grieve. Be angry. Have your arguments with God. He can take it. Then, when you are ready to talk, the tender mercies, the people and circumstances that support and protect you, will become visible again and true healing can occur.

The healing of grace.

Looking back, I'm overwhelmed by the love and tender mercies that God placed throughout my mission to motherhood. I don't see how anyone can look at all the pieces of my story and come to any conclusion other than that God was with me, loving me, supporting me, strengthening me with the village He formed around me to help smooth out every step of the way. Gradually, I learned God had a bigger purpose for me, too.

To share my story with you.

I hope my words don't sound like a sermon or like trying to evangelize a specific religious doctrine. I don't want to overstep the bounds of our girl talk. I'm not here to convert anyone, and I'm certainly not holding myself up as a pinnacle of virtue. Faith is a personal decision and comes in all different forms. I hope you will take away what is helpful and leave the rest behind. I hope your mission to motherhood will go smoothly and as happily as it can—and if it doesn't, I hope you know now that you are not alone in your struggle. I hope you will seek out and find the tender mercies hidden like Easter eggs along your path.

CHAPTER 22

A GIRLFRIEND'S ADVICE ON WRITING YOUR OWN FAIRY TALE

MY EYES SCANNED THE GRASSY LAWN TO SEE IF I COULD spot someone I knew. I walked through the grass, still moist from the spring shower that had just passed through. A pageantry of wildflowers and live oaks graced the grounds. The air was filled with the laughter of children and their parents' calming voices trying to keep them in tow. I was in the middle of a child's fantasy land—superheroes posing for pictures, a moonwalk bouncy house, a bushy-bearded man making balloon animals, and a petting zoo complete with baby goats, pigs, and miniature cows. I dodged the bubble machine as it hurled hundreds of iridescent spheres into the air as a group of toddlers ran frantically to catch and pop them. I passed impressive displays of childhood delicacies including cotton candy, snow cones, and decorate-your-own cupcakes guaranteed to cause a blissful sugar crash in about an hour.

This scene feels familiar, I thought with a smile. Only this time, it wasn't a dream. It was the annual Baby Reunion being thrown by my fertility clinic. This year, they were celebrating twenty-five years in practice and twenty thousand babies delivered. *Twenty thousand babies!* The number was staggering.

"It's the size of a small town," confirmed Dr. Babymaker, when I walked up to greet him.

"It must be so gratifying for you," I responded, placing my hand on his shoulder. The last ten years had made Dr. Babymaker look more frail than I remembered, but he still had that contagious charm. "Think you'll ever retire?"

"Not anytime soon," he said with a grin. "I'm having too much fun."

The scene filled me with awe. Families totaling twelve hundred strong filled the Hill Country retreat to celebrate all the little lives Dr. Babymaker and his team of physicians and nurses helped to create. As I looked around, I saw a melting pot of parents from all walks of humanity—White, Hispanic, Asian, Black, Indian, and more. I can only imagine this group represented a rich blend of religious and cultural beliefs, too.

It was such a joyful scene. *How could God NOT be a part of something this beautiful?*

"Hi, Mom," I heard in chorus, as Lauren and Brayden walked up to me with a snow cone in one hand and cotton candy in the other.

"Hey, kiddos, having fun?" I asked.

"Yep, heading over to the bouncy house next," they shouted as they ran away.

Mission accomplished, I thought, reflecting on my journey to motherhood. My fairy tale of family finally came true.

From one girlfriend to another, I hope my story helps you navigate the obstacles better and avoid some of the painful walls

I ran into. By all accounts, my mission to achieve motherhood was messy. But an important element of motherhood is selflessness—a willingness to endure hardship and sacrifice oneself to create and raise a healthy child. My mission carried many sacrifices, but in the end, they proved my mettle as a mother.

I wouldn't wish my journey on anyone, not even my worst enemy. No one should have to go through all the pain, suffering, and loss that my family and I endured. I wish I knew what faced you in the days, months, and years ahead. Perhaps you'll tell me. Perhaps you won't. But either way, I hope that your mission will be easier. That it will not involve disappointment or pain. That it will be free of betrayals, trauma, or jolting curve balls. That you will be better prepared for your mission than I was.

Looking back, there were a few things that would have lessened the sacrifices if I'd seen the landmines before I began my journey. If I could go back in time and speak to my past self, here are some words of wisdom I would share.

MAKE PEACE WITH YOUR PAST.

Even with the best parents, most of us bear scars from our childhood. That's because we are all imperfect, and sometimes parents say and do things that leave a mark. If you don't make peace with your past, it will haunt you. Even worse, those scars may derail and delay your mission, potentially sending you down the wrong paths. Do your best to identify and heal the wounds of childhood, especially those inflicted by your parents and siblings. I strongly advise doing this with a trained therapist. With several. They can help you confront your trauma safely and give you tools to manage it. Otherwise, unresolved trauma from your youth can hinder you from creating the family you want.

BE INTENTIONAL ABOUT YOUR PRIORITIES AND TRADE-OFFS.

As women of the post-feminist era, we've been told we can have it all. And we can. It's just extremely difficult to have it all at the same time. Nurturing a high-powered career and being a highly involved parent simultaneously is fraught with trade-offs and compromises. Have a keen sense of the nonnegotiables for your career and for being a mother. And do sanity checks to make sure your expectations are realistic. There aren't enough hours in the day to equally serve two all-encompassing masters. At some point, this will require sacrifice of one or the other.

THE BIOLOGICAL CLOCK IS REAL. BE MINDFUL OF IT.

Women are sold a bill of goods that they have all the time in the world to become a mother. It's simply not true. You don't have unlimited time, regardless of how many options exist to plan your career or become the person you want to be. Biology is not on a woman's side. The older you get, the steeper the fertility climb becomes. If you want to preserve your options for a child that shares your genetics, I recommend freezing your eggs before the age of thirty. It's a routine procedure now and readily available in most urban areas. This financial investment can buy you valuable time.

AVOID FORCE-FITTING THE FAIRY TALE.

I picked the worst possible man to marry simply because I thought it was a necessary component to have a child. Don't rush into relationships because you think you need a man to fill the daddy box. In trying to ensure you find the right guy to have kids with, you invariably pick the wrong one. The question for choosing a life partner shouldn't be: Who would make the best father/mother for my child? Instead, the question should be: Who is my best partner for life? Choose a partner for the right reasons: compatibility, trust, common goals, and physical attraction. And don't skimp on the vibrator, as even the hottest relationships cool off. Any partner that's a match for you will be a match for your kids. A good partner will make your life feel easier to live, not harder. You'll be a team, no matter what route you need to take to create the family you both want. You'll troubleshoot obstacles together, support each other, and not be afraid to show each other your authentic selves—scars, sweat, silliness, and all. If you're considering someone who falls short in meeting your needs as a partner, take a pass—your future children will thank you.

FOSTER PARENTING CREATES BEAUTIFUL FAMILIES. JUST NOT EVERY TIME.

If fertility processes aren't viable due to biology, financial considerations, or personal preference, then foster parenting and adoption are good options to be considered. If you go down the foster parent road, go in with your eyes open and recognize that disappointment exists there, too. But there are so many children in the foster care system in need of safe and loving homes. I guarantee the impact you make on a young life will be eternal and irrevocable.

FERTILITY IS A PRODUCTIVE BUT ROCKY ROAD.

Advancements in fertility options are changing the game for women who have difficulty conceiving naturally. If you decide to head down this path, it's important to understand that you will be surrendering control of your own body and reproductive system—the most intimate parts of you that normally only a mother or lover touches—and it will be mentally and emotionally taxing in a way most women are ill-prepared to handle. You must literally gird your loins to let go of your privacy and bodily autonomy. Elevated hormones will send your body into a tailspin, so laugh, cry, yell, do whatever is necessary to get through it. Trust me, the end result is worth a few dozen lab coats knowing what your vagina looks like. To help decrease your risk of tragedy, insist on getting a comprehensive genetics test done for you and your partner (any donor should already have this screening, but double check). Even if your doctor doesn't require testing the man because his family history doesn't suggest genetic risks, the price of a test is far less than the price of unidentified genetic defects and the catastrophes that can follow.

SPERM AND EGG DONORS CAN MAKE FAIRY TALES COME TRUE.

Whether you have concerns about the vitality of your own eggs or are in need of a yin to complete your yang, donors can pave the way to a healthy child. There is plenty of superhero sperm out there you can find through handy, searchable banks—some might even look like George Clooney.

And sperm isn't the only genetic material you can get. Egg donor agencies have increased in number, and your fertility doctor may offer egg donor options, too. If you're over the age of thirty-five, consider whether using an egg donor is right for you. It can serve as a fountain of youth and dramatically increase your chances of having a healthy child.

HONOR AND GRIEVE THE LOSSES.

There is just as much possibility for heartache as there is for joy on the motherhood mission. No one likes to speak about it, and many pretend the choices are easy—but they are not. Life—creating life—can be complicated, traumatic, and sometimes dangerous. You may lose a baby. There, I said it. *You may lose a baby.* It will rip your heart, relationships, and faith apart. But loss doesn't have to be the end of your mission. If you are one of the unlucky ones to suffer the death of a child, whether in or out of utero, it's important to honor that life and grieve it. The support of family and friends may be enough. If it's not, a grief counselor or therapist can be helpful as you walk through the pain.

DON'T PUT BLIND FAITH IN THE OPINION OF EXPERTS.

Doctors' expertise gives them an amount of power over life and death, but that doesn't mean they aren't immune to poor judgments, biases, or misinformed perspectives. It doesn't mean they aren't human and fallible. We can respect doctors, as we do other highly educated professionals, for their knowledge and experience, but let's not revere them to the point that we ignore our own intuition. Specialized education does not make them gods. As a mother, you cannot check your own judgment at the door. Resist putting blind trust in the hands of doctors, therapists, lawyers, or anyone, really. Trust your gut. Push against people of authority, if necessary, to protect yourself and the best interests of your family. No one cares about the health and well-being of your child and your family more than you. Be your child's advocate at all times even if it means ruffling some feathers along the way.

DIVORCE IS BRUTAL. BEING PROACTIVE MAKES IT BETTER.

If you're going through a breakup of a marriage, try for an agreed or mediated divorce if you can. This minimizes the conflict and cost and can help preserve a positive relationship between co-parents. However, if your partner demonstrates behavior that suggests he or she is unethical or untrustworthy, then they probably are. If they have broken agreements with you in the past, it's likely they will do so again. As painful as it may be, pay the price for a good attorney early on to fight it out. If you wait, it can get worse both emotionally and financially.

Get a good divorce lawyer to draw up legal agreements, especially when it comes to custody and parental rights. You'd be amazed how quickly handshake and verbal agreements go out the window when a marriage starts to crumble. I'm a fan of prenuptial and postnuptial (yes, that's a thing) agreements on matters of property, which protect you if significant changes occur, like getting an inheritance or starting a new business. This is good practice even if the marriage is happy, as it spells out in detail who gets what and when in what circumstances.

CAREFULLY GUARD THE INTERESTS OF YOUR CHILDREN FROM WOLVES.

If you're a single mother, be very, very careful who you let into the lives of your children. If you allow someone to live with your child or children, allow them to provide financial support for your child, or allow them to be called Mom or Dad, your conduct may put you at risk if that person claims visitation and parental rights after you break up. If you used an anonymous sperm donor or have a blank in the daddy box, you're especially at risk. For all our advances in women's rights, the system is still set up to be misogynistic. It wants someone in the daddy box.

NOT FEELING THE FAIRY TALE? CONSIDER SINGLE MOTHERHOOD.

If the fairy tale isn't finding you, perhaps it's time to ask yourself a different question: Do I even need a partner at all? If the glass slipper doesn't fit, why do you even want to wear it? Barefoot will get you there, and probably much more comfortably. More and more women in their twenties are choosing to do motherhood solo. These young women are deciding early to ditch the old motherhood rules and make up their own. So if divorce, fear of commitment, or other challenges have made finding the right companion difficult, consider going it alone instead of force-fitting someone into the co-parent box.

Being a single mother takes courage. Some of the saddest women I've ever met are those who wanted to be mothers and let it pass them by due to fear of doing it alone or succumbing to societal standards. That void creates a despair—a deep, soulful regret that follows them for the rest of their lives. Weigh your options. Be brave.

TRUST THAT LOVE WILL FIND YOU IN ITS OWN TIME.

There is no hard and fast rule that says you must fall in love with an adult partner before you can fall in love with your child. No matter how many failed romantic relationships you've had, don't give up on the idea that your person is out there. Sometimes, you've got to rewrite the traditional fairy tale and let love come to you on its own terms. When you're really ready to pursue love for the right reasons, love will find a way.

IT TRULY TAKES A VILLAGE. CHOOSE YOUR VILLAGERS WISELY.

I know it's a cliché, but sometimes clichés convey a universal truth. Your motherhood mission isn't only about creating your children; it's about creating your entire family. If you're going to pursue motherhood on your own, you'll need a village to help you—your blood family, your friends, your neighbors, co-workers, people from church, or other single moms. Look at the people God has placed in your life. Spend time taking stock of the people who are committed to supporting you. It's important to evaluate who can assist with various kinds of needs: physical, emotional, financial, logistical, and spiritual. The website Single Mothers By Choice (singlemothersbychoice.org) is a good resource.

Not everyone will fit in your village, even if they technically hold the title "family." Choose villagers who provide love, support, and affirm your self-worth and values. Sometimes, you have to let go of people who don't embrace your vision of family. Blood doesn't make a family. Values make a family. Those who share your values will find you and stick with you.

CONSIDER THE CREATOR'S ROLE IN YOUR MISSION.

If you are a person of faith, know your higher power wants you to have the desires of your heart. It will be there to love and support you through your mission and will send the people you need to get through it. I believe creating life is something that is best done in partnership with your Creator, which is the source of love, not in isolation.

Motherhood is a sacred journey. As stressful, difficult, and painful as it was, I've come to realize that God was with me every step of the way. He was bigger than my doubts. I always wanted a big family, but never thought I'd have it. I was wrong. God's plans were more grand and perfect than mine.

I'm sure there are some who question the morality of my choices. If that's you, I hope it won't cause you to miss the lessons of this book. Sometimes God uses the most unlikely and flawed messenger to send the biggest message.

WILL YOU ACCEPT THE MISSION?

There's a grief that came when I realized the stereotypical motherhood fairy tale wasn't going to happen for me. But that wasn't the end of my story; it was the beginning. If the existing fairy tales, from either side of the political spectrum, weren't going to work for me, I knew I'd have to write a new one. As real women, our truth is always somewhere in the middle and more complicated than politics or the media let on. This is the reality we have to work with, so this is the reality we must recognize and adapt to meet our unique needs.

I knew I had to become a mother. Failure wasn't an option.

If this sounds like you, know that your dream of motherhood is possible, though it may not look like the storybook. There will be opportunities in things you can't control. Past pain will need to be released so you can open your mind and your heart to new possibilities. Vulnerability can become strength when in the service of selflessness and love.

This is my story, but I also want to know yours, because I know there is a tender mercy bringing us together through the pages of this book. Where are you right now in terms of your mission of motherhood? What are your doubts? What are your strengths? What are your nonnegotiables?

We may know our mission, but we don't know the path we'll walk to accomplish it. Our job is to walk through it in love, perseverance, courage, and faith. If motherhood is your dream, then just like everything else you've fought for and accomplished in your life, it's in your power to get it. There is always hope, but only if you let yourself reinvent what it means to be a mother along the way. The key is understanding why you want to become a mother and then understanding your options so you can choose the best path for you. You have choices. You can write your own fairy tale.

Time to get the big girl panties on and get down to business.

And if you need help, a shoulder to cry on, or a fellow mother to share your mission with, I'm here for you. Check out the resources I have listed on **missionmotherhoodbook.com**. Drop me a line. I'm always up for a chai latte or a good Cabernet.

EPILOGUE

THE LAST FIVE YEARS HAVE FLOWN BY. EVERY DAY, WEEK, month, and year is spent seeking out new adventures for my blended family of ten: my mother, Art, me, four kids, Colleen, and two dogs (not to mention Faith, LeTroy, and their two children, who realized the importance of family and moved back to Texas). Sometimes it feels more like a zoo than a family—two senior citizens over eighty feels like two additional kids at times—but I wouldn't have it any other way. Sadly, we lost Uncle Johnny in 2023 and we are working to help all the kids deal with their first true loss of a grandparent. While blended families are never easy, I'm happy I get to make a positive impact on all their lives.

I don't have contact with my brother. He's still rooted in his beliefs, and I'm still rooted in mine. Unless something significant changes in one or both of our perspectives, there is no middle ground between us. I've had to release that notion of family. It's sad, but it's a choice, and an acceptance of something

I cannot change. The only thing I can do is protect myself and my children and not continue to battle against a hurtful world view.

My relationship with my ex continues to be rocky, but, after an official divorce, he can't hurt me anymore. I suspect he tries to assert control and exact revenge through Lauren, but I'm careful not to give away my power to him. We parent in parallel at this point. He has never apologized for the pain I felt he inflicted on my family.

As much as I love dancing, I put that passion on hold for the last decade to focus my energies on being a single mother. As my children have gotten older and Art arrived on the scene, my prospects for resuming adult interests are looking up. A couple months ago, I attended Derek Hough's incredible *Symphony of Dance* show and managed to get in a quick salsa dance with him. My mother even got in on the action. I expect to be dusting off my dance shoes on a more regular basis very soon.

I continue to work at my high-tech job when I'm not parenting or writing, but I never lose sight that my career is not the most important thing. Sometimes it's a struggle. I still take my children with me on business trips when possible. My mother goes on most of those adventures with us. My children are incredibly lucky to live day-to-day with a grandmother who is as loving, giving, and generous as my mother. My mother is still my rock, although as she ages, she leans on me more and more. I'm grateful I get to reciprocate the love and support she unconditionally lavished on me.

I cherish being a mother even on the toughest days. If I had to do it all over again, I would. I work hard to fill our days with love and adventure. One evening in October, I created a Disney watch party for *Zombies 2*. I had face painters and a house full of zombie decor. Let me tell you, it's a bit of a challenge finding age-appropriate zombie decorations. This wasn't a new thing for me, as I try to make a special occasion out of almost anything. My mother and I were in the kitchen, putting the finishing touches on green-and-black iced cupcakes, when she said to me, "You're always looking for ways to make life fun and special. I wish I had a mother like you." I almost cried on my cupcakes. It was the best compliment I could receive, coming from the woman who raised me.

Lauren is doing well. She has outgrown the majority of her health issues, although she still has a sensitive stomach and a cautious personality, and it takes time for her to embrace the new or unfamiliar. She sometimes struggles with the time she's required to spend with her father, but we continue to make progress. Priscilla still helps us navigate her path in the healthiest way. I'm reassured that God is in control and she will get important skills from her time with him. Self-reliance, resilience, the knowledge that people are imperfect, even parents. She's a star student and currently studying a year above her grade level. She's creative and kind-hearted, everything that I could dream of. She's living proof that miracles do happen.

Brayden is a gregarious bundle of joy and charisma. He's bright and has impeccable comedic timing that keeps us laughing most of the time, a trait his egg donor would recognize along with his still lanky and unwieldy limbs. Like his name says, he is brave, but he is also a sensitive soul who isn't afraid to show his emotions. I'm confident he'll be a very different man than the ones I grew up with.

At eleven and nine, my children are at ages where they still want to be with me. Sometimes they say, "You're the best mom ever."

"Well, you deserve the best," I always respond.

One evening, we were having one of those dramatic Texas

thunderstorms, the kind that sends dogs running under the bed. Suddenly, a bright bolt of lightning struck nearby followed by a loud clap of thunder that shook the walls. Then I heard another kind of thunder, the footsteps of my two children running toward my bedroom. They were huffing and puffing when they arrived in my doorway.

"Get in, you two," I said with a chuckle.

As they climbed into the Big Bed, one on each side, I snuggled them under one of my mother's afghans.

Lauren said what she always did, "I love you to the moon and back, Mama, more than yesterday and less than tomorrow."

"Thank you, Lauren. You are my special girl. There will never be another one like you."

Then Brayden asked, "Mama, will you marry me?" Which is something he often asks me.

I gave him my pat answer to this question: "Brayden, you can't marry your mother."

"Why not?" he asked, both innocent and puzzled. "You are the most beautiful woman in the world."

I kissed him. "You're such a wonderful boy. What makes you so amazing?" It was a rhetorical question, but nine-year-olds don't do rhetorical questions.

"My heart," he said seriously.

"Your heart, indeed." I hugged both my children as a happy tear slipped down my cheek. "You know, you both are my sunshine. Right?"

"Yes, Mama," they said together, "we know."

ACKNOWLEDGMENTS

THERE ARE SO MANY PEOPLE IN MY VILLAGE WHO WERE instrumental in helping me achieve my mission. I'd like to express my deep, heartfelt gratitude for the impact you've made on my life.

Thanks go out to:

My mother and lifelong cheerleader for standing by me through every crisis and every triumph. Everyone should be lucky enough to have a mother like you.

My children, Lauren and Brayden, for bringing immeasurable joy and meaning to my life. You make the journey worthwhile.

Rachel and Brandon, I wish we had more time together here on earth. I'm grateful you are free of pain, and I look forward to reuniting with you in heaven.

Nick and Madi for enriching my life and being open to the love I have for you. I look forward to having a front-row seat as you become the people you were meant to be.

My father for passing down his tenacity, humor, loyalty, and love of family. You gave me the things I needed to achieve my mission. I trust you are keeping things lively in heaven!

Art, my partner in crime. Thank you for being the first man to see the real me and appreciate my heart and my intentions. Your fervent belief in the vision for this book helped me keep the faith in moments of doubt.

My extended family—Colleen, Johnny, Faith, LeTroy, Eleanor, Sullivan, Steve, Gina, Ed, Olivia, Ryan, Alana, and Adele for giving me the big family I always wanted. Thank you for your unconditional love and acceptance.

JillEllyn for your encouragement and guidance about the art of writing and publishing a book. You are amazing and wise.

The amazing team of professionals at Scribe Media. Special thanks go out to Amanda for helping me hone my voice and share my story, Maggie, for your encouragement and advice, Emmy for keeping the project on track, and Anna, for bringing my creative vision to life on the cover.

Jason, my press relations and marketing collaborator, for helping bring attention to my story. I couldn't have done this without you.

Jimmy, Katherine, and the rest of my legal team for your passion and dedication to prevail in a case that defied common sense. You're the only people I would want in the foxhole with me!

All the fierce career women who have inspired me (you know who you are). I'm humbled to call you friends and am filled with admiration for your shining examples of what women can achieve. You are some bad bitches!

The friends, co-workers, and angels-on-earth who supported and held me up during the most difficult times of my journey to motherhood. You'll never know just how much your presence and kind words kept me sane when I wondered if I could go on.

Each of the incredible, talented, selfless doctors and nurses who helped me along my fertility journey and battled tirelessly by my side to diagnose and care for my children. We didn't always prevail, but your dedication meant the world to me.

The PEO sisters of Chapter GT. You are some of the most generous and remarkable women on the planet! You barely knew my family, but you stepped in wholeheartedly to prop us up in the most difficult times and celebrate with us in the joyous ones. You are heaven sent.

My mother's steadfast friends—Mary and the "Same Time Next Year" sisterhood—for supporting my mother and helping her through the darkest times.

All the therapists who guided my family through the most difficult trauma of our lives. We came out whole because of you.

The anonymous strangers who signed the Change.org petition and made contributions to GoFundMe. You are living proof that there is still love and humanity in our "take no prisoners" world.

Finally, I'm grateful to my Heavenly Father, for never giving up on me even when I gave up on You. Thank You for the abundant blessings You bestowed upon me.

ABOUT THE AUTHOR

CHERI BERGERON is an author, trained life coach, blogger, public speaker, and women's activist whose mission is to guide women to discover their unique mission of motherhood. A thirty-five-year veteran of the software industry, Cheri applies her business acumen, tenacity, and entrepreneurial spirit to inspire would-be mothers to understand their full range of options and seek unconventional paths to parenthood when traditional fairy tales have failed them. Free resources may be found on Cheri's website missionmotherhoodbook.com. Cheri lives with her beautiful, blended family in Austin, Texas.

www.ingramcontent.com/pod-product-compliance
Lightning Source LLC
Chambersburg PA
CBHW030509080526
44586CB00011B/129